STILL STANDING

For Dorian, Olivia, Alice and Harriet

STILL STANDING

A MEMOIR

Anna Crighton

CANTERBURY UNIVERSITY PRESS

UC

UNIVERSITY OF
CANTERBURY
Te Whare Wānanga o Waitaha
CHRISTCHURCH NEW ZEALAND

First published in 2024 by
CANTERBURY UNIVERSITY PRESS
University of Canterbury
Private Bag 4800, Christchurch
NEW ZEALAND

ISBN 978-1-98-850341-7

A catalogue record for this book is available from the
National Library of New Zealand.

Grateful acknowledgement is made for permission from
Faber and Faber Ltd to use the extract from the poem
'The North Ship' by Philip Larkin.
The poem 'Noel' by Barry Cleavin was first published in
takahē 23 (Spring 1995).

Book design, layout and printing:
Caxton, Christchurch, New Zealand, www.caxton.co.nz
Editor: Anna Rogers

Front cover photograph: the author in 1955

Contents

Acknowledgements

For reasons of length – my first draft was considerably larger – material about my ancestry, which was really only of interest to family members, ended up on the cutting room floor. I am grateful, though, for the assistance of Kaye van Grunsven at Christchurch City libraries in helping me to research my French and British roots. My thanks, also, to Mark Greenwood from the Photo Lab, who converted historic photographs and 35mm slides into reproduction quality images.

I would like to thank the following for their information from specific archives: St George's Hospital, Princess Margaret Hospital and Christchurch Public Hospital, who provided me with medical records and details (I am grateful to Dr Alistair Humphrey for checking my account based on these); Professor Ros Ballaster, Mansfield College, Oxford; Inka Bertz, Head of Collections/Curator of Art, Jewish Museum, Berlin; Louise Davison, Business Operation Officer, Human Resource Service Centre, New Zealand Defence Force; Fraser Faithfull, Archivist, Good Shepherd, Melbourne, Australia; Tim Jones, Librarian, Christchurch Art Gallery Te Puna o Waiwhetū; John Leamy, Department of Home Affairs, Australian Consulate General, Auckland; Sarah Murray, Curatorial Manager, Canterbury Museum, Christchurch; Karen Needham, Attendance Officer, Christchurch Girls' High School, Christchurch; Mel Rissman, St Andrew's College, Christchurch; Jane Smallfield, Library Manager/Archivist, Otago Girls' High School, Dunedin.

For their generous time and assistance with behind the scenes details, I thank colleagues past and present: Professor Conal McCarthy, Victoria University of Wellington Te Herenga Waka; Robyn Ussher; Associate Professor Linda Tyler, University of Auckland Waipapa Taumata Rau; Gareth Wright, Heritage Team, Christchurch City Council; Jenny May, Heritage Management Services.

I have known each of my close friends, Millie Ford, Merilynne Evans, Barbara Davies and Kathy Hamilton, for more than 50 years. Writing this book brought further opportunities to reminisce, with tears and laughter, over shared adventures, and provided details often missing from my own recollection. My friend Hamilton Baxter, a master hoarder of records, sent me letters I had written to him between October 1964 and June 1967. They seemed so confused and emotional, but in them were incidents that had completely escaped my memory. Special thanks go to Tony Allan who, more than five decades since our relationship, agreed to meet with me and gave his approval for me to tell our story. Being able to talk about those times allowed any lingering mental suffering to evaporate.

I owe a great debt of gratitude to Mike Crean, who was a journalist at the *Press* during my years as a Christchurch city councillor, for his independent and objective overview of this part of the book. His research and comments were invaluable. Former city councillor Alister James also checked the details in Part Three in his inimitable way and suggested corrections, which were truly appreciated. Max Robertson, another council colleague I had first met back in 1960, also shared hilarious memories, though not all were suitable for publication. I am most grateful to my friend and former PhD supervisor, Dr Mark Stocker, who read earlier drafts of the book and showed patience, humour and only occasional irritation in contributing insightful changes.

Throughout the writing of the book my son, Dorian, endured more hours of listening to and commenting on aspects of our shared past and my impossible behaviour than I had a right to expect. He gave me his love and understanding and permission to expose the less conventional details of my past. His support for me to tell my story in such an honest way was reassuring. Other family members, Lesley Moffitt, Nova Hichens, Alan Bower, Jeannette Kwant and Gwen Searle, and my friend Judith Ritchie, were also generous with their time and shared memories. Mark Gerrard kindly read and approved the parts of the book concerning our years together.

I was lucky with my editor, Anna Rogers, who respected my voice and how I felt throughout the text. My publisher, Catherine Montgomery, was professional yet sensitive to my emotions. My thanks, too, to Katrina McCallum, at Canterbury University Press.

Introduction

My life seems to be neatly compartmentalised into three distinct phases.

After I left childhood I was unaware that I faced a choice about who I would become. Maturity brought a greater understanding of consequences. My relationship with my parents troubled me: I realised that I did not love them as a daughter should, but I was dutiful nevertheless, despite the lack of affection I received. I continually played down my lonely battle with depression, keeping my low spirits to myself and later channelling them into a restless search for knowledge.

There were happy times and extraordinary experiences in the next phase of my life and I forged precious, lasting friendships. I still suffered from low self-esteem but when beset by melancholy found the strength to pull myself through. I was unprepared for the hardships in life and astonished that I did not perpetrate even more calamities than I consciously or unconsciously did. Nevertheless, by the time I had a public life, my difficult experiences enabled me to see how others struggled, and I never forgot this or them.

The third phase of my life took me down the route of public life and unexpected fulfillment. I completed a PhD (with Distinction) at the age of 68 and received a damehood in 2020. But most of all, I had the joy and pride of being a mother and a grandmother. My love for my son Dorian, and his for me, has sustained me; he is the one constant in my life. He has grown to be a loving person and a role model as a father, son, companion, friend and colleague, with a strong sense of right and wrong.

This is my story in my words but it has relied on recollections from family members and in a few instances it incorporates memories from others who have shared experiences with me, especially my close friends Millie Ford, Merilynne Evans, Barbara Davies and Kathy Hamilton. I asked many questions and sent for records and files from various institutions. Since I was a young girl I have gathered all sorts of historical family records, photos and letters, and from time to time over my life I have written down my feelings. Scraps of my past had been flung into a box which, as I moved from flat to flat, house to house, country to country, and through stormy relationships and earthquakes, has somehow survived.

My father kept meticulous records. The lists, photographs and papers that fell into my possession after his death in 1997 have been an invaluable source of information on his life, some of which I had never been aware of. And I was really excited when my friend Hamilton Baxter sent me letters I had written to him between October 1964 and June 1967. For many months I wrestled with how much I should say about the horrors of my marriage. After 50 years, after all that time, when the door to the room of those memories was finally unlocked, the silent tears began to flow. The more I remembered, the bigger the dilemma grew: whether to write of those appalling times, or to stay silent. I was concerned about how my son would cope with the knowledge that I was referring to his father. Finally I decided I must describe it, but without opening all the doors within my mind. I have not told everything.

As a hypersensitive introvert I have spent most of my life not revealing the true nature of my feelings and experiences to others, and so my desire to write this memoir was baffling and required thought. I like to think that this book comes from the heart, with occasional assistance from the head. Yes, there is probably a bit of the 'My Way' in it, though I hope I have enough humility to avoid saying 'Je ne regrette rien'.

PART

ONE

The Hard Years

CHAPTER 1

Made in Linwood

I was born on top of a sandhill, in the Glendower nursing home on the corner of England and Gloucester streets in the Christchurch suburb of Linwood, a relatively substantial 8lb 2oz baby with a mop of dark hair and cerulean eyes. The date was 12 January 1944. My mother, Noeline Hichens, had walked just a few houses to the nursing home from the large villa at 487 Gloucester Street where my parents and my older brother Ralph were living with my maternal grandparents, Joseph and Lillian Searle. I was called Shirley Anne, but known by my second name.

My mother, quiet and very beautiful, appears to have been born with the ability to attract attention with little effort. Those who knew her as a young girl and later unanimously agreed that she was lovely but overindulged and pampered. And as the youngest daughter of five children, she was spoilt – by her two older sisters, May and Alma, who were already at high school when she was born, by her doting big brother Henry and certainly her parents. Noeline and her younger brother, Roy, were raised together almost as a separate family to their three siblings. My mother's reports from her years at Avonside Girls' High School reveal her to be an intelligent and diligent pupil. In her first year, 1933, for example, she came first in history, bookkeeping and arithmetic and second in geography and was placed second in her class of 25.

Many suitors called at the Searle house to woo the young Noeline, but it was tall, handsome Noel Frank Hichens, whom she met at a dance, who won her heart. When they married on 30 December 1939 at St John's in Latimer Square, she was just 20 and he 22. She was as strikingly beautiful as he was tall and handsome. He put her on a pedestal, where she perched for the duration of their marriage. To my father she was always 'Princess'.

The young couple moved into the back half of her parents' house for financial reasons and also because, being so young, Noeline needed the comfort of being near her mother, especially during the war years.

Noel was born in Christchurch on 7 September 1917 to Frank Nicholls Hichens, a builder, and Edith Gertrude George. He was the third of four children, after his older sisters Daphne and Vera and before his younger brother Ray. The family lived in a terrace house at 111 Kilmore Street on a site replaced first by the *Christchurch Star* building and later by the Convention Centre built in the 1990s. Opposite was the Limes Hospital, where the Christchurch Town Hall now stands. The neighbouring Avon River, with its bulrushes and flaxes, provided an exciting wild playground for Noel and his siblings, all of whom attended the Normal School just down the road on Kilmore/Montreal Street corner. In 1930, aged 13, my father left with a Certificate of Proficiency, which was awarded by school inspectors to Standard 6 (Year 8) pupils who passed in a certain number of subjects. It also meant two years of free secondary schooling, in Noel's case at the Christchurch Technical High School where he excelled. His report for the first year, when he was second in the class, read: 'A really excellent result. A fine worker and a splendid type of boy.' He matriculated in 1933, which was equivalent to the later University Entrance. The following year, in April, on annual pay of £112, he started as a message boy at the Post and Telegraph Department, where he would spend a good deal of his working life as an engineering draughtsman. He was promoted to cadet in October and by 1940 was a junior draughtsman.

My father was not called up for military service until 1942, when he was 24. Thanks to what his army medical record describes as fibrositis characterised by spontaneous pain, especially in the lumbar region, he was not chosen for active service or regarded as suitable for the Home Guard. His skills as a draughtsman were useful, however, for mapping duties and in June 1943 he worked alongside his near contemporary, the celebrated artist William (Bill) Sutton, in the District Camouflage Section. Making full use of Sutton's artistic skills, they concealed and disguised gun emplacements and bomb stores with gusto. As Sutton later recalled in Pat Unger's book, *Bill's Story*, 'I remember we disguised an airfield at Taieri, Dunedin, by extending the appearance of paddocks and hedgerows into the airfield itself ... with bleaches for grass and manure to intensify the colour ... it was so good, our chaps couldn't find it.' On the recommendation of a medical board Noel was discharged on 9 October 1943 with the rank of sergeant, having served just 15 months.

In 1963 he was admitted as a registered engineering associate with his experience and responsibilities in the practice of telecommunication engineering draughting. In his last role, as the inaugural inspecting draughtsman at Post Office headquarters, he was instrumental in unifying and standardising drawing office methods and procedures throughout New Zealand, which entailed travelling and liaising all over the country. He was also responsible for a 1969 report that introduced microfilming into the New Zealand Post Office. When he retired, in October 1974, on a respectable salary of $5258, he received the usual letters of 'sincere appreciation' and 'valuable contribution' from the director-general and postmaster-general.

My brother Ralph Frank was born in Christchurch on 18 August 1941. A quiet and reserved boy, he was especially spoilt by our maternal grandmother, Lillian, whom he adored. Since Lillian preferred boys to girls, a fact she made obvious, Ralph enjoyed outings with her to town, to the horseracing (a passion of Nana's) and visiting relatives. I was not taken on such occasions.

On 10 January 1945 I was admitted to Christchurch Public Hospital where I spent my first birthday and where I uttered my first words: 'Stand up.' Mum had taken me that day for a visit to her sister May's house in Edgeware Road. While the two women nattered and enjoyed their lunch I crawled over to the bench, found an enticing cord hanging over the edge and pulled a full kettle of boiling water over myself. My screams were horrific, as the torrent of boiling water poured down one side of my body, catching the side of my neck but just missing my face. To relieve the excruciating pain, my Aunt May patted great handfuls of flour onto my burns. I was bundled up and taken straight to the hospital where I stayed for six weeks. It took several decades for me not to feel self-conscious about the lumpy scars and hideous mounds of flesh pushed into place to form some semblance of smoothness. I cried piteously when I was left at the hospital and the nurses advised my parents not to visit me as it would be too upsetting. The result was that after my six weeks in the children's ward I did not want to go home and clung crying to the kindly nurses, wanting to stay with them. It was to be my first experience of feeling rejection – twice.

The accident was reported in the *Press*, under the heading, 'Child Scalded'. So, at eleven months of age I hit the media for the first time.

My early life was fairly orthodox for its day. My parents provided the necessities of life but found it difficult to show affection. They appeared cold and distant. My father was authoritarian while my mother was self-absorbed and not exactly a true maternal presence, then, or indeed throughout my and my brother's lives. Dad set strict rules for his son and daughter. For example, when I was reluctant to eat tasteless, watery cabbage that had been boiled until it went pink then strained to ensure any remaining goodness went down the plughole, my father would tie me to the chair until I ate the offending mass, no matter how long it took. In one of his perceptive columns, Joe Bennett once wrote: 'Cabbage is the food of misery ... It's the food of Siberian gulags, the epicentre of man's inhumanity to man.' I agree totally and have never cooked it, let alone eaten it, since. I recall, too, Philip Larkin's apt observation, in his famous poem about parents, that misery is handed from one generation to the next.

Mum's cooking was legendarily bad in the early days of her marriage, but it did improve over the years. Sadly, the love of food associated with our French ancestry was lost on Noeline, who inflicted on us the English culinary inheritance at its worst: endless roast lamb Sunday dinners followed by days of cold lamb with mashed potatoes, beetroot and peas, or, even worse, bubble and squeak. I have fond memories, though, of the puddings, which I loved: rice, sago and tapioca (frogs' eyes), milk puddings, junket with nutmeg sprinkled on the top, apple dumplings, bread and butter pudding, banana custard, jelly and, of course, steamed puddings, smothered in sweet white sauce, custard or cream. But my all-time favourite was Christmas pudding covered in brandy sauce. The rich mixture, containing dried fruit and wrapped in a cloth, was placed in a pot of simmering water until cooked. Hidden within our helpings would be threepenny and sixpenny pieces, in those days likely containing real silver, and with shrieks of joy Ralph and I would tally up our winnings.

I felt wrong and out of place, merely tolerated. This deficiency of love eventually led to feelings of insecurity and isolation in both Ralph and me. Did we not deserve to be loved? I do not recall any physical affection, nor much laughter at home. It was the extended family living around us that made it a happy place. Where Ralph was quiet and reserved I was contumacious. Often mutinous and always adventurous, I would embark on my 'travels' from the time I could walk. Being dressed in the morning was a ritual. My upper body was covered so that the burns were not exposed and my arms heavily bandaged to restrain me from scratching the eczema that spread in the crooks of my arms. Once I was dressed, Mum would pin onto the back of my clothes a notice that gave my name and address so that I could be returned, like a piece of human lost property, should I be found wandering. In retrospect it seems comically Lewis Carroll-like, but it didn't feel like that then.

My sense of heritage and tradition came from living in my grandmother's villa. I have happy memories of this magical house full of exquisite objects, from the endless clocks ticking, the antimacassars covering the backs of the chairs and the doilies on every flat surface, to the colourful and exotic plethora of decorative arts, the potted palms, the richness of the velvet curtains and the elegant dark Edwardian furniture. The ornate cornicing and the large airy high ceilings with their roses gave the house a sense of grandeur. In the Victorian chromolithograph of *Mary, Queen of Scots, and her forbidden love*, which hung in a prominent position above the fireplace, Mary was descending the stairs with her entourage to find her private secretary, David Rizzio, apparently asleep at the foot of the stairs with his mandolin. Her jealous husband Henry Stewart, Lord Darnley, had had him murdered. The picture now hangs in my house. On the walls of the hallway on my grandmother's end of the house, beyond the border of the elaborate plaster archway and thick red velvet curtains, hung two large chromolithographs of the Battle of Waterloo. Beneath these violent images of Napoleon's defeat stood occasional tables often sporting bowls of fresh flowers from the garden.

After Joseph's death in 1949, Lillian created for herself a small bedroom in a closed-in veranda on the sunny west side facing the orchard and an even smaller kitchen, the larger one being at the back of the house where our family lived. A long table sat in the front window of the drawing room, where meals were enjoyed, with my grandmother always seated at one end where she could observe passing life on the street. Visiting the front of the house, and tentatively parting and walking through the dividing heavy velvet curtains, fascinated me. I remember standing and just gazing. That is when my grandmother would get me to fetch and carry for her, explaining to me why she couldn't do it herself: 'I have a bone in my leg.'

Lillian's end of the house was very different from ours, which faced north and was always warm and sunny. Grandeur was non-existent there, replaced by the more modern furniture of the time that Noel and Noeline preferred. Ralph had the sunroom as a bedroom; my room was screened off by a curtain from that of my parents. The rear windows and doors opened onto the expansive back garden. An orchard of cherry, plum and apple trees stood in a kitchen garden containing all sorts of delights, including gooseberry bushes and raspberry canes. It was an idyllic playground that I relished exploring, climbing trees, making huts and even, on one occasion, setting fire to the hedge while having a tea party. I have a vague and distant picture of sitting in a gap within the hedge, with matches to light a fire and boil the kettle, but then the hedge started flaming and the fire brigade had to be called. I was so frightened that I hid under the bed until I was cajoled out. I can vividly recall my father's wooden spoon punishment.

When I turned five in 1949 I was excited to be going to school, taken there by my big brother. Before leaving each day we had to line up at the kitchen table for a morning ritual: a spoonful of the hated and nasty-tasting Lanes Emulsion. However, as I gagged and somehow swallowed, I could look forward to the sweetener that followed – a tablespoon of gooey and gorgeous Maltexo.

The primary school I attended, Christchurch East, was within easy walking distance from home, requiring only the crossing of Stanmore Road on the way. A long line of single-storey weatherboard classrooms, modern for their time with fully glazed north-facing walls, looked out onto an asphalt playground. The access corridor, where we were allocated named hooks for coats and bags, ran along the south wall. There was no hall then; we would all stand outside for assembly in any weather. The school has grown over the years, roll and buildings, but most of the original classrooms have survived. I loved school from the start and never tired of learning. It seems I displayed endless imagination, and the teachers encouraged me with my reading, writing and drawing.

Searle family picnics were legendary and something to look forward to. Favourite places, all within a 40-kilometre radius of Christchurch, were Coe's Ford (there was a rope hanging from a tree over the river on which we would swing), Motukarara, Sumner Beach, Spencer Park, Woodend, Pines Beach and Waikuku. The mothers would chat and produce food while the fathers, beers in hand, got the thermettes primed and lit to boil the water for the tea. We cousins ran amok, making up games, swimming and exploring – it was action-packed and thrilling. We would go home sunburnt, often covered in sand, tired but happy.

Often on a Saturday night the Hichens family would go to the Aranui speedway to watch my father's favourite rider, Ronnie Moore. I remember the smell of the cinder track, the roaring of the motorbikes, running around with Ralph and being carried over my father's shoulder back to the car. There were also Sunday dinners at one another's houses. When it came to our turn, the families would gather at the front of the house and sit at Nana's big table. Singing around the piano was always a highlight: 'The White Cliffs of Dover', 'Pack Up Your Troubles in Your Old Kit Bag', 'It's a Lovely Day Tomorrow', 'Bless 'Em All', 'You are My Sunshine'.

Because I was just six, I did not understand the significance of December 1950 for Christchurch and Canterbury – the centennial of planned European settlement in the province. There were public events aplenty, including an open-air church service in Cathedral Square attended by over 30,000 people. And fittingly, Harewood, opened in 1940, became New Zealand's first international airport. There was a procession watched by over 100,000, the Canterbury Centennial Games were held and a new Centennial Pool was built in Armagh Street facing the Avon River. Every school child received a medal with a black and red ribbon. One side, depicting a pilgrim family with the first four ships in the background, read: 'The arrival at Lyttelton 1850'. The obverse read: 'Canterbury 1850–1950 New Zealand Centenary'.

Then in 1951, when I was seven years old, the Hichens family left their home in Gloucester Street, Christchurch, and all that was familiar and comforting, for a new life in Dunedin.

CHAPTER 2
Last Years of Innocence

We moved south because my father was transferred for work. His office was in the impressive chief post office building situated in The Exchange, Dunedin's historic business centre. For the next seven years our parents appeared settled and both Ralph and I were happy making new friends through our involvement in dance, tennis, music and at school.

Our home in Forrester Avenue, Pine Hill, was a modest but new two-storey weatherboard house on the proverbial quarter-acre section. We were forbidden to talk to the boys who lived on one side because they were considered 'too rough and common', but allowed to play with the children of the other neighbours because their father was a teacher. Three doors up the hill I made friends with Carol Smith, the same age as me and in my class at Pine Hill School. She was an epileptic, sometimes falling to the ground and writhing. I was terrified the first time I witnessed it but her mother kindly explained to me that it was best to leave Carol alone until the fit ended and to keep a watch on her so she would not hurt herself. I protected her when the boys at school cruelly made fun of her.

I have warm memories of Pine Hill School, which was reasonably new and within easy walking distance of home. On Mondays, when the bread was stale, Mum would make us tinned salmon sandwiches for our school lunch because it helped to moisten the bread. As a treat once a month we were given a shilling each for a pie from the school shop. And there was the school milk, a bottle each at morning playtime. Most of my schoolmates did not like it, especially if it had become warm and creamy after being left in the sun, so I had their share as well. Some mornings I might drink up to six bottles. I did well at school but when it came to jumping a class, as recommended by the headmaster, my parents did not agree. They did not want me going to high school out of my age bracket. As a result I spent two years in Standard 6 (Year 8) before going to high school. I found that boring and even though I produced a report card at the end of the year showing a row of As and A+s, my father berated me for getting one B+.

I started at Otago Girls' High School on 5 February 1957. Founded in 1871, it was the first state secondary school for girls in the southern hemisphere and reputed to be the fifth oldest in the world. Its motto was 'The right education makes the heart as strong as oak'. In the third form I took Latin, French, history, English and maths. The more relaxing classes of art and embroidery rounded off the curriculum. I especially and fondly remember Constance Lascelles, the embroidery teacher. I still have the sampler bag I made with rows of different stitches neatly displayed. Our first sewing lessons were to make navy bloomers for physical education. These were unsexy, shapeless and unspeakably ghastly. I well remember, too, the glamorous Latin teacher and endlessly intoning verbs and conjunctions from pluperfect tense to present, and Grace Johnstone, my French teacher, with her long skirts, knitted cardigans and brogues. I loved drawing lessons outside and visits to the Otago Museum but, to my father's great disappointment, loathed algebra and calculus. I was near top in just about everything else, however. My favourite hobby was illustrating my exercise books, especially the history ones. I spent hours in my room sketching and painting watercolour images of medieval halberdiers and castles. The lack of immediate relevance to mid-century New Zealand never occurred to me and never bothered me.

But Wednesday afternoons were something to look forward to. Girls' High girls and Boys' High boys would meet after school in a downtown studio, under strict supervision, to learn ballroom dancing. The typical scenario was girls on one side of the hall and boys on the other. When the music started, the more adventurous boys would cross the room first and ask a girl to dance – always the prettiest ones first. Others would tentatively follow. I was very shy and reserved but always felt pleased when approached. I was enthusiastic about the seamless choreographed movements of the Maxina, but my favourite was the figure-dance, when we would glide around the room in pairs, hand in hand. Then there was being swept around the dance floor for the Gypsy Tap, quicksteps and foxtrots plus the reels, especially the eightsomes, with lots of laughter when we became muddled about where we should be.

Those afternoons showed me that dance was special but my love for it did not stop there. I was allowed to start Scottish country and Highland dancing lessons held in the little hall in Gladstone Road, Dalmore, not far from home. I practised and practised my footwork technique until I mastered it. Mum made me a white dress, I had a tartan sash and a pair of dance pumps were purchased second hand. Then on a Saturday night there was the dance – the reels, jigs and the strathspeys. I always came home exhausted, but exhilarated.

Fridays were also something to look forward to. After school I would go to Preens Drycleaners in the Octagon, take off my gym frock for pressing and wait in a booth for its return. Then I would meet up with Ralph and my parents – Dad would finish work early – and we would be off to the five o'clock movies. Fish and chips on the way home finished off the evening.

And there was tennis. I learnt to play at school and joined a Saturday tennis club. I became quite proficient and won several cups. Ralph learnt the banjo and guitar but, to my sorrow, I was not allowed. It was explained to me that because I was a girl and would marry and have children, a rounded education and music lessons were not so important. Other parents took the opposite line – a charming musically accomplished girl would surely make a good wife! To compensate I was given a mouth organ. which I taught myself to play, but my heart and mouth weren't in it. Ralph was diligent, not only spending hours practising his banjo, but also making balsa wood models. He was so proud of his efforts, which he would string up in his bedroom, but often our father would interfere, tell Ralph to pull them to pieces and start again and make them perfect next time. His offer to help never eventuated.

Our parents' indifference to their children's lives became more apparent during sports days and prizegivings. Neither of them attended, even though I won quite a few prizes, often carrying home a pile of books. I would go straight to my room, sit on the bed and relive the moment with enjoyment and pleasure as I reread the inscription on each flyleaf. I enjoyed my solitude at such times. My bedroom became my happy place and one I retreated to willingly. I was an avid reader. I enjoyed the Regency novels of Georgette Heyer, the author of young dreams, but my favourites were the 'Wells' series of ballet books by Lorna Hill. I kept these until the 2011 Canterbury earthquake wiped out most of my library.

Ralph had built himself a crystal set and he would listen to that in his room but I was pleased to have my own maroon-coloured mantle radio, which pre-dated the move to Dunedin. When I was younger, in Christchurch, I would ensure I was in bed by seven every night so that I could listen to *Night Beat* with Randy Stone, the proverbial tough and streetwise reporter who covered human interest stories for the *Chicago Star*. I loved counting the pips at the top of the hour and waiting for the last one, which was slightly longer. There was also *Life with Dexter* and when I was home from school sick – I frequently suffered from migraines – I would listen, as Mum did, to the morning soaps, *Portia Faces Life* and *Doctor Paul*, and the legendary Aunt Daisy.

Ralph and I loved the summer breaks. Down the gully from our house was a forest and creek where the northern main highway in and out of Dunedin was later created. With our friends from the neighbourhood we would spend hours down at the creek catching tadpoles, freshwater lobster and crabs. Then there were the games – hide and seek, who could climb highest in the trees, playing cricket on the street outside our homes. Further up the hill there was a farm where we picked gooseberries and raspberries, filling our buckets and earning a penny a pound. On Sundays, in good weather, the family took off for the traditional run in the car for either a picnic lunch or afternoon tea. On a visit to Larnach Castle I was enchanted with the historic character of the building even though it was almost derelict and the gardens were overgrown. I dreamt of owning it one day and quietly restoring it to its former glory. Even at the age of 12 I was conscious of tradition and the past. We would often drive further afield to Karitane or Waikouaiti and there was always the peninsula and Port Chalmers.

During the summer holidays, too, our family would go camping. This annual tradition had started over the Christmas and New Year of 1946–47 and the family group in those earlier years often included our maternal grandparents. My birthday always fell on a day when we were away but I still got presents, a cake with candles and the inevitable song in my honour. There was a charm about the tent, even the rickety and uncomfortable camp beds (scrim stretched over a frame), and the smell of wet canvas when it rained. I am not sure if Mum enjoyed preparing the meals but she seemed to manage with the camp stove. I can still smell the aroma of the burning twigs in the thermette blending with the burning of the toast over the flames. Because of the lack of refrigeration while we were camping, Mum would preserve eggs in a tin. They were disgusting.

Most meals, though, included easy to cook sausages or chops – my favourites in that carnivorous era.

We would travel all over Central Otago, each annual holiday to somewhere different – Wanaka, Queenstown, Alexandra and so on. And sometimes we would venture further north, to Murchison, Nelson and our favourite spot of all, Kaiteriteri, a very long way to go in an non-airconditioned car. On long trips our father would stop at the occasional pub for a beer and bring out a glass of sarsaparilla for each of us as a treat (no stopping in Oamaru, though, which enforced prohibition). Today we would have been labelled freedom campers for we would pitch the tent anywhere on impulse – beside a lake, river or forest, and sometimes even in a camping ground. Our camping equipment had progressed from a bell tent to a square tent, with a flap on one side that could be elevated on poles to form a porch. For the journey all our camping equipment was packed into a lidded trailer with high sides. When we made camp this became my bed: I would climb in and the lid would be slightly elevated to let in air. I felt isolated from Ralph and our parents, who all shared the tent, and would have liked the comfort of being with them rather than in a coffin-like box. Nevertheless, they were happy times.

During our 1953–54 Christmas holiday travels, we purchased a miniature smooth-haired dachshund with the rather regal kennel name of Gold Mohr of Brote. We called her Penny, which matched her colour. The backyard, made dog proof, was Penny's domain. Because my father wanted to breed from her, only select pedigrees were allowed anywhere near when she was on heat. I was in awe at the determination of the local hormone-addled canines to sniff out and jump the fence. My father solved part of the problem. First, Penny had to wear a nappy sort of arrangement but where do you put the tail? Second, he ran a wire round the top of the 1.8-metre fence and connected it to a switch placed inside under the window facing the yard. We were on watch duty when Penny was allowed outside. If a dog infiltrated the yard one of us would run out to frighten it off while the other would flip the switch, thus electrifying the wire. On its exit jump, the dog would invariably catch a shock and yelp horrendously as it retreated. Few dogs ever returned. Penny did have a litter of pups, an arranged copulation with a suitable sire. We kept one. She was named Queen.

My father had two collections to which he was devoted, one of antique clocks and one of old gramophones and polyphones. Every Sunday all the clocks would be wound ready for the cacophony of midday gongs and chimes. It was deafening and created much excitement. Another Sunday morning passion was playing records from his considerable collection of LPs and 78s on a large console radiogram that took pride of place in our sitting room. His favourite was the Trinidadian pianist Winifred Atwell, who was popular at the time, and played such numbers as 'Black and White Rag', 'Somebody Stole My Girl', 'The Sheik of Araby' and 'The Poor People of Paris'. Rock'n'roll it was not.

When I was 14 and in the fourth form at Otago Girls', our father received yet another promotion, to manage the 40 or so draughtsmen in the Christchurch drawing office. Our mother, who had barely tolerated living in Dunedin, was pleased to be going home. After the blue skies of Christchurch, she had found the grey days down south execrable and her mother had died in 1954, three years after our move to Dunedin. Mum missed her and would often suddenly burst into tears and would frequently be in bed in her darkened bedroom when we returned home from school.

My mind is completely blank when I attempt to recall actually leaving Dunedin, though I know my last day at high school was 9 May 1958. None of the friendships from those seven years were ever rekindled later. As he would do later with his gun collection, my father disposed of his unique clocks and gramophones and polyphones rather than let anyone else own them. I do not recall our family pets being part of the move north either. It was almost as if we stepped out of our Dunedin life, shed all that it had given us and moved into another zone. Neither Ralph nor I wanted to leave a place where we had been so happy and fulfilled. As we packed our bags, for me sans dance pumps and tennis racquet, we were also saying goodbye to our childhood and taking our first tentative steps towards a life neither of us would cope with well. The years of innocence were over.

CHAPTER 3
Gone Feral

Ralph recalled the move as the beginning of the worst period in his life. At least he was old enough not to have to go back to school, I thought to myself. Mum told me many years later that she had asked Dad to leave me in Dunedin at boarding school so as not to disrupt my schooling. He refused. My life would have been so different and perhaps much happier if only he had agreed. Ralph had aspirations to be an architect but Dad had decided he was to be an auto-electrician. Given no choice, he was taken to Young Bros and signed up for an apprenticeship. He did not particularly like his job but stuck at it, and did it well.

We moved into a new weatherboard house in Avonhead Road, a modest three-bedroom, one-bathroom abode planted in the middle of fields, a good distance from Yaldhurst Road, the main road into Christchurch from the west. The isolation was a shock. Gradually houses started to appear around us and we found ourselves on a back section in the centre of them, with a long drive to upgraded Avonhead Road.

The colourful interior of the house was a feast to my eyes. The cupboard fronts in the open-plan kitchen and bathroom and laundry were painted in alternating shades of pastel pink, chartreuse green and pastel turquoise blue. The floors in those rooms were lino of black and white squares; the rest of the house was carpeted. Dad spent most of his weekends installing high fencing around the property. Potatoes were planted over the whole section to break up the soil, and paths were laid to the front and back doors. Mum, apparently much happier, set about decorating with a new chrome and Formica table and chairs in the kitchen, and contemporary furniture in the sitting room and bedrooms. My aunts would come and gush over the house, saying how lucky their sister was. My mother enjoyed those visits after being 'in the wilderness', as she put it, far from her relatives. Ralph was allocated the smaller bedroom off the kitchen while I had the larger one next to my parents' room. Facing north, it was sunny and comfortable and I spent most of my time there.

While Ralph reluctantly trod the path decreed by his father, I had to return to school. My parents had enrolled me at nearby Riccarton High School, but when we went to visit we found that it was still being built and would not be completed or taking enrolments until the following year. Mum and Dad panicked and I felt stranded. They eventually found me a place at Christchurch Girls' High School in Cranmer Square, in the city centre, and after frenzied preparations I started there in my new uniform at the end of May 1958. Because of the erratic bus service (there was none down Avonhead Road), I cycled to and from school every day, via Yaldhurst Road, Riccarton Road and through Hagley Park to the Armagh Street entrance of the school – a long distance. On cold, frosty mornings I would pedal like crazy to get to the park gates as quickly as possible, because by then my frozen hands would start to tingle and become warm. Any chance I could get, I would go after school to Dad's office in St Elmo Courts, a block away on the corner of Hereford and Montreal streets, sit at a spare desk to do my homework and get a ride home. I did this regularly, especially if it was raining or a nor'wester was blowing.

Ever since I was a toddler, I had enjoyed exploring and during the Christmas school holidays of 1958–59 I did just that. Running through a culvert under Avonhead Road, about halfway between our house and Yaldhurst Road, was a creek that was the source of the Avon River, and I would sit there most days, reading or drawing. One day I met a new friend who had brought her horse down to the water for a drink. She promised to meet me there the next day and bring a horse for me. That was the start of my relationship with Sandy. There was no saddle or stirrups but I would spend hours riding Sandy bareback round the paddocks. Oh, what sheer joy and exhilaration. I was sorry when the holiday ended and my friend disappeared, along with Sandy.

Another animal experience about this time said a lot about my increasingly rebellious attitude. A fellow student arrived at school with some white pet rats to give away, ugly specimens with long pink tails. 'I'll have one,' I said. My plan worked a treat. When I came home from school, my mother was in the kitchen preparing our dinner. I said, 'Look, Mum' and took off my hat. Sitting happily on its haunches on my head was the rat. She screamed and yelled at me to get rid of it, which my father later did. It had been worth it, though, to see the look on her face.

Because I had been in the top stream at Otago Girls', I was placed in a similar class in Christchurch. But there I struggled. It was the middle of the school year and though I did my utmost to catch up with the other girls, the work was so different. I struggled, too, with the environment at home and at the new school, and with loneliness and feelings of failure. And, like my brother, I missed my Dunedin friends. I could not keep up, and I did not have the will to do so. It was all too overwhelming.

Christchurch at the end of the 1950s spawned two distinct species of teenage schoolgirls. The first, prim, proper, Anglican and virginal, aped their mothers and would never be seen in public without hats, gloves or handbags. They spoke properly, they stood up for 'God Save the Queen' at the cinema (but then I did too) and they probably had grandmothers who wore twinsets and pearls and spoke fondly of 'Home'. The second were tearaways who bubbled with sexuality and rebelliousness, and in cinemas pursued complementary activities to those of their straighter sisters, preferably in the back rows. In a Darwinian way, they tested themselves and tested the system. I ended up as one of the latter group, and it felt good.

Unlike naive me, they talked openly of sex and boys, and would rush home after school to change out of their uniforms, then meet up at a milk bar. The favourite was the Milky Way in High Street and there was also the Dainty Inn, with its pulley system that took orders to the kitchen. We would cram into booths and order milkshakes. If one of us had the money, we would play the jukebox: Elvis Presley, Bill Haley and the Comets, Little Richard, the Everly Brothers and Ricky Nelson. And it was the place to see boys.

Then I met Maurice. Maurice was older, in his twenties, and had a motorbike. He wore a leather jacket and jeans and reminded me of Marlon Brando in *The Wild One*. I was smitten. He would meet me after school on his motorbike. I would hear the loud revving as I tore down the corridor to the main entrance on Armagh Street, hid my bike and satchel behind the school fence for retrieval later and then leapt onto the pillion seat and we were off. The sense of freedom was exhilarating. We would hang out at his place and play records. Inevitably the casual friendship morphed into his relieving me of my virginity. I didn't really understand the act but I went along with it, enjoying the sensation of being held and cuddled more than anything else. The most formal sex education I had ever had was being given a book to read by my mother with no following discussion. I learnt more from the girls at school.

Inevitably, the school complained to my parents about my sullen and wild behaviour, especially the decline in quality of my schoolwork – I habitually did the least amount required – and my lacklustre attitude. At a round table discussion with the headmistress and my parents, I said I wanted to leave school, and my wish was granted – in the middle of the first term in 1959, when I was 15. I also left behind my short-lived relationship with Maurice. I had been at Christchurch Girls' High School for less than a year.

But leaving school was conditional. Mum insisted I attend the Digby's Commercial College, in Worcester Street, to learn shorthand, typing and bookkeeping. My class was at 4.30 for two hours once a week. I hated it, especially the shorthand, but typing was okay and once I had mastered bashing out 120 words per minute on the manual typewriter I considered myself good enough to get a job. I often bunked off to a 5 o'clock movie or a show at the Theatre Royal. All I could afford was a seat in the gods on the steeply raked third-floor gallery, but the shows were great no matter where you sat. I distinctly remember enjoying *Annie Get Your Gun*, and biking along Riccarton Road belting out 'Doin' What Comes Natur'lly', which suited my mood. After some months, the college contacted my mother and enquired why she was paying fees when I had stopped attending lessons. She was very angry with me but I was determined not to return to the monotonous and repetitive classes at Digby's. Mum said I must get a job and so I complied.

I had no idea what I wanted to do, and advice was lacking from any direction, but after scouring the ads in the *Press* my eye fell on Garrick, Cowlishaw and Clifford, Solicitors, who were requiring an office administrator. I thought the name of the firm curious and therefore decided to apply for the position. When I arrived for the interview I discovered there was only one partner, solicitor Ogilvie Garth Clifford, and no other employee. I was appointed on the spot and that was that. I could not believe that at my age I was sole charge of an office. Ogilvie Garth was a stern character, always dressed smartly in a three-piece checked suit, who arrived at the office around 10 a.m. with his morning tea and left at 5. He drove a beautiful Lagonda, which I would gaze at in awe. I was also struck by his magnificent moustache. My role was to open the office at 9 a.m. and close it at 5 p.m. If Ogilvie Garth was not in the office at lunchtime I had permission to close it for my break. My dreams of learning about the law and maybe even becoming a lawyer were dashed. Apart from some filing and tea making, my main task was to take money from a constant stream of tenants, from the multiple properties he and his mother owned, calling at the office to pay rent, write receipts and sort out the banking.

I quickly learnt that Ogilvie Garth was the only surviving child of Annette Mary Clifford, aka Ma Clifford, an eccentric who had a reputation as both an exploitative property owner and a provider of cheap accommodation. Despite this, her biographer, Margaret Lovell-Smith, has recorded that she had a motherly attitude towards her elderly tenants and would remind student tenants of the need to write home and to remember their mothers' birthdays. No one really knew the extent of their holdings but in 1962 it emerged that she and her son owned a total of 47 properties and that between 1950 and 1958 she was receiving rent from up to 550 tenants.

I was unaware that the endless pages of text I was given to type related to a civil claim by the Inland Revenue Department for alleged arrears of income tax, which Ogilvie Garth was opposing on his mother's behalf. In 1962 she was charged in the Christchurch Magistrate's Court with wilfully filing false returns of income over a nine-year period, involving a total discrepancy of £238,613. The high-profile case resulted in a conviction on all tax charges and a draconian fine of £100 for each year a false return had been filed. The verdict was later upheld by the Court of Appeal.

The work was tedious and became downright boring but it gave me the means to have a good time and buy the latest clothes. The only entertainment for my age group was going to the movies on a Friday night in Cathedral Square, hanging out at milk bars or going to the Saturday night rock'n'roll dance. When allowed, I would tag along to dances with Ralph and his friends or get a ride into town in my brother's car. On one occasion he was caught using Cathedral Square as a race track in the early hours of the morning and subsequently fined. A small piece describing his delinquent behaviour appeared in the newspaper. Dad was not pleased.

There are no movie theatres in Cathedral Square now but in the 1960s, when going to the pictures on a Friday night was de rigueur, there was one in every corner. That was also the night the shops stayed open until 9 p.m. and so the square was an exciting, colourful and lively place, the true hub of the city, where the buses, in their red livery, came and went, and the buildings were still dwarfed by the cathedral spire. Adding to the glamour of the cinemas were their elaborate façades and extravagant interiors, and their seductive neon signs. I remember the Savoy (formerly the Liberty, with two sets of futuristic neon rings cascading down the centre of its white façade), the Tivoli (once Everybody's and later the Westend, next to Chancery Lane), the Regent with its distinctive dome, the Embassy. … But my favourite was the Crystal Palace, tucked into the corner of the north-west quadrant. its entrance marked by a 32-metre tower that was illuminated at night by powerful floodlights. (It became the Carlton in 1963 but for me it was always the Crystal Palace.) In 1986 I decided to go and see the last movie there before the theatre was demolished. My love of history did not prepare me for what I was about to see. *Caligula*, all about the wicked Roman emperor, was full of violent and hard-core sex scenes; no wonder it drew an audience of men in beige raincoats. I left quickly.

When the controversial film *Ulysses*, based on James Joyce's 1922 novel, came to New Zealand in 1967, I saw it at the Plaza Theatre, which had once been the Strand. It had been banned in Ireland, and would be for decades, and though shown in Britain, it was significantly amended, thanks to the Board of Film Censors. It was released uncut in New Zealand but with the requirement that the audience was to be segregated. So, I attended a women's session. The *Evening Post* thought that those after 'sheer pornography' wouldn't find 'much to feast on', though women would be shocked. Frankly, I was underwhelmed. The word 'fuck' was not foreign to me. So, sex on the screen and a description of oral sex by one character? What was all the fuss about?

The novelty of returning to Christchurch and the new house soon wore thin for my mother. If she had been depressed in Dunedin, she became more so at Avonhead Road. It was usual, once again, to find that she had taken codeine and gone to bed in a darkened room. Then, out of the blue, she seemed to rally, took driving lessons and used her mother's legacy to buy herself a car, a Ford Prefect. This allowed her to get out of her isolated environment while the rest of the family was at work or school. She then aspired to really break free of what she saw as the housewife trap and talked of finding a job. My authoritarian father firmly forbade his wife to go to work, insisting her place was in the home, but my mother courageously, or perhaps desperately, disobeyed him. She wished to broaden her new-found freedom and did so, finding a manual job with an engineering firm. That was when the cracks started to appear in the marriage.

Mum's brother Roy was also experiencing difficulties in his marriage. After returning from a trip home to Italy, wife Ada refused to occupy the same bedroom as her husband: she had fallen in love and was having an affair. Ada ordered Roy out of the house; the marriage was over. Roy retaliated, successfully petitioning for divorce on the grounds of Ada's adultery and gaining custody of their two children, Josephine and Stephen. The affair had been conducted over a long period and was proved to have broken up the marriage.

My own parents' marital troubles intensified, with fights and arguments, and Ralph and I became collateral damage in the war between them. To complicate matters, I became even more wayward and adventurous with boys. Mum and Dad did not have the skill or the will to cope with me but it was I who was the victim – a wild child with self-destructive traits. Considered to be in moral danger, I was admitted to the gated Mount Magdala Convent for the Sisters of the Good Shepherd to 'straighten me out'. I was 16. When Ralph asked our parents, 'Where has Anne gone?', the reply was, 'She's gone away'. 'Is she having a baby?' 'No.' And that was all he was ever told. My parents would never talk to me about this episode, which affected my life so deeply. It was not, it seemed, a subject worthy of discussion. Had I really lacked a moral compass? Did they ever regret sending me to such a place? I hoped so but even in their old age, it remained unmentionable.

The harrowing 2002 film, *The Magdalene Sisters*, set in Ireland in 1964, told the story of so-called 'fallen' women who were considered sinners and must be redeemed by being sent to work at a Magdalene laundry. They were not 'bad girls': one was raped by her cousin, one was 'too beautiful and coquettish', another was an unmarried mother and the fourth was an intellectually disabled unmarried mother. The film detailed their lives while they were inmates, portraying their harsh daily regimen and the squalid living conditions at the laundry. I went to see the film with some trepidation but found that, even though many of the scenes related to my stay at Mount Magdala, I felt distanced from it all. I did wonder, however, who would have thought that such a laundry had been established in Christchurch, New Zealand.

The Catholic Sisters of the Good Shepherd, four sisters from Angers in France and two from Australia, had arrived in Christchurch in 1886. Two years later a large residential facility was opened in Halswell for women and girls suffering 'disadvantage'. Despite the place name, the asylum, as it was called, stood on 80 hectares of flat, featureless farmland off Lincoln Road. As a 1903 description put it, 'the noble women who have voluntarily relinquished the pleasures and the allurements of society, in order to devote their lives to the reclamation of their fallen sisters, have laboured assiduously in that cause'. The Good Shepherd Sisters left Mount Magdala in 1968 after 82 years' service and eight years after my own incarceration. All that now remains is a private cemetery in a paddock and some street names in the nearby Aidanfield subdivision.

The Catholic church had collaborated with the courts, sifting out the 'wayward girls', as the locals called them, who were rebellious, who ran away and who were deemed uncontrollable by their parents. These were the pickings for the Magdalene laundry. However, some Magdalenes were placed in the hands of the church by their own families, even if they were non-Catholic. I was one of those and, as it turned out, the only one at that time – a dubious distinction. I could not understand why I was sent to such a place. I did not consider myself bad and still cannot think of any particular incident that precipitated this decision. Those I lived and worked with during my time at Mount Magdala were wards of the court. They were tough but understandably so: they came from abused backgrounds and from Catholic orphanages where they had also been abused.

I arrived in my best dress, not fully comprehending where I was being placed – only that it was some sort of a correction facility, whatever that meant. I had packed a little box of treasures as a comfort and my favourite book, *Pride and Prejudice*. These disappeared from the locker beside my narrow bed within hours of my arrival. The dormitory was shared with nine other girls, as was the ablution block. This unfamiliar institutional environment was austere, the routine regimented, the meals plain, the twice-daily trips to the chapel for prayers somewhat consoling and the long hours of working in the hot, steamy laundry physically exhausting. We would launder and starch sheets, towels, napkins, tablecloths and bedspreads from various city hotels, such as the Windsor, the Excelsior and Coker's. The giant mangles were hard work but because I was not as strong as some of the other girls, I rarely worked on those and would do the sorting. There were only two words to describe the laundry, hard labour. The sisters were kind to me, though, and I was not punished like the other girls. This set me apart, which made it difficult for me to befriend those sent by the court. Withdrawn and shy, I kept to myself most of the time and sat alone. I was miserably unhappy in these alien surroundings.

Most of the girls had no personal contact with their families but I was allowed a weekly visit on a Sunday afternoon. Each time my parents came I pleaded with them to take me home. They refused. Most of my thoughts then turned on how to end this nightmare. I meticulously looked for and planned ways to escape. It was at this stage that I befriended Julie, one of the court wards. She was a rebel and fell in easily with my idea. After much plotting, we decided on a day and during the compulsory evening chapel service we slipped out and made a run for it. We had to scale two high fences to reach the outside. Once there, we just ran and ran across paddocks until we came across a small creek, where we settled for the night. Fortunately, it was a warm November evening. We decided to make our way across the paddocks the next morning to Lincoln Road to hitch a ride. After that we would play it by ear. But we only had about 12 hours of freedom. The police had been alerted and tracked us down. We could hear their dogs getting closer but had left it too late to run. By then we were tired, not having slept well, and hungry, having devoured the small amount of food we had smuggled out of the kitchen.

It was only after that episode that my parents, alerted to the breakout, relented and took me home. A week later I was a bridesmaid at my cousin Barbara's wedding, a grand family affair with no expense spared. After my recent bleak incarceration, I loved every glamorous moment of it. I had entered the convent on 27 September 1960 and was discharged, 'absconded', on 21 November 1960.

I remained utterly unconversant with reality, unconnected, and my loss of innocence exacerbated the strain of melancholy in my personality. I took refuge in sex. I was craving to be touched, to receive affection, and sex made me feel wanted, even if it was only fleetingly. My parents, concerned about my disreputable behaviour, sent me to a psychologist. 'No good will come of it,' he told me. 'You won't find love between your legs.' This phrase stayed with me for the rest of my life, and proved perceptive. I was acting without a sense of consequence but my neediness led to instant gratification and intense but temporary happiness. All the while I remained unaware of the difference between love and sex.

Ralph was also going through a rebellious phase but his was subtler. He felt lonely and depressed. Any help from his father would have been a miracle. He would often be reduced to tears of frustration and loneliness and if found crying would be told to man up. Our father called him Mannie, which he hated. This was when Ralph joined the Avonhead Rugby Club – an old-fashioned prescription perhaps but the best thing he could have done, for that was where he met his three best friends.

Before rock'n'roll hit our shores in the 1950s, and teenagers embraced the exciting post-war American culture, there was no television, few cars, life was local and the drinking age was 21 and over with six o'clock closing of the mostly squalid pubs. Dances were organised and attended by thousands of people up and down the country. For teenagers and 20-somethings it was pretty much the only form of entertainment, apart from movies. Ralph, three years older than me, was already part of that scene. He loved his music and always bought the latest rock'n'roll 45s, EPs and LPs and played them consistently. I remember his first purchase – 'Rock Around the Clock' by Bill Haley and His Comets. He wore that record out. He wore the latest bodgie gear – winkle-pickers, a long lurex jacket in dark blue, black string tie and black stovepipe trousers. He grew sideburns, and slicked his hair into the DA (duck's arse) style. I thought him so handsome. Elvis Presley's DA was legendary, and I was a fervent Elvis fan right from the first song I heard, 'Love Me Tender', in 1956. I would buy as many of his latest records as I could, then play them full blast and dance and sing along when my parents were not at home.

And there was dancing. Initially, while Ralph 'grooved' at the rock'n'roll dances, I attended the staider affairs at the Latimer. For me it was happily reliving those Wednesday afternoons in Dunedin: foxtrot medleys, the Gay Gordons, the Gypsy Tap, 'Hands, Knees and Boomps a Daisy – all innocent, good fun. Eventually, though, I succumbed to the lure of the fully-fledged rock'n'roll dances. There were other dance halls in Christchurch, including the Hibernian, the Yaldhurst and the Caledonian, but the most popular was the Spencer Street dance in Addington, which would attract more than a thousand people on any one night (even though its capacity was under 400). Entry was 2 shillings and sixpence, and, as well as the music, there were three sittings of supper – sausage rolls, sandwiches, cake and a hot drink. Roles were clearly defined: women in the kitchen and men at the door strictly preventing the drinking of alcohol inside and policing any hooliganism outside, where beer was allowed. It was a very controlled operation. From the start of the 1960s Robert Consedine was organiser and MC at Spencer Street. Robert, only two years older than me, had grown up in Addington, and at that early age was already committed to community service. Many years later, when I worked at the Robert McDougall Art Gallery, all the staff attended a course on the meaning of the Treaty of Waitangi. It was run by Robert Consedine.

On a Saturday night, when the 'Top 20' was played between 11 p.m. and midnight, the hall was often so packed you could hardly move. I did not enjoy the squeeze, preferring more space to let rip with the exuberant moves I had learnt, including being pulled through a partner's legs and rolled over his back. I could keep this up for three hours straight before taking a break. The list of top songs was handed to the bands beforehand and the competitiveness between them gave the dancers a real treat. Johnny and the Revellers were the first band and others followed – The Downbeats with Johnny Parker, Max Merritt and the Meteors, Ray Columbus, Dinah Jacobs, aka Lee, all at the beginning of stellar careers. And everyone had a cigarette: a low pall of smoke hung in the air just above our heads.

My two months at Mount Magdala had not tamed me, but merely increased my unhappiness and my escapades. Dad continued to be very strict, waiting at the gate when I came home from a date to ensure I did not sit in the car snogging. It was easy to get around that one: the snogging would be done before the drive home. I was forbidden to go out with Catholics or Māori. No reason was given. I did not know any Māori boys until I saw a singer with the band at the Spencer Street dance who imitated Little Richard. He went by the name of Little Henry and he was brilliant. I had 45s of 'Tutti Frutti' and 'Good Golly, Miss Molly' by Little Richard, and to my impressionable ears Little Henry was his equal in singing those songs. But it was his rendition of Jimmy Jones's 'Good Timin'' – 'a ticka-ticka-ticka-tick timin'', complete with yelping falsetto – that was his signature tune. It was one of my favourite 45s and I hammered it.

One Saturday night, Little Henry singled me out and worked his charm on me. I would hang around while the band packed up for the night and go back to his place. In the United States the star quality of Little Richard meant that despite segregation – blacks on the balcony and whites on the main floor – the audiences would come together to dance. In Christchurch there was no such segregation but I did encounter my first taste of racism. After one very successful dance night Little Henry and I decided we would book into the Ambassador Hotel, which had a vacancy. But the man on the night desk took one look at my Māori friend and said, 'There are no vacancies for the likes of you!' I was even more astonished when he turned to me and added, 'But, Miss, you can stay here.' Instinctively disgusted, I said to Little Henry, 'Let's get out of here!' and we scarpered.

Home was not a happy place. Around this time our parents made no attempt to hide their terrible rows and Ralph and I would huddle together for comfort, our ears to a glass pushed against the wall to better hear the arguing in the adjacent room. Unless we had done that, we would never have known that the cause of the fighting was an affair my mother was accused of having. Ralph and I confided in each other. I felt so unloved that I had become convinced I was adopted. Ralph did not feel he was loved by Mum and found Dad overpowering. We talked of our Dunedin days and how happy we both had been there.

The consumption of alcohol became a new pastime for Mum and Dad. What began as a few drinks before and after dinner escalated alarmingly into riotous and drunken dance parties, very unusual for my outwardly conventional parents. These started off as small affairs, with just a few colleagues and friends, but over the years they became legendary, with the house open to all. And what parties they were – rock'n'roll played at full blast with much laughter, singing and yelling. My mother loved it all, and flirted outrageously, but I am not so sure my father was totally enamoured. I would observe from the door and sometimes join in but, in a strange role reversal, usually took myself off to my bedroom, though there was no way of getting away from the noise. And it was nothing for me to find a body the next morning sleeping it off on my bedroom floor.

Then I met Tibor.

In October 1956, thousands of protesters had taken to the streets in Hungary demanding a more democratic political system and freedom from Soviet oppression. In response, Communist Party officials appointed Imre Nagy as the new premier. He tried to restore peace and asked the Soviets to withdraw their troops. They did so, but Nagy then tried to push the Hungarian revolt forward by abolishing one-party rule. He also announced that Hungary was withdrawing from the Warsaw Pact. The response was brutal: on 4 November 1956, Soviet tanks rolled into Budapest to crush the national uprising once and for all. Thousands were killed and wounded and nearly a quarter of a million Hungarians fled the country. The New Zealand government agreed to accept Hungarian refugees and the first draft of what would be almost 1120 arrived by air in December.

One of them was Tibor Pataky, from Budapest. When, aged 16, I met Tibor at the Spencer Street dance, he was handsome, exotic, sweet-natured and had a cute accent. And I found his stories of street fighting against tanks and the Soviet army extraordinary and exciting, and admired his courage in leaving his homeland to live in a distant foreign country. There was an element of sympathy involved as well. Between May and July 1944, 437,000 Jews had been sent to Auschwitz from Hungary, most of them gassed on arrival. Tibor's mother was among them. From the outset he, like other young male refugees, was cheerfully resolved to settle and accept the society of his new homeland.

Tibor was gainfully employed by the North Canterbury Nassella Tussock Board, grubbing tussock. Every work day he would line up with the other members of the gang to be taken by bus to various farms near Christchurch. It was hard, back-breaking work but it gave Tibor a job and an income. His first ambition was to buy a car. It was some time after I met him that I saw where he was living and I was appalled. He had a bed in the space under the stairs of a run-down Ma Clifford house in Worcester Street. Think Harry Potter, but without even a door: Tibor had only a curtain. Basic bathroom and kitchen facilities were shared. No wonder he spent every possible moment at Avonhead Road.

Over the months we went out together he became besotted with me and I found my first true love. Our pet names for each other were Annikem and Tibi. We had many fun times and he made me happy. His proposal of marriage, however, came at an unexpected moment and I was taken aback. Even though the opportunity for escape was not lost on me, I knew I would need my parents' permission. This they granted with ease, my mother even supplied the engagement ring – a sapphire and diamond ring that had belonged to my maternal grandmother. The thought of freedom from Dad's strictures gave me a sense of euphoria, albeit temporary. In hindsight, however, I believe the arrangement meant my parents could get me off their hands and Tibi would have a secure future. To agree to marriage was an impulsive and surely naïve gesture on my part. I remained capricious and unsettled, ended my engagement and decided to leave Christchurch. I did, however, keep the ring, which I considered a family heirloom. When Tibor became engaged in 1963, I was happy that he had moved on. I had done so too. Sydney beckoned and I yearned to travel there to live and work. I was almost 17.

CHAPTER 4
In Limbo

My cousin Grahame, who was already living in Sydney, agreed that I could stay with him until I found work and a place of my own. This seemed to reassure my parents but Grahame was only six years older than me and even wilder. At that time you could travel freely between Australia and New Zealand, for a permanent or temporary stay, without a passport or visa. Too easy. I booked a passage and set sail on the *Wanganella*.

In Sydney I found office work and permanent accommodation at the Ashfield Private Hotel, which was actually a boarding house, where I enjoyed the company of the other residents. The owner and landlady was Millie Phillips, a feisty little Polish woman, who ruled the establishment with precision and efficiency. Every Thursday around 5 p.m. we would all queue to pay our weekly board, which included breakfast and an evening meal. There was a roomy sitting room where we could watch television – black and white, of course. The Flintstones seemed to be the most popular programme around dinner-time. Away from home for the first time, I really played up to being 'adult'. I started smoking; everyone did. Emulating Audrey Hepburn as Holly Golightly in Breakfast at Tiffany's, I bought a long cigarette holder. I was particular about what I smoked, though: Pall Mall for everyday use, menthol when I had a cold or just wanted a change. Saved for the very best occasions was the crème de la crème of cigarettes, Sobranies. Very strong, with a heavy tar and nicotine content, they came in pretty colours that I considered the height of sophistication. And they suited my cigarette holder.

But I became restless and homesick for familiar surroundings and decided to return home in time for Ralph's twenty-first birthday in August

1962. I found that Mum had changed jobs and was now working for Hugh B. Bower & Co. Ltd – and that she was having an affair with her boss.

Ralph was given a traditional party in the local rugby rooms with family and friends, live band and supper. Dad, however, could not help himself and took the joy out of the evening by announcing to everyone that his marriage to Noeline had ended. It was a shock to us all, especially my mother, to hear of this in such a public manner. Both she and Ralph were humiliated. It was one of many acts of cruelty by Dad that was hard to forgive. He appeared to relish spoiling and upstaging what should have been a happy occasion. Ralph could not leave home quickly enough. After the party he packed his bags and moved to Nelson, where he transferred to the local branch of Young Brothers to continue his work as an auto-electrician. He did, however, return for Christmas that year, which we spent together.

And then my mother left home too. As she frenetically threw together her clothes and a few belongings, and then as she put her bags in her car, I pleaded with her not to go. But she was determined to go. I ran down the drive, chasing her retreating car, tears streaming down my face. The sense of abandonment was enormous. She stayed with her sister May before moving into a flat with Hugh Bower. I was left at home with a distraught father to make sense of the situation in the way I knew best – badly.

I found a job as office manager for the newly opened branch office of the Department of Statistics, which had the job of compiling external trade statistics. My colleagues strongly resembled the astutely observed public service stereotypes portrayed in Roger Hall's *Gliding On*. His scripted office routines could have been taken directly from our daily interchanges. Max Robertson, 16 years old, newly married and an expectant father, sat in a back room working as a clerk. Our paths would cross again many years later when I became a Christchurch city councillor and he a council staffer.

It was a happy office. We had lots of fun and my social life was enhanced by dinners and movies with my colleagues. But living at home with Dad proved difficult. He was bereft and I was on the receiving end of his sadness, anger and intermittently strange behaviour. He brought home a pet magpie, named Daphne, who ran around the backyard squawking and attacking anyone, including me, who ventured into her area. I would dread having to hang the washing out if she was not in her cage. She also annoyed the neighbours. Because her wings were not clipped, she could fly up to their chimney, where she would sit, squawking loudly, until enticed back home. To keep me company, I acquired a lovely miniature black poodle I called Susie, who became my constant companion. But though I enjoyed my job I knew I could not continue to be a full-time housekeeper and cook for my father. I decided to request a transfer to the Wellington office. That way I would have a legitimate reason for leaving my father without hurting him further. The plan worked and my request was granted. In the middle of 1963, aged 19, taking Susie with me, I went north.

The office, on the second floor of the Progress Motors Building in Victoria Street, was a large room set up with about 40 desks and chairs plus a large section of metal shelving for storing the processed customs entries for the port of Wellington. My job was coding the licensed goods imported into New Zealand in that protectionist era. Although head office was so much larger, I made friends with some of my coding colleagues, particularly Millie Rogers, who kindly agreed to give Susie a home, and Mrs Melhuish, both of whom took me under their wing. Once a week I would go home with Millie for dinner. Her husband, Walter, was a prison officer and they lived in a prison house on Mount Crawford. These were happy evenings, full of family comings and goings, laughter and chatter. They also had a son about my age, who kept asking me out. And they had a television. My visits also meant time with Susie. Mrs Melhuish, who lived alone, wore deathly pale make-up on her very wrinkled face and used a cigarette holder, had been a proof reader at *Truth* before joining Statistics. She spoiled me, buying me presents – clothes and jewellery – every payday. The only way I could repay her kindness was to go home with her after work and cook a meal for us both.

My supervisor, Hamilton Baxter, would also ask me to his place for meals. A serious-minded young man, he was studying part time for a BA in English at Victoria University. I did not realise at the time that George, who shared his house, was also his partner. Hamilton and I would go dancing at the Downtown Club on Customhouse Quay and remained friends for the rest of our lives.

I rented a bedsit in a big old weatherboard house in Boulcott Street. I shared a bathroom and toilet with several others but my one room was

large enough for a single bed, a chair and table. I was supplied with a
hotplate and power point for a kettle and toaster. I loved it there. It was
an easy walk to work and I had a wonderful outlook over the remarkable
St Mary of the Angels church and beyond to the central city. The bathroom
contained a large, stained, oddly coffin-shaped bath with a califont gas
water heater, an enormous contraption of pipes which, when coins were
inserted into the box on the wall, would rattle and shake and produce a
gush of gorgeous hot water. I would lie in the bath, with the door locked of
course, dreaming and planning and occasionally topping up the hot water.

Then, after answering an advertisement, I moved into a flat in
Majoribanks Street, Mount Victoria, with three female flatmates – a teacher,
a nurse and what was then called an air hostess. It was a wonderful time
and our parties became legendary. We were also close to the darkened and
atmospheric central city coffee shops, complete with chianti bottles with
dripping candles. My beau of the hour, lovely, caring English-born Gerry,
turned out to be more permanent. We became engaged – my second fiancé.
Because he was close to his parents, and mine were enmeshed in their
own lives, I was happy to agree that we should marry in England. To raise
the cost of the fare I worked Friday nights and weekends as a waitress at
a Greek café in Lambton Quay. I was there when the terrible news came
through that John F. Kennedy had been assassinated in Dallas.

CHAPTER 5
A Kiwi OE with a Difference

In May 1964, aged 20, with a brand-new passport and a wallet of travellers' cheques, I embarked at Wellington on the *Fairsea* bound for England, where Gerry would be waiting for me. We would marry in Selsey, a quaint seaside town about 12 kilometres south of Chichester in West Sussex. In my luggage was the something 'borrowed' – the wedding dress of Gwennie, my Uncle Roy's much younger second wife, whom he had married the previous October and which fitted me perfectly. There had been another family wedding just a few weeks before my departure: in March I had been a bridesmaid when Ralph married Janice Caesar. I was happy to learn that they had decided to settle in Christchurch.

In the waving crowd on the quayside below me was HB, as Hugh Bower was known, my mother and Gwennie, who had all travelled up from Christchurch to see me off. As the ship slipped its moorings and edged slowly away from the pier, a band struck up 'Now is the Hour', made famous by Vera Lynn and often played when New Zealand soldiers left for the Second World War. I stayed at the railing as the gap widened between ship and shore, tears streaming down my face as Wellington slowly receded into the distance. I felt excited about what lay ahead and not at all fearful for my journey to the other side of the world – it was a moment of total self-reliance.

My cabin mate was a middle-aged woman who did not approve of me coming to bed at all hours of the morning and then sleeping through most of the day. It was an unfortunate coincidence that she also knew my father. I hardly saw or spoke with her. Also on board was a close friend of Ada's, who had been on the same war bride ship to New Zealand. Tina and I met up from time to time but generally I made the most of the freedom of this wild shipboard life, unlike anything I had encountered before.

I did not want to bypass Egypt and lose the opportunity of seeing its ancient treasures and so on 9 June, instead of proceeding through the Suez Canal on the ship, I caught a bus across the desert to Cairo. Because my time was short, I had to be selective about what I would see. Missing ancient Thebes with its necropolis was unfortunate but a camel ride tour to the pyramids at Giza more than compensated. I was able to climb up the outside of the Great Pyramid and then down, rather nervously, into the dimly lit inner tunnel that led to the burial chamber. I tried to imagine how Howard Carter must have felt in 1922 when he discovered Tutankhamun's nearly intact tomb with over 5000 artefacts. The next visit then had to be the Cairo Museum to see the boy pharaoh's gold coffin and famous mask of gold, and other remarkable and unique treasures.

Then I fearlessly, but foolishly, explored on foot areas of the city where tourists were forbidden to go. The Suez crisis of 1956 had passed but Britain had the right to station peace-keeping troops in Egypt for the defence of the Suez Canal and they had a strong presence in Cairo. The British patrol caught up with me, sitting cross-legged in a back street, having joined a circle of seated Arabs who were taking turns at smoking a hubble bubble pipe. It was particularly unfortunate that I was caught just as I was about to indulge. I was thoroughly reprimanded, then bundled onto a rather rickety bus that was travelling north to Port Said on a narrow road by the banks of the Nile. The Egyptian countryside was riveting, the green strip where the Nile flooded dotted with white villages and beyond, as if nature had drawn a line, the dry and biscuit-coloured desert. Farmers were ploughing with oxen and the country villages and farm buildings looked so quaint to my imperialist eyes. It was not an easy mission for me to board the *Fairsea*, which had already left but had weighed anchor, waiting for me to be transported across by boat. I was unceremoniously taken on board and the trip across the Mediterranean began. I promptly took ill. Feverish, achy and suffering from dreadful headaches, I was confined to the ship's hospital. What I had managed to contract from my experience in Cairo was a dose of malaria.

Also travelling on the *Fairsea* was a young Italian, Vincenzo, who swept me off my feet with his Latin charm. Thousands of miles from home, on the open ocean. This was the loving relationship I had always dreamed of. I fell madly in love. When it came time for him to disembark at his hometown of Naples, he asked me to go with him. My spontaneous decision was 'yes' and so on 12 June 1964, without another thought, not even of my fiancé, I stepped onto Italian soil. As I was leaving the ship, a crew member asked if I would take a parcel on shore for him. Of course I obliged, without knowing what was in it. In the very cavernous shed on the wharf where customs was situated I was assailed by a cacophony of excited Italian voices, loud, laughing and happy, as people went about their chores, greeted relatives and friends and moved baggage and cargo. As I was walking towards the customs bench, dragging my luggage behind me (no wheels then), one of my stiletto heels broke. To my amazement, I was besieged by a pack of young Italian men wanting to assist me, the customs officer waved me through without a care and suddenly I was outside in the sunshine staring at the city of Naples, waiting for Vincenzo. It did not enter my head that I could have been stranded there. I sent a telegram to Gerry saying I was stopping off at Naples with a friend to travel around Italy and I would let him know in a few weeks when I would be arriving.

After staying for a few days with Vincenzo's non-English-speaking family in their apartment – an experience that fed my nascent addiction to central-city living – he and I spent idyllic weeks touring Naples and its environs in his Bambina, sleeping in little villages along the way. I learnt what a real Italian pizza looked and tasted like and how to eat spaghetti with just a fork (Neapolitan style), I was serenaded by charming violinists at restaurants and of course I worked on my Italian vocabulary. After just a few days I became quite fluent. It was all so easy and romantic but the longer we were together the more I identified a streak of jealousy and possessiveness in Vincenzo's make-up. He would make ridiculous scenes if I even looked at another man and accuse me of flirting. Feeling I was too young to cope with all this, I made the decision to continue my journey to England. After all, I had some explaining to do to my fiancé. Leaving Vincenzo, however, turned out to be decidedly difficult. He did not want me to go and at one stage I thought he might even try to physically stop me. But I caught trains from Naples to Calais, a ferry over to Dover and then a train into London, where loyal Gerry was there to meet me. I was so happy to see him, even if suffering a little guilt at my deception. By the time we had travelled by bus from London over the Sussex Downs to Selsey, I was exhausted.

At Gerry's parents' house I slept in a very pretty attic bedroom, with a handbasin in the corner, which had obviously been redecorated specially for my arrival. Gerry and I got to know each other again and became intimate for the first time. This did not, though, improve things on the home front. His parents were polite but there was an undercurrent of hostility from his tight-lipped mother, who was as stony as the local beach. His father was quite different, a quiet and reserved man who was obviously dominated by his more vocal wife. She accused me of wanting to marry her son to get a British passport. I was stunned that she should think that and showed her mine, which said 'British subject and New Zealand citizen'. But then some of the questions she asked astonished me with their ignorance. Were doctors in New Zealand? Did the natives wear grass skirts? Gerry was apologetic about his parents but I had had enough of hostilities and living in a tense household and had no wish to invite more grief. A long-term relationship was not going to work. I moved further down the road to board with their neighbour Doris. Gerry and I remained good friends and I would see him from time to time even when he returned to New Zealand to live.

Doris bred and showed cocker spaniels and they and their hair were everywhere in the house, which reeked of dog. But Doris was kind and welcoming and very excited to have me as her paying guest. She was a little upset, though, when, at breakfast, I would slather great chunks of butter on my toast. I had not realised that she had bought New Zealand butter to please me and that it was an expensive luxury. The butter soon disappeared to be replaced by margarine – a new experience for me. I found work at the local hotel, where I seemed to do a little bit of everything, mostly waitressing and reception, except cooking (like my mother, never my strong point). Doris owned a magnificent Bentley S2, which was kept in pristine condition in the garage – no dogs allowed – and was hired on a regular basis, among other clients, by a wealthy film producer's elderly mother, who lived in Selsey for the benefit of the sea air. She would be driven several nights a week to a small local casino, where she gambled and drank. I became her handsomely paid companion, escorting her into the casino and leaving her to enjoy herself while I waited at the bar. I did not drink much then but I do recall imbibing the occasional Scotch. When she was ready to leave I would accompany her home, prepare a night-cap and help her undress and get ready for bed. At the hotel I met a gorgeous young Irishman called Ronan and we soon became lovers. He was living with his sister in Selsey and I was boarding with Doris so there were some very romantic beach encounters under the stars.

One day a delightful young German family – Jürgen, Henrietta and their two little girls, Heidi and Jenny – arrived for a holiday and I offered to babysit so the parents could have evenings out. The girls adored me and we became so close that Henrietta said, 'Come back with us to Germany as our au pair.' I gave notice to my employer, who was not pleased I was going so soon, said goodbye to Doris and the pooches and climbed into the back of the family car with the girls to begin the journey to the cathedral city of Cologne.

I loved the German lifestyle, and the girls, and my German vocabulary increased steadily. Jürgen worked at the Ford Motor Company through the week and I would assist Henrietta with housework and child-minding. Their upstairs apartment was large and I had my own room. I loved sitting on the fire escape outside my window, enjoying a cigarette and gazing over the city, especially at night. But then Jürgen spoilt it all. He started to become just a little too friendly. I would have to push his hand away from my knee when he reached under the table during dinner. I resented his advances and certainly gave him no encouragement. On one occasion there was a flaming row about me and Henrietta threw a glass of water over him. He quietly left the table with his hair dripping. I was so embarrassed that he found me sexually attractive. I would tell him that I was not interested but his lack of control overshadowed my life. Do men not realise that it is in a woman's DNA to detect unfaithfulness?

The final straw was when he offered to keep me in my own apartment so he could visit me there. He told me I was beautiful, vivacious, funny and intelligent but his intentions were more than clear and I would have none of it. I adored Henrietta, Heidi and Jenny. I knew I had to leave. I was truly sad to go; being part of a happy family had meant so much to me, even for such a short time.

On my return to England, I settled in Chichester, rented a bedsit and found a job. Then I discovered that I was pregnant, having conceived sometime around early August. I was bewildered. Although I had a sketchy knowledge about contraception, I was incredibly naïve and relied on my partners to be enlightened and take the necessary precautions. This was the swinging sixties, when the pill revolutionised sex and society, but like poor old Philip Larkin and sexual intercourse, it came too late for me. I did not consider having an abortion because I had no knowledge of such a procedure.

Men often told me that I was attractive, but such compliments meant nothing because I did not feel like that inside. I placed no value on myself and, more than anything else, simply felt detached. Life was one big party and lessons were hard learnt.

I went to find Ronan to tell him he was to be a father, but he had left his sister's house and moved elsewhere – she would not tell me where. Then Vincenzo came over to England to ask me again to marry him and live with him in Naples. He was very hurt by my refusal. There were many things in England that I, accustomed to 'colonial' prosperity, could not comprehend – the family of one work colleague did not have a bathroom but brought a bath into the house on a Sunday for the family to take turns to bathe – but the free National Health Service was excellent and looked after me well during my pregnancy.

I had written to Mum with my new address and it was a revelation to receive a letter. It told me that her decree absolute had been awarded on 16 December 1964. She was finally freed from my father and took no time in formalising her de facto relationship with Hugh Bower: they were married on 11 January 1965. The following day, alone in a bedsit in Chichester, five months pregnant, I celebrated my twenty-first birthday. To mark the occasion I bought myself a silver cross and chain from the jeweller just around the corner. My loneliness and even homesickness were overwhelming, though they were interrupted from time to time by a kindly traffic planner in another bedsit, who would invite me for the occasional meal. Other than that, I watched television and walked. Financial survival was difficult as I had had to give up my job. Christchurch beckoned.

I needed to tell my mother I wanted to come home and why. (I had no idea where my father was at this stage.) This time I flew, which took days. After the plane left London on 5 February it stopped to refuel in Rome, Beirut, Karachi, Bangkok and then Singapore. When I fell ill on the leg to Singapore, the airline sent a message to my mother and Hugh. Through his network of contacts, Hugh arranged for me to be collected from the airport in Singapore and chauffeur driven to a private hospital, where I spent a luxurious and relaxing four days. The medical care was excellent and when my health recovered I was able to continue my journey. (Somehow my passport had gone missing, but I was able to return home without it. It was eventually returned to me by post.) The tears began to fall as I left Sydney and did not stop until I landed in Christchurch. My dry-eyed mother and HB were at the airport to meet me.

CHAPTER 6
Out of the Frying Pan ...

While I awaited the birth of my child I went to live with my mother and HB
in their Kilmore Street apartment. It was his decision to 'take Anne in', as
Mum put it. Despite this kindness, it was a time for reflection and sadness.
The dilemma of whether to keep the baby or have it adopted was never
far from my mind. Mum was staunchly for having the baby adopted – to
give it a better life 'than you ever could'. She made it quite clear to me how
ashamed she was of having an illegitimate grandchild. In those days the
stigma attached to being an unmarried mother was strong and the shame
palpable. But I was not keen to decide just then. The days of waiting seemed
endless. I had to keep to my bedroom most of the time so that no one,
especially visitors, would see the obviously pregnant unmarried daughter.

There was time to prepare. Knitting was one of my favourite ways of
relaxing and the needles clacked continuously as I made layettes, booties,
hats and little matinee jackets. The sewing basket made an appearance too
as colourful smocking was added to plain nighties and little embroidered
rosebuds to the finished knitted garments. I was also able to help Ralph,
who was frantically trying to finish his bright red hot-rod for the speedway's
new racing season. My contribution was keeping the bodywork clean –
washing and polishing.

The contractions started around 5 a.m. on 10 May 1965 and I was fearful.
By 7.30 they were much stronger. It was a Monday and my mother said
she would drop me off at the hospital on her way to work. And so she did,
leaving me to face the birth alone, entirely without comfort and support.
The nursing staff at St Helen's Hospital (later Christchurch Women's
Hospital) were professional but distant. It was a lonely and frightening
experience but I had no choice. After all, this must be a punishment for

my misspent youth. I decided that my mother must be right – it was the best thing for the baby to be adopted and to be part of a family with two parents. What could I do as a young unmarried mother with no money and no family support? I had no qualifications and there was no domestic purposes benefit in those days. Finally convinced it was the right thing to do, I made the final decision. The staff had been alerted and preparations were made for the baby to be adopted. Labour was a long and lonely experience. As the baby's head was crowning, a pillow was put on my chest so that I could not see the baby when it was born. The child was whisked away immediately. All I was told was that it was a baby girl and that I was able to give her a name: I called her Pamela Anne.

Then I went home to Mother.

A wave of post-partum depression hit me. I was so mentally and physically exhausted I felt I had nothing more to give. It took some weeks of recuperating at Kilmore Street before I felt able to function again, but the wounds from that experience have taken a lifetime to heal. I was not unaware that my daughter, once she learnt that she was adopted, might also feel betrayal and pain.

In 1992 I was able to see the adoption order for Pamela Anne Hichens, dated 4 February 1966 and made in the Invercargill Magistrate's Court. The surnames of the adoptive parents were redacted but I learnt that they had called the baby Jeanette Ulla. I also learnt that my daughter had weighed 7 pounds (3.2 kilograms) and had no physical defects. My not unflattering description read: 5' 7", slim, light brown hair with auburn tinge, blue-grey eyes, fair skin, freckles. Reserved and refined girl.' I noted wryly that baby Hichens had been conceived in England with an Irish father, born in New Zealand and until their marriage her adoptive father, Clifford, had been a British citizen resident in New Zealand, her adoptive mother, Helga, a German citizen resident in Switzerland. After the parents' divorce, Helga and Jeanette went to live in Munich.

My mother made it clear that I should move on and find myself a place to live and work. She wished to return to the familiar life she had been enjoying with her new husband without me under her feet. I, on the other hand, was forced to weigh the need for solitude against facing the world again. I located a bedsit on the first floor of a huge old house on the corner of Hereford Street and Rolleston Avenue, now the site of the YMCA. The large, sunny room had a picture window looking out over the Botanic Gardens and the back door off the galley kitchen opened onto a fire escape that reminded me of Cologne. I could sit there quietly smoking and gazing at the neo-Gothic wonder of the University of Canterbury buildings and the multiplicity of roofs beyond. I started as a novice law clerk at a local solicitors' office an easy walk away in Cathedral Square. Although it mostly entailed typing legal documents and wills, I enjoyed the work. However, one of the partners consistently pinched my bottom and made salacious remarks every time I entered his office. I complained but when nothing changed I moved to an importing company, where I worked as a clerk and played goal shoot in their netball team.

The days passed pleasantly enough. I enjoyed the odd date, but I did experience periodic loneliness and looking back, I can see that I used mindless diversion to alleviate the lingering emotional pain. On days when I would withdraw into myself and evaluate my life, thoughts of my baby's adoption would overwhelm me and I would struggle to keep the gathering melancholy at bay. I did decide to take driving lessons, get my licence and buy my first car. It was truly an old bomb, a 1948 Ford Prefect sedan, painted an unpleasant green and selected for me by Uncle Roy, who gave it a good inspection before I paid for it. I named it Maud (rhymed with Ford). Its dodgy clutch was tricky to coordinate with the gears, which led to much bunny hopping until I mastered it, but it was great for getting to the beach. It was not long before I traded Maud in for a dark green 1952 model Triumph Mayflower, making a £15 profit on the deal. It was a dream to drive and had demisters, heater, indicators that worked and a column change. Its name? Petal. I had to stop hiring a TV in order to meet the monthly payments on the car but I considered it well worth it. On Friday nights I worked as receptionist at my sister-in-law Jan's hairdressing salon; she and Ralph were expecting their first child and she needed the help.

In 1966, too, Dad met and began to live with Joan Tibbots. I liked Joan and she was good to him, and to me, and an excellent cook. After two months in Australia, where my father worked in Brisbane and Melbourne to upskill and gain overseas experience, he and Joan shifted to Wellington, where Dad had been offered a very senior position with the Post and Telegraph Department. After that move he and I lost contact for a long time.

❖

My love for dance sent me in two very different directions: I joined a dance troupe for cabaret shows and was also hired as a part-time go-go cage dancer at the Plainsman Nightspot in Lichfield Street. The former I joined after seeing an advertisement that said 'little experience required as lessons will be given in jazz dance'. Judy, the principal, was a talented professional dancer who set about training a chorus line for the burgeoning Christchurch night club and cabaret scene. She did everything – the choreography to her chosen music, the costumes, the bookings and the teaching. I passed the audition and with two others and Judy, made up a small group to be hired for cabaret engagements. The rehearsals were brutal. It was practise, practise, practise every night until we got a routine right. Judy did not let us rest until we were step perfect. My favourite piece was our routine to the Henry Mancini theme music for the TV show, *Peter Gunn*. The finale for each show was the cancan, with its famous high kicks. To relax, we would often hang out at the Flamingo in Hereford Street, the Embassy in Manchester Street or the Albatross Coffee Lounge in the Square.

And then there was the go-go dancing, in a cage, a craze imported from Europe. Rather than being suspended from the ceiling, two cages were elevated on plinths, one on each side of the band, with flashing lights trained on the dancers inside. All this was new and exciting to me, dressed in my mini-skirt and knee-length, high-heeled boots. It would certainly send a very different message today.

For New Year's Eve 1966, my friend Jacqui and I decided to celebrate in Timaru. It turned out to be a nightmare of a trip. Petal blew a head gasket just before reaching Ashburton. I tried pushing the car while Jacqui steered but it was too heavy for me. Two young men, Ian and Peter, on their way to Timaru for the same reason as us, stopped to help and said they would tow us on to the next garage. Ian sat on the bonnet of my car holding the rope on the bumper with his feet. The rope caught around his ankle and he was dragged off the car and along the road. The seat of his jeans and underpants were ripped out and he was bleeding profusely. Fortuitously, Ian's aunt lived nearby. She patched him up and the boys towed my car to her place.

Then the four of us resumed our journey to Timaru in the boys' car. Suddenly, though, it stopped – a broken back axle. I blacked out at that stage and started to bleed badly all over the back seat. A passing car stopped and took me off to the Ashburton hospital, where I spent New Year's Eve, while the others slept in the car by the side of the road. I had apparently damaged my insides when I was attempting to push the Triumph. I was let out of hospital the next day with instructions to rest. We had two broken-down cars, a public holiday, no mechanics on duty and no tools. What to do? Ring Uncle Roy. He and Gwennie said they would come to our rescue but they arrived in a taxi – their car had broken down as well. After three days, thanks to makeshift repairs, one car was finally able to tow another. The third was taken back to Christchurch by a tow truck.

Nineteen sixty-seven began with a constant round of dancing, parties and sunbathing, but it was also a time to reflect. I wanted to do something worthwhile, but what? I had always been interested in politics but I also had a hunger for knowledge. Therefore, as I was over 21 and eligible to enrol, I decided to go to university and study English. Support for my decision came from an unexpected source – my mother. She even encouraged me further by offering to pay my admittedly then very modest fees. In a letter to Hamilton I proudly announced my first mark of 16/20 on an essay about 'The moral psychology of Henry Fielding's *Joseph Andrews*'. The lecturer did, however, add that 'your grammar leaves much to be desired'. The arts faculty of the university had not yet moved to Ilam and the lectures were still held on the city site. I loved being a student there – the romance of the neo-Gothic architecture, the cloisters, the clattering of shoes on the wooden floors, the lecture rooms with initials carved into the lids of the desks, even the smell of wet clothes flung over the radiators to dry during lectures. I revelled in the campus atmosphere and loved the learning but I felt alienated and lonely there. Despite my attempts to educate and better myself, my unsettled state got the better of me and I did not continue my studies or complete the year.

No one had any idea of my deep longing to belong somewhere, to be loved and even married, with children. I covered it well. Maybe Mum was right, all I was good for was marriage. All my friends and work colleagues were either married or about to be married. At 23, and single, I was an oddity. The search for love did not dominate my life but there was always a glimmer of hope that one day I would find the right man. Then I met and fell deeply in love with M. He was tall, blond, charming and English.

The courtship was fairly standard – getting to know each other and having fun. I was open and transparent about myself, but he was very tight-lipped about his past. I did learn that his father was a seafarer who had lived in the large seaport of Grimsby in Lincolnshire, where M was born. He, too, went to sea and when I met him he was a petty officer on an English cargo ship. He loved boxing: his nickname, for obvious reasons, was Canvas-back Crighton. He obviously relished his long periods at sea, and I did too. Having fended for myself for so long, and always enjoyed financial and social independence, it was refreshing to have time to myself when he was away. But because he was absent so much and when he was home there was just the two of us, I did not often witness how he interacted with others. Looking back, I realise I never got to know what kind of a person he really was.

Our marriage took place in the Christchurch Registry Office just before Christmas 1967. I do not have a photo of what seemed a genuinely happy day: I subsequently destroyed them all. There was no reception to speak of, just a few drinks and basic catering with friends and close family in HB's factory staffroom, and no honeymoon planned. We rented a flat in Geraldine Street and my married life began. It was there I received my first beating. We were not even fighting when it happened and I was shocked at his anger. My misdemeanour? I had washed one of his jerseys and shrunk it. He was, of course, sorry afterwards and pleaded for forgiveness. And I gave it. It would never happen again, he said. But the beatings continued at unexpected times. His rages came to dominate the marriage.

Unsure what to do, and never having been subjected to physical force, I put up with this pendulum of uncertainty. I stoically carried on, not wanting to cause a fuss and certainly not wishing to prove, so soon after the ceremony, that my marriage was a mistake. But with each beating I became more withdrawn and subdued. After I discovered a hand gun in his possession I panicked and unthinkingly threw it and the bullets into the fire. I then had to dive behind the couch as the ammunition started exploding around the room. Needless to say, I was severely thrashed for my action, which only exacerbated my already fraught state of mind. We had to move flats twice because of the rows. Neighbours would complain of the raised voices, of the beatings and my crying and screaming. It was all very embarrassing and humiliating. M did not live in the third place for long as he was away at sea, but Ralph came to stay for a short time when his own marriage was in strife. My brother spoke of his problems but I was not prepared to share my own pain.

I carried on as best I could under a cloud of inadequacy, insecurity and ever-diminishing self-esteem. Then M bought us a house in Waltham. This gave me a chance to do some nest building while I pretended to be happily married. It also meant we were distanced from neighbours. While my husband was away, I pottered quietly around home and garden and went to work, but it was at this house that M's behaviour became even more extreme. His violence arrived from nowhere – no pattern, no warning, no reason. On one occasion when he tried to strangle me, the bruises around my neck were so bad, and I was so frightened, that I went to the police. Their only advice was for me to make a formal complaint against my husband but I was too scared to do that. One of the officers said he would drive me home and have a few words with M, but I implored him not to as the ramifications for me would be worse. M had already threatened to kill me if I ever told anyone. I was so numb to the abuse that I believed him. It was then that I realised I had no one to protect me. I really was on my own. The first women's refuge in Christchurch was not opened until 1973 and I knew of nowhere else to go.

Once, when I was having a bath, he tried to push my head under the water. As I struggled, my toe caught on the chain to the plug and pulled it free, letting the water escape. Badly bruised and terrified, I simply could not understand why he would do this to me. It seemed all so surreal that I even started to doubt that it really happened. I carried a fear of drowning in the bath for most of my life and would draw only a shallow one unless I could lock the door to the bathroom.

Oh, how isolated I felt, physically, mentally and emotionally. After each abusive session I would plan to leave, but where would I go? Admit to my mother I had made another dreadful mistake? And would she believe me if I told her what I was being subjected to? Would anyone believe me? I would leave for a walk or a drive in the countryside but I always went back, and back again, after each bad experience. I did think of a plan to leave him but these were fairly loose thoughts and did not amount to anything definite. It seemed that every time I came to the end of my tether he would either threaten to kill me or, confusingly, become loving and agreeable.

Lacking the energy or the will to resist or fight this coercion, I retreated into myself.

Helpful and reassuring for me was the presence of a neighbour, Margaret Payne, who lived alone in a little cottage with a beautiful garden. She was so charming, and a great cook, and we became friends. She proudly told me over a cup of tea one afternoon that she was the mother of Alison Holst, the celebrated food writer and television chef, Patricia Payne, the well-known operatic mezzo-soprano, and food stylist Clare Ferguson. I visited Margaret often and turned to her at difficult times. She offered tea, warmth and sympathy but of course there was little she could do for me.

Then I found out that I was going to have a baby. This led to a change in my husband's behaviour when he came home on leave. Fleeting moments of happiness lulled me into a false sense of security and my pregnancy gave me an inner strength that had been lacking up until then. All I knew was that the beatings stopped.

But a more insidious practice was in store for me. It was only much later that I learnt what it was. M served me Mickey Finns – drinks doctored with chloral hydrate, commonly used in sexual assaults and then readily available at chemist shops. I did not drink alcohol at that point but was very partial to Lemon & Paeroa. M would pour me a drink, add chloral hydrate and once I was suitably mellow sexually violate me in unspeakable ways. This happened often. (It was still legal at that time to rape your wife.) I felt totally powerless and bewildered but inwardly my resolve to leave him was gaining momentum.

My life revolved around my baby. For the birth I booked myself into the maternity wing of Calvary Private Hospital in Bealey Avenue, a handsome building I had always admired. There, on Friday 19 September 1969, Women's Suffrage Day, after a difficult birth, my son was born. When he finally emerged, he was wrapped in a caul or amniotic membrane, a soft, jelly-like bubble. This rare thing of beauty happens in only one in 80,000 births. Possession of a baby's caul was said to bring its bearer good luck and to offer protection against death by drowning. Cauls were therefore highly prized by sailors. The irony of this was not lost on me. Those born inside their amniotic sac are considered lucky, special or protected. I gazed at my baby in wonder, counted his fingers and toes and declared him perfect. It was a euphoric moment. I would love and protect him for the rest of his and my life.

This birth was so different from the distressing and traumatic time I had experienced four years earlier. Now I was able to indulge myself fully in the wonderful sensation of having a baby I could keep and cherish. Although, as with my daughter, I went through this experience alone because M was away at sea, I was glad. This was the happiest day of my life and would prove to be a prodigious turning point.

Until July I had been working as PA to the director of fishing company P. Feron & Son Ltd and these pay packets had allowed me to shop for my baby. Excitedly, I purchased a bassinet, a cot and high chair in the colonial style, plus a pram and all the accessories required for a new baby. Everything I had lovingly sewn and knitted for my daughter I now repeated for my boy. My love of the classics led me to call him Dorian, after the dominant people of ancient Greece around 1200 BC. The Dorians influenced Greek art through, for example, their composition of choral lyrics, which were sung at festivals. I was so happy. My son was the centre of my life.

I saw M rarely after the birth because he was away at sea most of the time. In 1968 my brother had moved to Auckland with his new partner, Nova, and Dorian and I went to visit them at their home in Royal Oak. I was in a fragile state and found it comforting being in a normal environment. Although I missed my brother and felt sad that he lived so far away, I was delighted to see him in such a loving relationship. While I was up north M returned on leave, thought I had left him and begged me to come home. When I got back to Christchurch he greeted me with a new car – an MG sports. The next time we saw each other was to be the last.

Just after Dorian's first birthday, I refused to swallow a drink that M gave me. On this occasion I sensed something amiss. It was his insistence that made me suspicious. He became angry and violent and tried to force the liquid down my throat. It was a long struggle but I fought back. Somewhere in the background I heard 'Mama'. Terrified and with my heart pounding, I finally freed myself, grabbed Dorian, who by then had been thrown against the wall, and desperately ran across the road to my neighbour. That was the tipping point. I waited until M left the house, dashed home while my neighbour kept watch, packed as much as I could, rang for a taxi and left. The violence against my infant son finally gave me the strength to leave.

Protecting him was all that mattered. I was determined that Dorian would have the love and stability that had eluded me. I did not want him to be any part of his monstrous father's life. Neither of us ever saw M again.

My main focus now was Dorian and being with him for his formative years. I would have to find work to support us. Not having any qualifications and certainly not wanting to leave Dorian in the care of others, I had only one choice – a live-in job somewhere. My mother, with whom we had stayed after I left M, tried to talk me out of it. 'You should find a proper job and put Dorian into day care. He'll thank you for going out to work for him.' But I remained adamant. Also M had frequently threatened me with his intention to leave the country, taking Dorian with him. The best plan for me was to get out of Christchurch and that was just what I did. In the *Press* one day I spied a live-in position, housekeeping for a country doctor. Perfect. After being interviewed by Dr Pat Cotter, on behalf of his colleague, Dr Alan H. Meikleham, aka Meik, a GP based in the North Canterbury town of Waikari, I was offered the position which I gladly accepted.

I whispered to Dorian, 'Well, my boy, you and I are off together on an adventure.'

CHAPTER 7
Adrift

Waikari was a sleepy little town. At the end of the road that branched inland from the main highway, Meik's house and surgery stood on a rise, with a magnificent view over the valley from the bay window of the sitting room. In the long window seat were hundreds of bottles of whisky accumulated over the years, each presented to the doctor on the birth of a baby. Meik did not like whisky. The house was peaceful, it was cosy, it was safe and it was a haven for Dorian and me. My job as housekeeper was to cook, clean, run the surgery and 'man' the radio/telephone, used to communicate with Meik when he was travelling on his country rounds. (The practice covered an area from Waiau in the north to Leithfield in the south and the lakes district in the west.) I had one day a week off but rarely took it.

Meik's runabout was a Ford Escort in which he clocked up an average of 64,000 kilometres a year, but at the weekend he would bring out his 'Sunday car', which was always the latest Mercedes, and take us for a drive. I enjoyed the relaxed atmosphere of Waikari and threw myself into country life. When the local drama group advertised that they were entering a play in a national competition and needed volunteers, I thought, 'I'll have a go at that.' I had no aspirations for an acting role but was happy to work backstage and became the props person for the production of *Billy Liar* that won us third place for our category.

Mum drove up to visit me quite often. We were almost friends by now and, like most grandparents, she was indulgent with her little grandson. Ralph called in as well before he went off to Bougainville to ply his trade at the copper mine and save for a house in Auckland. I loved seeing him again and was tearful when we parted. I also made a new friend. Millie Ford was one of Meik's patients and he had said to her, 'You'll have to meet my new housekeeper. Her skirts are as short as yours.' So she rang and invited me for afternoon tea. We struck up an instant rapport that was the start of a very special lifelong relationship. Millie would visit me most days, walking the short distance between our two houses, and Meik would join us for lunch. Millie was a tall, strikingly attractive and elegant young woman. Although she was pregnant when we met she dressed with style. She and her husband Keith, a gruff, no-nonsense man of few words, had a son, Michael, who was 10 days younger than Dorian. Millie and I would often stroll around Waikari with the boys in their pushchairs and on really hot days would stop at the pub for a shandy, sitting on the porch in the sun, chatting happily.

Since I had some time off over the New Year of 1971, a family summer holiday was planned in Havelock, at the head of Pelorus Sound. HB, with Mum, sailed his yacht *Safari* north from Lyttelton, Ralph and Nova came down from Auckland, HB's children, Alan and Lea, came from Palmerston North, and Dorian and I drove up from Waikari. I had arranged for Dorian to be christened at St Luke's, a cute little 1950s church at Linkwater, not far from Havelock. Sadly, Dorian was too big for the christening gown that Lea had made, but I dressed him in white and he looked beautiful. Nova, Ralph and Lea became Dorian's sponsors and with the five other people in the congregation to swell our party of eight, it proved to be a joyous occasion. The following night Nova, Lea and I slept on *Safari*. Cyclone Rosemary was imminent and the boat rocked, creaked and groaned all night. We all drank far too much beer and told spooky stories. When it came time to pee we simply hung our bare rear ends over the side.

The holiday, designed for our newly blended families to get to know one another, was not a great success. The weather was terrible. My headaches and rash, the usual signs of tension and worry for me, had returned due to the edginess in the atmosphere. Ralph did not like HB and wanted to leave early but Nova insisted he stay the distance. We did our best but the occasion was never repeated and over the ensuing years the step-siblings and I drifted apart.

I decided to apply for a legal separation. I could not consider even the thought of a taxing court case when I felt so fragile and vulnerable, but my solicitor did his work well. Proceedings would be on the grounds of M's adultery, committed with two women who had laid complaints with the police of being drugged and raped by him. In hindsight it beggars belief that M got away with what he did to women for so long – the others before and after me, who kept quiet through shame and fear. After I discovered I was pregnant, I had received a phone call out of the blue from a woman who told me that M was the father of her daughter's baby. I did not believe it at the time, but later learnt that she and M eventually came together and had another son as well. This woman had a horrific time with M, who abused her to such an extent that her life was ruined until he died. Unlike me, she did not have the courage to leave him.

The police were able to satisfy my solicitor that the allegations were well founded. It provided a good negotiating base. Because of his history of violence and his threat to take Dorian out of the country, I would not agree to M having any access at all. My solicitor successfully negotiated a separation agreement and my custody of Dorian. The terms of the separation were not defended. Like all doctors, Meik received a monthly update from the Department of Health in Christchurch. The report dated 1 April 1971 included the following statement: 'The latest drug to come to our notice recently as becoming popular on the local scene is chloral hydrate. Various criminal acts after using a "Mickey Finn" on unsuspecting customers have been reported.' Chloral hydrate was subsequently removed from the market.

Living in the same house with Meik inevitably led to a close relationship. On the night in May that Millie's daughter Tracey was born, Meik returned from the hospital after the delivery and we celebrated the birth in the time-honoured way. Our relationship was a happy and companionable one, something alien to me. Meik's career had been unusual. He had given up his career in teaching to enter the medical world and for him being a country doctor in North Canterbury, where he had been since April 1953, was a dream come true, providing the challenges he was looking for. Meik was so successful and popular that in 1978 he was recognised for his work with an MBE. Taking inspiration from him, I decided to do something about my own qualifications. So, starting from where I left school at 15, I enrolled to study for School Certificate through the Correspondence School. I enjoyed it immensely and at the end of the year, as the only adult, I attended Papanui High School to sit the exams and passed with flying colours.

Then, Meik asked me to marry him. I was touched, felt his loneliness and need, but just could not agree. The age difference did not worry me but it had been such a short time since my disastrous marital experience.

Although I realised I would be loved and cared for and have financial security, it was too early for me to contemplate that then. Sadly, when I refused his offer he was very hurt and from then on, our relationship cooled. It was time for me to move on, but where?

I was very fortunate. The Maruia Springs Hotel, further north and inland from Waikari, in the Lewis Pass National Reserve, needed a manager. And the owner, Murray Free, was a friend of HB's. Aware of my plight, HB spoke to Murray, who visited me at Waikari and I was offered the job, complete with salary, accommodation and all meals plus assistance to move Dorian's cot and all his other toddler paraphernalia. I accepted without hesitation.

The hotel was in the middle of nowhere in an idyllic spot overlooking the Maruia River among native bush and beech tree woodland. My accommodation was an L-shaped room, with Dorian's cot tucked around the corner. Running the hotel was easy. Gerry, a rotund and cheery ex-army chef, was in charge of the kitchen, Rex managed the bar and I oversaw the housekeeping, bookings, engaging staff, accounts and other general duties. Once a week Dorian and I would drive to Christchurch in the hotel truck and do the rounds of the suppliers for fish, meat, vegetables and anything else that was required. Hiring staff was easy as there were always international hitchhikers making their way around New Zealand who were eager to be employed for temporary kitchen, waiting and cleaning duties. There were also local staff: Eunice Hunter and Josie Blackadder from the valley were regulars. The few huts not accommodating employees were always filled with men from the road gangs or geologists in the area for survey work, who would winter over.

Despite Maruia's remoteness, lunchtimes were a lively affair with coach tours, road gangs, locals and passing tourists calling in. In winter, the vast fireplace with its roaring fire was a drawcard and the off-duty staff and I would skinny dip at night in the hot springs, leap out and roll around in the snow and then repeat the fun. Pool tournaments and possum hunting were also popular nocturnal pursuits. The power supply was driven by a generator at the top of the hill that regularly got blocked by a dead possum, which stopped the water flow. This always seemed to happen at night and required traipsing up the hill to dislodge the obstacle. Two pigs housed in a pen at the back of the hotel were fattened on kitchen scraps, then butchered for meat and bacon and replaced with piglets to start the cycle again. Dorian loved to feed the pigs. After our arrival Gerry named one for me and one for Dorian by painting our names on their backs.

Dorian had the run of the hotel. At mealtimes I would sit him in his high chair in the kitchen and Gerry would ply him with food. His favourite was a cooked chicken placed on his tray. He would expertly and quietly work his way through the entire bird, sucking loudly on the bones. His first words were 'More meat'. I did not take many days off but when I did I would take Dorian down to visit Josie and Aftie Blackadder's farm at Springs Junction. He loved it there where he could feed lambs and chickens, chase ducks and play. Although Dorian was a favourite with all the staff, and very happy, I felt the hotel environment was not conducive to his upbringing, especially when I found him in the bar sampling the wares. It was time to move on. I had gone on to do University Entrance by correspondence, and this gave me confidence and options for the future. I handed in my notice and decided I could now return to Christchurch.

I found a little flat in Woodham Road that consisted of a large front room big enough for Dorian's bed and mine, a very small sitting room, an even smaller kitchen, with a wringer washing machine in the corner, and a shower room and toilet. There was hardly any outside space. But I could just afford the rental of $12 per week from the $28 unemployment benefit I had applied for. I turned down most job offers because I would not leave Dorian. But I learnt very strict budgeting as the $16 left over had to cover all other expenses. It was not easy. My doctor was concerned about my weight: I ate very small portions to ensure Dorian had the healthy meals he needed. When I told Mum, who had a very well-stocked linen cupboard, 'I don't even have pillow cases', she offered to show me how to make some. She was still fond of saying, 'Well, you made your bed so now you have to lie in it.' Apparently without pillow cases. They were hard times.

But others were generous. When I went out to see Millie, by then living in Darfield, she never sent me home empty-handed. There was always home baking, vegetables and fruit from the garden, treats and she would press a dollar note into my hand for petrol. One day when I was feeling particularly overwhelmed, a letter arrived from Ralph, enclosing a cheque for $100. I was so overcome by this unexpected and thoughtful windfall that I immediately burst into tears. I rang him to thank him but all I could do was sob out my gratitude. In his usual quiet way Ralph said, 'I sent it to make things a bit easier for you and so you can treat yourself. Why are you crying?'

Because I had a lot of spare time on my hands, and a meagre income, I enrolled with a recruitment agency for temporary and part-time office work and was lucky to get a one day a week position with David Watson, who owned a farm at West Melton but lived in Ilam. He was a Nuffield Scholar and one of my tasks was typing up his very lengthy scholarship report. I worked for him for around three years, typing, keeping wage records, paying accounts and doing general administration. I was able to take Dorian with me and he played and slept while I worked. David's wife, Maisie, helped too. I also bought a cheap tennis racquet and joined a weekly women's session at the local club.

Then I resolved that any future study would be to further my love of art. I decided on the fine arts preliminary exam as an entry to the University of Canterbury School of Art and enrolled for night classes at Papanui High School. There I met Margaret Dawson, who was there for the same reason and had a son, Jeremy, who was the same age as Dorian. A friendship evolved that lasted for the rest of our lives. Because our tutor was enjoying a very torrid affair, either in the back of his car or in the school toilets, he spent more time out of the classroom than in it and we did not learn much. In fact neither of us passed the entrance qualification but we felt sufficiently enthusiastic to try again the following year, 1974, and this time we lucked onto the excellent tutorship of Ray Neuman at a Hillmorton High School night class. We each chose a topic for our entry – Margaret the sunflower and I the pine cone. I dissected pine cones for drawings, painted pine forests, made a contemporary sculpture from a copper toilet cistern ball with spiralling copper wire attached, designed graphics for labels such as pine-scented disinfectant, and filled sketchbooks with drawings. Dorian and I spent hours in the Botanic Gardens, where he played while I sketched. Margaret and I both passed the entry exam this time.

So the days at Woodham Road ticked by and I found a modicum of contentment. Dorian was such a delightful child, so easy to love and mother and we enjoyed each other's company. But a change of flats was inevitable. As a fast-growing boy, Dorian needed his own room, and so did I.

My mother, Noeline Searle, fire station dance, 1939.

My father, Noel Hichens, 1927.

Noel and Noeline as a courting couple, c.1938.

The wedding of Noel and Noeline, 30 December 1939.
The bride's father, Joseph Searle, is second from right.

Anne at 11 months, 1945.

Anne, aged three, as flower girl at a family wedding, 31 January 1947.

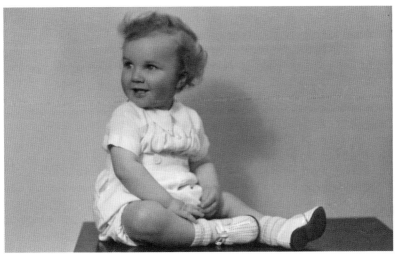

My brother, Ralph, at 11 months, 1942.

When my Uncle Roy returned from the war he lived with my grandparents
in the front of their house. His Italian war bride Ada arrived in 1946 and
Josephine was born later that year. Anne and Ralph, with Ada holding
Josephine, 487 Gloucester Street, 1947.

The Searle sisters, Alma, May and Noeline (front),
and Joseph having a snooze, at Sumner.

Anne and Ralph, 1950.

Anne, 1955.

Leaving Eglinton Valley in 1957, during our last camping holiday.
Note the box trailer which converted to my bed at night.

The adorable Penny settled in well with our cat Tippy.

Anne and Ralph, March 1958.

Anne on Sandy, Avonhead, 1958.

Anne as a bridesmaid, 28 November 1960, a week
after being discharged from the Magdalene laundry.

Anne and Tibor Pataky, 1960.

Ralph's twenty-first birthday. Presentation of a key was traditional,
but the posed photo does not hide the family unhappiness.

Hamilton Baxter and Anne, Wellington, 1963.

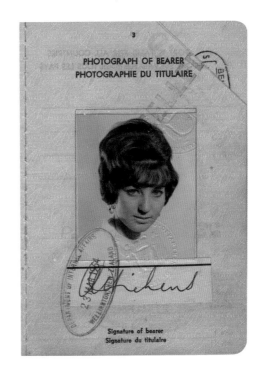

My passport photo –
British subject and
New Zealand citizen.

Anne embarking on MV *Fairsea*, May 1964.

Celebrating the crossing of the equator, with King Neptune in the starring role, was a new and hilarious experience. The party went on for days. Anne, dressed as a mermaid, standing second from left.

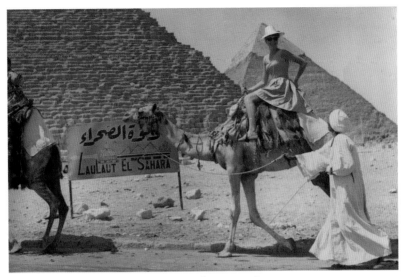

En route to the pyramids.

Anne and Doris at Selsey with two of the spaniels.

Anne on a seawall at Selsey Bill.

Defying the ban on pets at my bedsit,
I bought a cockatiel named Peanuts.
He was amazing company and I
chatted to him a lot, even teaching
him to say a few words.

A modelling assignment – this one
was for bamboo and rattan products.

One of the regular spots for the cabaret dance
troupe I joined was the Christchurch Airport
Lounge – Judy, the principal, at the front,
Anne at the back.

Enjoying the summer, 1967.

Our first Christmas – with Dorian at my
mother's place in Idris Road, 1969.

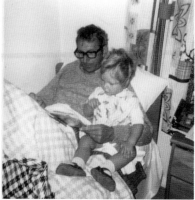

LEFT: Dorian and Ralph, Havelock, 1971. RIGHT: Hugh Bower (HB)
reading a story to Dorian, 1971. – *Bower family archives*

Dorian's christening, 3 January 1971. Noeline, Anne holding Dorian, Lea and Nova, with Ralph, HB and Alan in front.

Millie Ford with Michael and holding Tracey, Anne with Dorian, Princes Street, Darfield, 1972.

LEFT: HB, Dorian and Anne, 1973.

RIGHT: Tony Allan on *Rebel II* before leaving for the start of the trans-Tasman race. I designed and painted the skybird on the hull. – *Christchurch Star, 6 April 1974. Christchurch City Libraries. CCL-Star-1974-2272-016-024N-02*

I thought I had the overgrown section sussed by borrowing a sheep from David Watson's farm but Ee-wee (Ewe), as Dorian called her, ate everything except the grass. Leinster Road, December 1974.

There was, however, one snag about leaving: Dorian had adopted an old stray cat, Dougal, whom he loved, but no pets were allowed at our new place. I rang my father, whom I rarely saw unless I needed something, and asked if he would come around when we were out, collect Dougal and have him put to sleep. He agreed, but when we arrived home Dougal was still there. I rang my father to ask why he had not done the deed. 'But I have,' he said. Two days later our neighbour knocked on the door and asked if I had seen their cat.

Our new home, in Carlton Mill Road, was in a block of relatively new flats, and it felt so good to be away from an old, cold house that received little sun. Being on the first floor was not ideal, and there was no garden, but it was sunny and warm and Dorian and I each had a bedroom. I came to an arrangement with the owner that, in return for cheaper rent, I would do his laundry.

HB's yacht *Safari* was usually moored in a berth at Naval Point in Lyttelton Harbour near the modernist Banks Peninsula Cruising Club building designed by Peter Beaven. It was a very social club and gatherings in the bar at the end of sailing days and regattas were lively. HB and Mum had joined the club and I would sometimes go along with them. There I met Tony Allan, an attractive, broad-shouldered, happy-go-lucky, very blokey guy, who owned the trimaran *Rebel II*. My heart thrummed when we were introduced and we started going out together, which meant most of our spare time was spent at Lyttelton on *Rebel II*, either sailing or just chilling or me watching his races. It was all so different, and almost peaceful.

Then Tony told me he wished to realise his ambition to enter the 1974 Solo Tasman Yacht Challenge, which started in New Plymouth and finished at Mooloolaba, Queensland. He wasn't interested in just competing – he wanted to win. I was totally supportive. It was summer and the weather perfect when *Rebel II* went into the yacht club haul-out area for maintenance. I have never done so much wet and dry sanding. My main contribution, however, was to design and paint a skybird graphic on each side of the bow on the main hull, inspired by *Jonathan Livingston Seagull* and Neil Diamond's 1973 album. By this time Tony had moved in with Dorian and me. He was always short of funds so HB gave him a night shift job at the factory. Catching up on sleep and working on his yacht were day-time essentials. I particularly enjoyed going with Dorian to Tony's South Brighton family home for visits and meals. It was such a happy and carefree family atmosphere.

Once the race had started, in April 1974, I left Dorian with my cousin Lesley and flew to Mooloolaba to meet Tony on his arrival. It was thrilling to watch the yachts coming in. Tony achieved a creditable third in 11 days and 13 hours; I was very proud of, and for, him. He was exhausted but exhilarated. I stayed with Tony on *Rebel II*, an idyllic few days sleeping on the deck in the warm evenings and exploring the Queensland sea coast. I would gaze into the clear water for hours, fascinated by the polychromatic scales of the fish. It was not easy to leave but I needed to return to my boy, leaving Tony to bring *Rebel II* home.

My memory of the next period of my life was completely blank. I felt a sense of dread, a nebulous apprehension that something had gone very wrong. I could, however, vaguely recall having been a patient at Princess Margaret Hospital around that time and so requested my medical record for 1974. The file arrived with a covering letter stating that all hospital records before 1975 had been destroyed but there was a copy of my psychological medicine record – exchanges between the doctor at the University of Canterbury Student Health Counselling Service and a Canterbury District Health Board psychiatric physician – as well as clinical notes for Princess Margaret and Christchurch Women's hospitals. It was enough for me to establish an outline of what had happened. A cursory scan of the notes and correspondence left me literally breathless and my heart pounded so much I thought I was about to have a coronary. I was so devastated I quickly hid the file under a pile of books as if it was on fire. Only days later was I able to read it in detail and make further sense of the contents.

I discovered that Tony and his brother Chris had attempted to return to New Zealand with *Rebel II* after the race but this was aborted as time was running out for Chris to get back to work. Tony stayed on at Mooloolaba, living on his yacht and picking up odd jobs until December 1974, when he decided to return to New Zealand. In the meantime we exchanged phone calls and it appeared that the relationship, although tenuous, was not yet over.

Back in Christchurch I was attempting to cope on my own once again. Then I discovered that I was pregnant. I don't recall how or when I informed Tony of this, if, indeed, I did. The medical notes were telling:

> She came to such a point of desperation that she swallowed the contents of a bottle of Mogadon tablets.
>
> Her appetite is variable, and her mood definitely worse in the mornings, improving as the day goes on. She has been in this state for some months.
>
> She has managed to be fairly independent by denying dependency needs.
>
> She became anxious when she took the risk of involvement in a relationship.
>
> She needed someone to rely on but soon found he was very unreliable.
>
> The relationship with Tony was getting unbearable – the two sides fighting – it was affecting Dorian.
>
> Mrs Crighton feels that she could not possibly go through with the pregnancy.
>
> Mother remarried, distant, selfish, felt neglected at times, 'she drinks a lot which upsets me'.
>
> Looks to men with a childish dependency.
>
> Seems slow and rather vague.
>
> Social adjustment precarious.

And the referral to Christchurch Women's said: 'In my opinion she is only on the verge of surviving at the moment, having little inner sense of security and a rather tenuous adjustment to family and social surroundings. I think that if she has to go through the pregnancy she is very likely to suffer a good deal of depression and would certainly have to give up care of one, or both children.' The pregnancy was legally terminated on 17 August 1974. On the 30th I was admitted to Princess Margaret, where I gained some relief from my stress, and was discharged on 2 September. According to the last clinical notes, dated 8 October 1974, even though I was drifting with no aim in life, I 'wasn't depressed – just mixed up'.

Two months later Tony, on *Rebel II*, embarked on what was to be a disastrous return journey. When his yacht overturned only days after leaving

Mooloolaba he drifted in the Tasman Sea, cramped in a life raft, for 20 days before he was rescued. The story of his survival and fortuitous rescue is recounted in *Alone in the Tasman*, published in 2018. Understandably, a different person eventually came back to me in January 1975. Not long after his return he packed his bags and left the flat, though not for long. I then suggested that we rent a house, with a garden for Dorian, and start again. Tony agreed. However, I was slowly recovering from my breakdown and depression, and the emotional impact of the termination, and Tony had just survived an extraordinary emotional experience that had left him scarred. We were both vulnerable and the relationship was doomed to fail.

Even so, we moved the furniture from the flat to the house I had rented in Leinster Road, which had a large backyard immediately adjacent to Elmwood School. But Tony did not move in with us. He told me he was leaving because he loved me, that if he didn't leave me he would hurt me more. 'I'm a loner,' he declared. I was bereft, bewildered and despairing. The feeling of rejection was overwhelming but I needed to recover and build my life for myself and Dorian. I set about turning a big, run-down weatherboard villa into a home.

The kitchen, which had not been updated since the house was first built, included, in one corner, an old wringer washing machine. To drain the water all I had to do was put the outlet pipe into a hole in the floor. My bedroom, at the front of the house, was dark, thanks to densely planted trees, and when a breeze came up the branches scratched at the windows, which meant wide-eyed alertness and sleepless nights. I always slept better when I had boarders or others staying in the house. Sometimes, for company, I would bring Dorian in to sleep in my room.

I was still working for David Watson and then I picked up further part-time work for an architect friend of my mother and HB. I spent a lot of time at the Coffee House in narrow and charming Chancery Lane, which ran from Cathedral Square to Gloucester Street. Through my connections there I found Warren, whose parents had thrown him out when they discovered he was a covert cross-dresser. He was a delightful young man and I was happy for him to be my boarder on one condition, which he readily and respectfully accepted: he was not to appear in his outrageous female outfits and make-up until Dorian was asleep. He looked very beautiful when he did appear dressed in his full regalia, and I told him so.

I had moved again, to a flat in a newly built block in Holly Road, by the time my decree absolute, just before Christmas 1974, legally and emotionally closed a part of my life that I was happy to consign to the grave. (Unbelievably, the tenant on the ground floor was Gerry, my second fiancé. We caught up amicably on our respective lives, mine heavily redacted, then went our separate ways.) I was still feeling unsettled but now, and significantly, my dream of buying a home became a reality. By cashing in the family benefit, I had enough for a deposit to purchase a modest property – a north-facing private back unit of a row of six new townhouses in Picton Avenue, Riccarton. The rent I was paying at Holly Road would more than cover the mortgage payments, insurance and rates. I enthusiastically set about planning the garden and the interior. I had the bathroom window lowered so that I could lie in the bath and look out at a wild garden of natives, fernery and ponga. I now feel somewhat embarrassed to confess that I installed white shagpile carpet in the sitting room and up one wall, and for the kitchen–diner I bought a copper-topped table with carved wooden pews on each side. William Morris would not have approved but it was the 1970s, after all. It was a happy place and Dorian settled in well. In the six years since his birth, we had lived in nine 'homes'. We would be in this one for the next five.

CHAPTER 8
Soaking up Knowledge

At Elmwood School Dorian was in an experimental open classroom of approximately 60 pupils, with two teachers. Because he was a reserved little boy, he would sit at the back of the class and not interact; I could see from the schoolwork he brought home that he was not progressing satisfactorily. Though the school seemed to think he would settle in eventually, I was not happy to wait. For me, education was significant and essential. I conferred with Mum and HB, who immediately said he would pay for Dorian to attend St Andrew's College. I took up his kind offer with gratitude.

Dorian enjoyed the smaller classes, which suited him. He immersed himself in the curriculum, played cricket and rugby, took up swimming and made many friends. I also encouraged him to learn a musical instrument, something that had been denied me. He chose the flute. Difficult as the decision was, I let Dorian start biking to school. I went over the route with him several times before allowing him to go alone. For the first few times, after I waved him off, he was unaware that I followed by car to see for myself how he managed. He did well but I worried nevertheless. They were the first steps of my boy's independence and my first step in learning to let go.

It was Deiniol Davies, from his class, with whom Dorian played most after school. He and I came to know the whole Davies clan, Trevor and Barbara, Ben and Tom, for the rest of our lives. The four exuberant boys could be a handful and Barbara and I would devise ways to mop up their energy. One was swimming, which led to my involvement with the New Zealand Amateur Swimming Association. As well as serving in various roles, I obtained over $1000 of sponsorship for the 1979 National Swimming Championships in Christchurch and was swimming official at the 1981 New Zealand Summer Games. Over the summer of 1978-79

Barbara and I took the lease of the busy café at the Centennial Pool, selling pies, savouries, sandwiches, ice creams and confectionery. It was hard work at the shop but our boys thought it great: they played and swam at the pool all day. After the café closed for winter, I took a year's lease on a gift and stationery shop just down the road from St Andrew's. After school Dorian would either help me in the shop or sit out the back to do his homework. The shop produced a liveable income but it was a tie and I missed my freedom. But into our lives came tubby and cheerful Tom Burtt, a friend of HB's, who owned Lace Web Furnishers and offered me the job of office manager. Tom had been a New Zealand cricketer who played in 10 tests from 1947 to 1953 and Dorian, enamoured with cricket, was spellbound by his stories.

When the Davies left in January 1979 to live in Auckland, Dorian and I missed them terribly. I had envied their family life and loved being a small part of it. When he went to the Davies in school holidays Dorian was treated as one of the family, even lining up with Ben, Dan and Tom when the pocket money was doled out. This was a new experience for him.

HB had always acknowledged and recognised my potential, and had asked me many times to work for him. I finally succumbed and became the company's office manager. I was sad to leave Lace Web but I needed a fresh challenge. Mum committed to collecting Dorian after school and minding him until I finished work. It was a good arrangement for all of us: it enabled me to work and it brought Dorian and his gran closer.

Behind the Victorian facades of H. B. Bower & Co. Ltd was a 24-hour seven-day-a-week manufacturing business. The factory produced extruded plastic garden hose exclusively for Arthur Yates & Co. Ltd. There were also looms to weave rattan and bamboo for blinds, and the company owned import licences for the sale of bamboo garden stakes and costume jewellery and objets d'art, a lucrative side business. HB and I were involved in another ambitious project, recycling plastic polythene bottles, such as detergent containers, and making a wide variety of products such as mudguards or septic tanks from the chipped plastic. Parts of the recycling plant had unlikely origins. The large stainless steel washing baths came from the Kaiapoi Woollen Mills, the dewatering fans from the old Christchurch Gas plant and the gear boxes to drive the fans were originally part of the system that hoisted the Auckland Harbour Bridge extensions into place. The project was extremely ambitious and well ahead of its time. To me it seemed an overwhelming task but, undeterred, HB battled on, with me as his sidekick. We worked closely with the natural resources division of the Department of Trade and Industry, the Department of Scientific and Industrial Research, the Christchurch City Council and environment groups. However, batch testing and maintaining the quality required for reliable extrusion would have made the products too expensive, and New Zealand did not have a viable system for identifying plastic. The scheme fizzled to a standstill.

It did not take me long to get the office organised and life settled into a reassuring routine. I was appointed executive director in March 1976 and took over several of the large manufacturing contracts. Cash flow was my responsibility and I had to coordinate expenditure with the income I was negotiating from large as well as smaller contracts. The business was successful but the buck, as I was regularly reminded, ultimately always stopped with HB. He became increasingly anxious and the high doses of Valium he was prescribed over a long period of time started to affect his personality. He and my mother were going through a rough patch. While HB worked long hours, Mum was enjoying the financial benefits and, characteristically, having a good time. Cracks began to appear in the marriage. HB also became jealous and resentful of my success with clients and the contracts I had gained and maintained. He undermined my authority and took away from me the powers he had previously bestowed. I understood HB's anxiety and moods but the tension and atmosphere became unbearable. After four years with the company I had no option but to leave. I was not alone.

In July 1980, in order to be closer to Dorian's school and friends, I sold Picton Avenue. I was sad to leave the first home I had bought, described by the real estate agent as 'A very special unit with a most delightful little garden and terrace. Completely private. No traffic noise. Very sunny. Artistic, tasteful décor. Good living space.' After searching for a house within my price range and closer to St Andrew's, I found a place in St Albans Street that was perfect for our needs. It even had a tenanted flat at the rear. When Dorian and I moved in, that November, the large rooms and the garden felt luxurious.

In a weak moment I agreed that Dorian could have some pet mice, as long as they stayed in the double garage at the back, which he used as a rumpus room. Over time two became six, then 20 and before long hundreds. I quickly learnt that female mice can have up to 15 litters per year. All around the walls, sitting on benches, were boxes, cartons, cages – anything Dorian could lay his hands on. Nesting materials such as tissue paper, straw and anything else suitable disappeared into the garage. Dorian spent hours in there observing his pets, topping up water dishes and feeding them. All his pocket money went on food and toys. Entering the garage was like discovering a scene in a mad movie with mice frantically racing on wheels, copulating, twitching, jumping, chasing and climbing. The stench was terrible and I decided enough was enough. Dorian was concerned for their future but I had a cunning plan. One night we managed to jumble the seething mass into several large boxes, load them into the car and take them to the park just around the corner and set them free. They swarmed out in a fan and disappeared into the bushes. Dorian was happy with that.

One day he arrived home from school with a friend named Raphael. Through that friendship I met his father, Robert, who was studying for an MA at the University of Canterbury, his topic the 'Nibelungenlied', the German medieval epic poem that later inspired Wagner's Ring Cycle. Robert fascinated me. His intellect was extraordinary and he opened my eyes to unfamiliar music, poetry and literature that completely enthralled and absorbed me. We had great conversations and I was like a sponge soaking up the knowledge. He also introduced me to the metaphysical poetry of John Donne whose intense language entranced me. The first four lines of his deeply personal love poem, 'The Flea', remain in my memory to this day.

Eventually Robert and Raphael, and thousands of books, moved in to share the house with us. It proved to be a good arrangement. When I told Robert of my pathetic past attempts at tertiary study, he encouraged me to enrol once again at the University of Canterbury as a mature student. He ignited something in me. Something that told me I had a brain and should use it. So I did as he suggested. I was determined to complete a degree, but not at the School of Fine Arts. An impecunious artist? No thanks. I decided instead on a BA, ambitiously resolving to do a triple major in history, art history and classics. I was determined to make up for lost time.

Throughout the three years of studying, taking holiday work and being a mother I relished life as a student. My income was minimal but I survived with a scholarship, a holiday job during the May, September and Christmas breaks and my meagre savings. HB continued to pay the school fees for Dorian, who was doing well academically and enjoying cricket and swimming. 'I have a benefactor,' Dorian would explain.

My chosen majors combined my passions for art, history and architectural history. The two-year survey course, Art History 101 and 201, defined my understanding of the historical timeline of the periods of art, sculpture and architecture over the centuries, from Greek, Roman, Early Christian, Byzantine, Medieval, Renaissance, Mannerist and through the '-isms' of the nineteenth and twentieth centuries, and proved invaluable for putting art history into context. It was an in-depth academic survey, only available at Canterbury University, along the lines of Kenneth Clark's superb BBC TV series, *Civilisation*. I retain fond memories of my lecturers, in particular, Julie King, Jonathan Mane-Wheoki, Charles Manning, Geoffrey Rice and Regina Haggo. Charles Manning, a lecturer in the Classics Department, whom I politely called 'Sir', would later become 'Charlie' when we were fellow Christchurch city councillors. His colleague in the Classics Department, Charles Whittaker, was brought to Canterbury from Britain for a year and I enjoyed his different presenting style. I kept all my essays, either laboriously neatly handwritten or typed on an old manual typewriter, all, as prescribed, without mistakes. If an error was made, the whole page had to be redone. My grades were in the A+ to B+ range, mostly closer to the latter. One of the most frequent comments made on my assignments was 'mature'.

It was through Robert I met one of his fellow students, Kathy Hamilton. We became lifelong friends. Many years later, she recalled our first encounter at a St Albans Street party: 'Anne was tall with shoulder-length blonde hair that fell in waves. Slender, with what was and still is her trademark heavy eye makeup – that is with an abundance of blue eyeshadow that accentuated her cornflower blue eyes. She had a somewhat bohemian air about her, which is hard to explain – she wasn't bedecked with the stereotype strands of necklaces and flowing colourful robes, but there was something terribly interesting about her.' Kathy remembered, too, how after I had thanked her for bringing a plate and a bottle of wine, 'both were tucked away in the cupboard, never to be seen again, at least not by the guests. I learnt that she had been raising a child on her own for many years and those early struggles had made her conserve whatever food and wine came her way to be consumed later.' The other thing that stood out for Kathy was the house: 'I had never seen a freestanding fireplace with an enormous copper hood in the middle of a room before, and with artwork decorating the walls, it just felt so unconventional.'

The student parties were somewhat wild, as were those Kathy and I attended at the home of university English lecturer, Rob Jackaman. The wine was plentiful and we, like everyone else, imbibed more than was sensible. Getting home was interesting. Being in no fit state to drive, Kathy and I worked cooperatively as usual. This meant I would sit in the driver's seat and work the pedals and Kathy would steer from behind sitting on the back seat and issuing instructions when to stop and go. Somehow, we always made it home.

Kathy, also a solo parent, and I tried to make the best of the time and resources we had. We managed to have days out, to the Groynes, Diamond Harbour, Akaroa and so on, giving her three daughters and my Dorian happy experiences on a small budget. Picnics were always chaotic with our children and others, food and wine and a wind-up gramophone playing old 78s of 1940s songs. Those occasions had a Swallows and Amazons quality, a kind of innocence of lost summers.

A few doors away in St Albans Street lived Robert Erwin and his long-time partner, Lawrence Baigent. I ultimately met these cultured men, who became my good friends. Both were urbane intellectuals with an obsessive penchant for collecting modern New Zealand art, and to me their modest house, crammed with paintings, rare books and a collection of ruby glass, was a wonderland. The garden was bursting with exotic flower varieties as Robert was a sensitive and creative gardener, both as cultivator and designer. Visits there were never dull, always genteel, though there could be amusing hints of domestic disharmony. Once, when I noted that the washing was being done in the bath – sheets, towels and everything else – Robert grumbled, 'Lawrence will not have a washing machine in the house!'

I was enchanted with and inspired by their way of life and the seriousness of their day-to-day conversations. Robert was reference librarian at the University of Canterbury for many years and Lawrence, considerably older, had retired from a distinguished career in which he had been editor with the Caxton Press, novelist, reviewer and university lecturer in English. They both loved poetry, literature and classical music. Robert, because of his extensive knowledge of European art, architecture, literature and music, was engaged part time as a tutor and lecturer in the art history department. His insightful lectures frequently combined music with art, a combination that enthralled me and indeed most students. I had started painting again in a perfunctory way when I moved into St Albans Street and Robert, on one of his visits, said he wished to purchase one of my works. We agreed on a price. I was delighted and certainly flattered by my first sale to such a refined and sensitive man.

I would drive home in the evening from late lectures, in my dark blue Volkswagen Beetle, the tyres making a smooth and comforting swishing sound. On dark wintry nights the streets would be deserted but the lighted windows of the houses, even with drapes pulled, made a kaleidoscope of muted reds, oranges, and greens. I pictured the families inside, happily going to bed, preparing for the next day or sipping hot cocoa round an open fire. They would all be peaceful – children asleep, no sounds of arguments or unpleasantness. With my enjoyment of university, and Dorian happily established at school, I should have felt sure of life, but I could not escape the apprehension that nothing was certain. I may have seemed settled, but I felt adrift. A long poem I wrote at the end of 1981, titled 'Wasps, Wasted Years, Vespucci', summed up my uncertain mental state, as these lines show:

> I am in a black hole
> I feel myself falling
> I am fighting to get free
> But my strength is waning
> I am crying out for help
> But no one hears
> My pleas are silent
> So no one cares
> All too busy, busy, busy.
> Please, please help me.

PART

TWO

The Road From
Obscurity to Damehood

CHAPTER 9

From Anne to Anna

I did manage, somehow, to rise above the severe bouts of depression that still often plagued me, calling on my sense of fun to help me survive difficult situations and downsizing my domestic life to just Dorian and me. I sold my house in St Albans Street in April 1982. I had been doing temporary work, but, following a request from Tom Burtt, I returned as a consultant to Lace Web to computerise their card-based customer system and revamp the office to work more efficiently. With the house sold, I was desperate to find another one quickly. Kathy had had an offer accepted on an 1879 worker's cottage in Armagh Street but it had not gone unconditional. She said to me, 'You buy Armagh Street. Your need is greater than mine!' I had seen the place briefly and declared it appealing, so I made an offer of $20,000, which was accepted. I had already decided that I wanted to live in the centre of the city, as I had in Wellington, Naples, Cologne and Chichester. It was a decision well made, in the sense that it was all I could afford, but bad timing because the interest rates for first mortgages then stood out at 18 per cent. In November that year, after months of admonishing bankers and finance houses to lower interest rates on mortgages, Prime Minister Robert Muldoon pegged the rates by law. It then became illegal to lend money on any building or land at more than 11 per cent for a first mortgage and 14 per cent for a subsequent mortgage. Unfortunately this came too late for me as I was locked into the higher rate.

When first built, the Armagh Street house was on a section owned by Alice Clayton, a widow. The title was changed to her new husband's name when she remarried. By the time I purchased the property, it was on a back section and in sorry condition. As Kathy and I approached it on moving day, we appreciated the faded charm but, as she has recalled, the interior was a different matter. 'It was so depressing, empty and dark and very obviously in need of renovation, and such a contrast to the house that Anne had sold in St Albans Street. Anne became visibly upset and retreated to the veranda. Fortunately, the kind previous owner, in anticipation of our despair, had left a bottle of wine. I can still see us on that rickety veranda, drinking the wine, laughing and crying at the same time, as we have many times over the years at our choices of men and houses and resulting predicaments.'

I did wonder what I had done. The small four-room weatherboard cottage, with a veranda at the front and the bathroom and kitchen at the rear, had a foundation consisting of large boulders, many of the sash windows not working (and most were covered with cardboard instead of glass), an outside toilet, broken-down fencing, the advertised 'secret garden' was nowhere to be seen and a pile of rubbish filled the inside of an old shed. The heating was from a coal range and open fires. Fortunately, in each room the original fire surrounds, which had been boarded over, still had their undamaged original Victorian tiles and grates.

It was daunting but a challenge as, stage by stage, I set about turning this ugly wee duckling into a swan. Using funds from the sale of St Albans Street, and as budget allowed, within 10 years the kitchen and bathroom were extensively remodelled. Then came the bonus of an inside toilet. Even later, an extension to the east side of the cottage, which I designed, was added, with a bay window and polished timber floor providing a large sitting room. French doors opened on to a sunny north-facing veranda and terrace. The fencing was all replaced and painted and the driveway upgraded. In my rare spare time I removed layers of linoleum, old paper and carpets to reveal the beauty of the kauri floorboards, which I then had polished, removed the unsightly panels from the 'modernised' kauri doors, stripped layers of paint and shellac, scraped, wallpapered and painted, created a garden with an herbaceous border, planted 70 trees and shrubs, laid brick paths and gentrified the quaint outside toilet. In the words of a poem I wrote at the time:

> Green sleeves from painting walls
> White fingers from skirting
> Paintbrushes hardening
> Pen pensioned.

At university, I decided to take the two-year option for my masters course – four papers in the first year and a thesis in the second. I believe this was the first year that art history qualifications were held at masters level, a programme instigated by Professor John Simpson. This suited me well. My papers covered New Zealand architecture, constitutional history, colonial history and the New Zealand Labour movement 1880–1900. For the thesis, I chose a biographical study of the life and works of William Henry Clayton, New Zealand's first, and only, colonial architect. There were only five of us taking the art history course at that level: Robyn Ussher, Linda Tyler, Conal McCarthy, Sarah Rennie and me. We were soon to be universally referred to as the Famous Five, a moniker bestowed on us by Robyn, and one we relished. Female students found art history lecturer Jonathan Mane, as he was then, attractive and many were a little in love with him. He had a perfectly pitched and melodious speaking voice and his lectures were always first class. Jonathan possessed a natural grace and decency and was always approachable. He never put people down and he was generous in recognising students' ability. He had not yet acknowledged his Māori ancestry but was proud of his maternal French roots. He did not then openly acknowledge his homosexuality either; the Homosexual Law Reform Act only came into effect in 1986.

In the middle of 1983, the Famous Five, sans Sarah, embarked on a field trip to Dunedin under Jonathan's supervision. He resembled a Pied Piper as he strolled ahead with us trailing behind. We assiduously studied the excellent examples of Victorian architecture on our walking tours of Rakaia, Temuka, Timaru, Oamaru and Dunedin – often in the freezing cold – and just as assiduously played up in our motel room at night. Opening the door to a loud knocking at 11 p.m. we were confronted by a very angry and stern Jonathan, in his monogrammed pyjamas, ordering us to keep the noise down. Robyn, Linda and I scarpered for the bedroom, leaving Conal to take the heat as Jonathan chastised us for our unseemly behaviour and pointed out that, as mature adults, we should have known better. That aside, the field trip proved to be thoroughly worthwhile. It made us all aware of the fabric of the past and the need to cherish it. For me it was the start of a lifelong love affair.

Jonathan and his recently arrived colleague Ian Lochhead clearly enjoyed the opportunity to present New Zealand architectural history as a fairly new discipline. The Famous Five went on to curate an exhibition under their supervision. *W. B. Armson, A Colonial Architect Rediscovered* included original drawings and plans discovered through our research, all now safely deposited in the Macmillan Brown Library archives at the University of Canterbury. The exhibition, which opened in December 1983 at the Robert McDougall Art Gallery, ran for two months. Armson, who followed the British trend and used both Gothic motifs and Venetian Renaissance design aspects, began the most productive phase of his career in Christchurch in 1870. Each of us wrote a chapter of the 30-page exhibition catalogue: I was allocated 'Armson and Bank Architecture'.

Despite his importance, my thesis subject, William Henry Clayton (1823–1877), had been sadly neglected and very few secondary sources were available. That made the project more challenging, which I relished. As well as making an immense contribution to the architectural Victorian history of Tasmania and New Zealand, Clayton had a life that was a lesson in social mobility. Born in Tasmania, the eldest of 12 children, he was the grandson of a transported convict but educated at an exclusive school, then trained in England, and subsequently had an extremely successful career at the top of his profession. His daughter Mary married the prominent colonial politician, Julius Vogel. Clayton designed churches, banks, mansions and bridges and later, as colonial architect, he designed and saw to completion 180 buildings, 80 of which were post and telegraph offices. He was responsible for many public buildings in Wellington, including the old Parliament buildings, but is best known for designing the Old Government Buildings, one of the world's largest wooden buildings. Once home to the country's public service, it now houses Victoria University's School of Law.

Dorian and I made research road trips to Dunedin, Wellington, Russell and Tasmania, where, in January 1984, we spent an eventful two weeks travelling the island, viewing Clayton's extant buildings and his house, Wickford, in the Norfolk Plains. The then owners kindly gave me a tour of the house. I also celebrated my fortieth birthday. To satisfy Dorian, there was a surfeit of cricket watching on the motel TV, plus visits to zoos, beaches and many restaurants.

After I had submitted my thesis, laboriously typed in triplicate on an old Remington manual typewriter, the results were quick to arrive. I now had a Master of Arts with Second Class Honours (Division One) in history. I had received B+ for my papers and A– for the thesis. I was not unhappy.

When Dorian and I were happily settled in our Armagh Street cottage we continued our quest for pets, with mixed success. We tried goldfish, but two grotesque and ugly axolotls introduced to the tank disposed of those. Then there were the cats. We picked up a kitten we found while on a bush walk, alone and meowing pitifully. Kalinka turned out to be wild – really wild. She got fed but spent most of the time under the floor of the cottage. Then we acquired the ugliest white cat I have ever seen, but he was loving and we both loved him in return. Dorian named him Oskar Kokoschka. Oskar and Kalinka learned to cohabit peacefully. I thought it wise to take the cats to the vet for inoculations. We rounded them up and because I did not have a carry cage decided to pack them into a suitcase, which took some time. When we were ushered into the surgery and when the lid was opened, Kalinka sprang out, ran up the vet's arm and attacked his face. Oskar just sat there mutely. Kalinka, swaddled tightly in a towel, was then given the required vaccinations by a shaken vet. On leaving, I sensibly purchased a strong cardboard cat carry case for Kalinka. Oskar returned home in the suitcase. Then there were the dogs. We decided on a German short-haired pointer puppy we called Brax. But one day I got home from work to find Dorian in tears: Brax had escaped and Dorian had found her dead just down the road. She had been hit by a car. He brought her home in the wheelbarrow. Then we got Ziggy, another dog of the same breed: she lived for 14 years.

Early in 1985 John Coley, the director of the Robert McDougall Art Gallery, wrote to tell me that I had been appointed to the permanent position of secretary/administrative assistant. I was elated. I was now only one step away from my chosen field and interest in art, registrar/collection management. I did have the advantage of a track record at the McDougall – all part of my big plan. Thanks to the Temporary Employment Programme (TEP) launched by the government in 1980 – subsidised schemes set up to counter high unemployment – I had been one of 13 temporary workers taken on by the then director of the McDougall, Dr Rodney Wilson. Two consecutive six-monthly contracts contributed immensely towards my understanding of gallery administration and governance.

My desk was in the basement, which I shared with Neil Roberts, the curator, and other TEP workers. With no window to look out of, I enjoyed, instead, Philip Clairmont's *Fireplace*, a big acrylic on unstretched hessian. Its presence warmed all of my senses. Sometimes I assisted the very efficient secretary, Dagmar Fischer. Dagmar was a strikingly good-looking, very efficient German woman, who wore her blonde hair twisted in a plait on the top of her head. Her upstairs office was so cold that she sat at her desk wearing a fur coat; the temperature in the basement was little better. When Dagmar did not need me, I worked for Neil, hand-writing accession cards from the original register of all the listed works in the collection. In 1985, I took over from the popular and valued Janet Callender, who had resigned to marry and live abroad. On handover day, Janet introduced me to Merilynne Evans, the gallery shop manager. Janet told me that traditionally she and Merilynne met each week for lunch. I liked Merilynne immediately and announced I wished to carry on that tradition. We became close friends and have remained so.

The family atmosphere of the gallery was certainly enhanced under the jovial yet intelligent directorship of John Coley, who had taken over the role in 1981. His warm personality, together with the deep loyalty to the institution shared by his colleagues, reinforced the sense of us being a kind of art family. John was a practising artist and art educator. He may have come under criticism in some elitist art quarters for his populist views, but he was under pressure from his boss, the Christchurch City Council, to get people through the door. He succeeded in achieving a good balance between exhibitions of contemporary and historical art, more accessible and popular 'fun' art and a staggeringly good selection of touring exhibitions.

I remained part of the McDougall family for the next 17 years. They were many of the happiest days of my life and I never felt alone or lonely. Because not many of the staff had partners, there were several single people or people who had freedom within their relationships to enjoy one another's company. It suited my single status and sense of independence.

The year 1987 was marred by tragedy. After his divorce, Ralph desperately wanted his daughter from his first marriage, Vicki-Anne, to live with him and Nova, and their children Latiesha and Daniel, but it was never to be. He saw her as often as he was allowed and had her to stay – they were happy times. Then on 27 February 1987, aged just 19, she fell to her death from Lion Rock at Piha Beach, west of Auckland. I was told that she had committed suicide.

Ralph opened up to me on one of his brief visits to Christchurch in September that year. He was understandingly distraught at Vicki-Anne's death and the manner in which it happened. Indeed, Nova told me years later that the unremitting pain never left him. As an adult, Latiesha recalled how grief stricken her father was when he returned from a visit to the cemetery. He was so particular about caring for Vicki-Anne's grave, even taking up a lawn mower with him. Latiesha declared that if anything happened to her, she was to be cremated, not buried like her poor sister.

But 1987 also brought *Te Māori*, which had already toured the United States from 1984 to 1986, and I was not the only one who felt they had experienced a cultural revolution. This extraordinary exhibition firmly established, for the first time, that traditional Māori art could be viewed not just as ethnographic examples of a way of life, something primitively anthropological or historical that belonged in a museum, but as works of art often with a powerful aesthetic resonance, or, as Māori would say, mana.

When the exhibition came back from its international tour to visit New Zealand's four main centres in turn, it visited Christchurch first. *Te Māori, Te hokinga mai – The return home* opened at the Robert McDougall Art Gallery on 14 March 1987. The fact that *Te Māori* was hosted not by Canterbury Museum but by the city's art gallery showed how profoundly perceptions had changed and what a turning point this was. The ceremonial tapu lifting and the speeches of welcome were described by Pat Unger in the *Press* as 'moving and impressive ... things would never be the same again'. She added: 'From the dawn ceremony, when the exhibition was opened, to the bustle and welcome of everyday viewing, the way of the Maori has become clearer. No-one stands taller than the Maori orator on his marae and no singing is more evocative than the women's waiata.'

The McDougall held a temporary marae status – the centre court became the paepae – for the nine weeks that the exhibition of the 173 taonga was open to the public. During that time, iwi took turns, for one week each, as guardians of the taonga, as the elders welcomed and hosted visitors. Each morning and afternoon those attending the exhibition were greeted and farewelled with a formal pōwhiri.

While the McDougall staff were coping with the record number of daily visitors to see *Te Māori* – a total of 147,012 came, with a phenomenal 6000 on the last day – I had to take time off early in April to have my gallbladder removed. The solitary gallstone that had caused me such pain was about 10 millimetres in diameter and a very pretty green; I later had it set in Perspex as a paperweight. While recovering in St George's Hospital, I read of Andy Warhol's death only two months before. He had required gallbladder surgery since 1973 but, phobic about hospitals, he continually procrastinated. Fourteen years later, when it was inevitable, he eventually checked into New York Hospital on 20 February. Two days after his successful surgery Warhol died from cardiac arrest. This was dispiriting, to say the least. My spirits lifted, though, when on the Saturday morning after my operation, Merilynne rang me and held the phone aloft for me to listen to the iwi handover ceremony taking place on the paepae in the centre court. Even from my hospital bed I could sense the significance of the occasion and my skin prickled.

There was much celebration in July that year when my long-awaited dream role of registrar at the Robert McDougall Art Gallery became a permanent position. The most recognised New Zealand art professionals after the director are the curators, who know all about their specialist subjects. The wider public is probably less familiar with the role of registrars. I felt little ambition to be a curator, although I did curate a few shows, but always aspired to be a capable and respected registrar. I slipped easily into the permanent role, but there was so much to learn and do. A registrar must be an expert in logistics and planning, and possess the organisational and frequently purely inventive skills required to assess the strengths, weaknesses and needs of the objects in their care. In New Zealand registrars seldom have staff under their direct supervision and so must rely on communication and liaison with their colleagues – curators, conservators, photographers and exhibition teams – and colleagues from other public art institutions.

I moved from my first-floor, north-facing, sunny office next to John Coley's in the administration wing back to the familiar territory of the basement, but this time to a different 'cave', near the northern area of storage racks. A small barred window at ceiling level let in some light from the carpark and I had a lockable door and windows from the corridor custom made, to increase the security. A fireproof safe was installed in my office for the storage of valuable records, information and gallery collection accession registers. I happily worked there until my retirement in 2002, when the McDougall closed.

For our 1988–89 Christmas–New Year break, Dorian and I travelled to Queenstown to stay with my mother and Sam, now well ensconced as my mother's partner, and walked the Milford Track. One evening over dinner in one of the huts I talked to a young French tourist who remarked, 'You don't look like an Anne. You are definitely an Anna.' His comment stuck. Yes, I thought, Anne belonged to a different life and to a different person. This would be a way of shedding the unhappy memories of my childhood, and beyond, when I had felt marginalised. After much thought, I applied to have a legal name change – from Shirley Anne Hichens to Anna Louisa de Launey Crighton. (I retained the surname for Dorian's sake.) It was officially approved on 30 January 1989.

It was one of the most satisfying acts of my life. I had been given a first name I was not comfortable with and from the outset my parents called me by my second. Now I chose a name to fit how I felt about my new life: Anna (not too different from Anne) and Louisa de Launey after my maternal great-grandmother, who had had French Huguenot ancestry. I felt spiritually drawn to Louisa – that she had been born in Victoria, Australia, and as an eight-year-old orphan sent to England with her sister; that as an adult she undertook another long voyage, this time from England to Christchurch; that she had married into the Kirk family, who stamped their name on the early history of Christchurch; and that she and her sister chose to vote in the 1893 New Zealand general election, the first in which women took part. I have tangible reminders of her life: a photo of her and her husband Isaac and another taken when she was elderly, letters that her uncle and grandfather wrote to her from London, and her silver pocket watch. I have never regretted changing my name, which I slipped into without effort. It afforded me self-esteem and increased my confidence and sense of belonging. As C. S. Lewis said, 'You can't go back and change the beginning, but you can start where you are and change the ending.'

The same month that I became Anna, my boy left home. He joined the Royal New Zealand Air Force and moved for training to the RNZAF Base at Woodbourne, near Blenheim. His letters initially showed signs of homesickness but he soon settled down and passed a tough range of physical and mental challenges with a mark of 90.5 per cent. Ecstatic, I immediately arranged to attend his recruit graduation parade, taking my father, Gramps, along for the experience. However, we found Dorian on crutches, thanks to a badly infected ankle, which meant we all watched together from the sidelines. My son had found his niche and I could not have been happier.

CHAPTER 10
Sadness and Joy

Staying with my mother in Queenstown, which I did every Christmas break, was always fretful. I was never quite sure what to expect. I relished the moments when she showed motherly affection and thoughtfulness, for example bringing me a cup of tea in the mornings when she would sit on the end of my bed and chat. But then I might arrive and find her with a black eye and bruising, where Sam had beaten her. At those times I felt really sympathetic – I had been there, but did not expect to see my now aged mother experiencing such violence. But then I would witness the drinking, which would begin in the afternoon and well into the evening, with dinner postponed until it was so late that I was no longer hungry. I cared for my mother and encouraged her to move back to Christchurch where I could look after her. She always demurred at such a suggestion. At the end of my Christmas 1989 visit, it was back to Christchurch and home without her.

When I answered the phone a few days later it was my distraught sister-in-law Nova ringing me from Auckland: Ralph was in Kaitaia Hospital and had only hours to live. I found the news difficult to comprehend. I had seen him only a matter of weeks before when I was in Auckland on business. We had breakfasted together at my hotel, sharing news of each other's lives and children. Afterwards Ralph had taken me for a tour around his Auckland haunts and then back home to see Nova, Latiesha and Daniel.

Ralph and Daniel had been driving north for their traditional father and son annual fishing trip to Spirits Bay. As planned, they stopped off at Ninety Mile Beach on the way and set up camp for a couple of nights. But Ralph suddenly felt horribly unwell and asked Daniel to get the camping ground owner to take them to Kaitaia Hospital. At first the diagnosis was a massive heart attack but this later changed to a burst aortic aneurysm. Daniel, finding the gurgling noise in his father's chest unbearable, got himself back to the camp. Nova received the call at 4 a.m. to tell her Ralph was dying. A family friend Keith drove Nova and Latiesha to the hospital, and then went to collect Daniel. They were all at Ralph's bedside for just 45 minutes when he died, aged only 49, on 5 January. Unbeknown to him, and to our family, he had Marfan syndrome, a genetic disorder affecting the body's connective tissue. Ralph happened to be the one in 5000 people to have the syndrome with the most serious complications, involving the heart and aorta.

Blameless, decent, loyal Ralph, my first best friend. After hearing this inconceivable news I sat in the corner of the carport in a foetal position, my arms wrapped tightly around my legs and just rocked backwards and forwards. The image of my dear brother's blood gurgling in his chest was so vivid in my imagination that it added to the grief in unspeakable ways and all my coping mechanisms evaporated. Once I had some control of my feelings, I had to tell my mother: Ralph had always been her favourite. We left immediately for Auckland, where I went to see Ralph for the final time, lying serene in his casket at the funeral parlour. Unconsciously I shrank back when I kissed his ice-cold face: this was the first time I had seen someone dead. Thirty years on, the tears are falling as I write this. I sat with him and talked of the happy and the difficult times we had shared and how we would console each other. I felt so alone. At Ralph's funeral I read Larkin's poem, 'The North Ship', with its wonderful final lines about the vessel, rigged for a long journey, sailing 'wide and far/Into an unforgiving sea/Under a fire-spilling star'. Ralph had requested that his ashes be returned to Christchurch and scattered from Cave Rock at Sumner. And so they were.

Needing to be alone and feel the enveloping comfort of nature, I decided to hike the scenic and less crowded Greenstone Valley Track. I sought solace and I found it. It took three days to follow an ancient Māori trail starting at Te Anau and finishing where the Greenstone Valley enters Lake Wakatipu. I then stayed with my mother before taking her back to Christchurch with me. Then, in May, I whisked her away to Norfolk Island for a week. To get away and mourn, together but apart, seemed to be the right thing, and Norfolk Island was the perfect place – peaceful, easy for walking, hardly any other tourists and for me a treasure trove of history.

There was even a link to Clayton, whose convict grandfather William had been sent there with his wife and son in 1812. When I was not scouting around ruins, my mother and I would go for a long walk every day in the very beautiful landscape. In the evenings we consumed great amounts of alcohol, which temporarily alleviated the pain.

In New Zealand at that time there was only one official full-time registrar, Geraldine Taylor, at the Auckland City Art Gallery. Our professional association began in 1986 when exhibition research brought her to Christchurch when I was acting registrar. Once my role was official, John Coley sent me to Auckland to learn as much as I could from Geraldine. She was a great teacher and the knowledge I gained was immeasurably useful.

I also became a member of the American Association of Museums (AAM). Registrars at American museums were considered a full part of the professional team, more so than anywhere else in the world. In June 1989 the Museums of New Orleans and the State of Louisiana was to host the eighty-fourth annual meeting of the AAM and I saw an opportunity to learn more about my new calling. The Christchurch town clerk turned me down for permission and funding, but I was determined to go. I took annual leave, and with financial assistance and support from Art Galleries and Museums Association of New Zealand, I paid for everything else and attended the conference. There were nearly 3000 delegates from all the American states and from as far away as Russia and Taiwan. I had the distinction of being the only New Zealander, and the delegate who had travelled the furthest. The work of registrars in the United States covered a wide range of areas: permanent collection records, supervision of storage facilities, location of objects, loans in and out, packing, shipping, customs, inventory, insurance and risk management, photography rights, automation of collection management systems, legal aspects and condition reporting. Their minimum qualification was three years' museum experience and a BA in art history. The sessions covered most of these responsibilities in detail and I attended every one. Later I was not only able to share the knowledge I gained with New Zealand art galleries but also to establish policy and procedures for best registration practice at the McDougall.

Instead of eating breakfast and dinner in the conference venue, I would take a tram into the French Quarter and eat at one of the little cafés. Everywhere I walked, jazz and blues would float from dark interiors, lifting the spirits and creating a sense of lightness I had never experienced before. Most nights I gravitated to Preservation Hall, where I sat cross-legged on the wooden floor losing myself in the joy of a band playing pure, traditional jazz. I became an avid fan and purchased many cassettes to take home.

One of my roles as registrar was to courier art works, whether as loans for exhibitions to and from lenders (both private individuals or public institutions) or for other reasons such as for conservation work (the gallery's preferred oil painting conservator lived and worked in remote Takaka), or to uplift acquisitions. The criteria for professional couriering of art works safely must be strictly adhered to. I enjoyed this aspect of my work, whether carried out locally, regionally, nationally or, in some cases, internationally. A gallery van was purchased and equipped with racks, ties and blankets.

Trucks could be hired for moving large works, whole exhibitions or for long journeys, but to drive one I would need a heavy vehicle licence. Undeterred, I took lessons and then, the day of my test, dressed to kill, I tottered into the waiting room in my stilettos and took my seat beside the waiting blokes wearing their ubiquitous black singlets, shorts and boots. They smiled benignly at me. There was a lifting of eyes heavenward and a shaking of heads at the thought that I was even considering obtaining a truck licence. When my turn came, I kicked off my shoes, slipped on my sneakers, swung myself up into the cab and with my examiner nervously beside me, received the command to go. The test went perfectly and it was with some relief to all that I returned the truck and the examiner in perfect condition, and gained my heavy truck licence to boot. I beamed all the way back to the gallery, only wishing that the despairing blokes could have shared my joy.

When moving art works by van or truck it is imperative, for security reasons, to have a dedicated driver and another person riding shotgun so that if one of you has to leave the vehicle for any reason, there is someone with the art works at all times. On my many trips throughout New Zealand,

I always took another staff member with me, usually Merilynne. Over the years we covered most of the country, from Auckland to Invercargill, and had many adventures. On one trip to deliver works to the conservator in Takaka, the van broke down in the Lewis Pass. Leaving Merilynne in the van, I hiked to the nearest phone, which was at Boyle, in the middle of nowhere. The closest garage was at Springs Junction: we had to wait for them to arrive and tow the van the 34 kilometres back to their premises. The repairs would not be finished until the next day. What were we to do with the art works, and indeed, ourselves? There is always a solution. My friend Peter Somerville, who owned and lived at Moonlight Lodge in the Maruia Valley, with his partner Margaret Foyle, came to the rescue. He lent us a ute and trailer which enabled us to continue our journey and get the works safely to Takaka.

A journey to collect exhibition loans from the Auckland City Art Gallery turned out to be a nightmare. On our way back to Christchurch we were caught in a deluge as we approached Palmerston North and when I checked the back of the truck I found it was leaking. I then had to find a warehouse large enough to shelter the truck while I plugged the leak and checked and repacked the art works. Mission accomplished, damage zero. I thoroughly enjoyed returning to Auckland the exhibition, *Colin McCahon: Gates and Journeys*. The huge panels required a Pantech truck and trailer for which I did not have a licence, but this time I rode shotgun. I loved the trip and the driver, who stopped frequently for sustenance – pies and Coke.

Sometimes transit further afield was required. John Coley maintained Rodney Wilson's policy of hosting and endorsing large-scale and high-profile blockbuster exhibitions. *A Century of Modern Masters* came in 1981, *Still Life in the Age of Rembrandt* in 1982, *Paul Klee* in 1984 and in 1986 there were three major international exhibitions: *Oro del Peru, Treasures of the Incas*, the *Buried Army of Qin Shihuang* and *Canaletto, Master of Venice*. When this last show, which consisted of five oil paintings, 33 etchings and seven drawings of Venice, had to be taken to its next venue in Auckland, I was the courier. It amused me when others thought I was lucky to have such a job. Hanging around overseeing the safety of the crates in freight sheds and runways in a cold wintry August was not remotely glamorous. Nor was sitting in a netting seat in the back of a cargo plane dedicated solely to carrying the crates of Canalettos as it thrummed its way northward.

The collection of special works from Australia was more enjoyable as I was able to discuss registration matters with my trans-Tasman counterparts. On several occasions I collected and returned loans from the Gallery of New South Wales in Sydney and from the National Gallery of Australia in Canberra.

When Dorian turned twenty-one on 19 September 1990, I was determined that he would celebrate in a style that had eluded me. Invitations went out to our immediate family and all Dorian's and my friends, and I booked Jean Pierre's Café on Norwich Quay in Lyttelton, with live music from the Doug Caldwell Trio. The delicious food and the wine were French; the beer was not. The fun and frivolity went on well into the next morning. As a present for Dorian, I chose a work by Blair Jackson from an exhibition called *War Birds* at the CSA Gallery (now the Centre of Contemporary Art, CoCA). As Pat Unger had written in her review of the show, small could be splendid – 'Jackson plays with mighty human themes and reduces them to presentation plaques of anti-heroic measure'. So my boy reached another significant milestone, and in style.

For almost 30 years I had been a two pack a day cigarette smoker. I had gone through a stage of rolling my own but soon tired of that. At home, everything was timed by cigarettes. Dorian would say 'When's dinner, Mum?' and my reply would inevitably be, 'After one more cigarette.' At the art gallery smoking was banned and I started to get used to not smoking for long periods of time. I decided it was time to stop. It was hard and I went cold turkey. Cigarettes were replaced with food and my weight ballooned. I knew it must have been pretty bad when I opened Dorian's Christmas present to me that year: *The Hip and Thigh Diet.*

A good deal happened in 1991: Robert Muldoon left Parliament, the Soviet Union as we knew it ended, Gorbachev resigned, Bob Hawke was thrown out – Paul Keating came in, the United States invaded Iraq, my mother had a stroke (not serious), Rashiv Gandhi was assassinated, Mount Pinatubo erupted, the All Blacks lost the World Cup to Australia, and Dorian, at Whenuapai, managed to break several ribs during a rugby game. Millie Ford and I had a long weekend in Melbourne to see *The Phantom of the Opera* and had a picnic at Hanging Rock. We did this in style with an Edwardian-style hamper filled with wine, food and all the trimmings and a tartan picnic rug. We did not disappear without trace, and did not even find the famous spot sinister, though I could understand why some would.

❖

It was time for another escapade in the northern hemisphere. Before leaving, I made a rough plan of which places I wished to visit. When I shop, I shop to buy. 'Window shopping' is anathema to me, time-wasting and vacuous. The same principle applies when travelling. Destinations must have a meaning, which is usually centred on my world of history, art and architecture. So I started at Bruges, relevant to my MA thesis on William Clayton as he spent time there studying architectural motifs that would inspire his own work. From there it was on to old cities, castles, churches, abbeys, palaces, baroque architecture and fine art – not difficult to find in Europe. Armed with a monthly rail pass, I would go to the local train station, look at the place names, do some back of the envelope research and decide where to go next, always staying at a humble (and cheap) local pension.

In Salzburg I stayed at a pension built against the cliff with bars on the windows and the interminable bells ringing from St Sebastian church across the road. No visit to Salzburg is complete without a visit to Mozartplatz in the centre of the Old Town, where the Wolfgang Amadeus Mozart monument by Ludwig Schwanthaler takes centre stage. On the day of my visit, though, there was little to see, only Mozart's head peering above a discordant pile of shopping trolleys. It was an artist's protest at the commercialisation of the composer and the journalism in Austria's major newspaper, *Kronen Zeitung*, which relentlessly marketed him.

Visiting any art gallery was always a solace. While at the superb Kunsthistorisches Museum in Vienna, the city of chandeliers, waltzes and polkas, Klimt and Hundertwasser, I did a double take when I spied, in one of the smaller galleries, Gerard Dou's *The Physician*. I had last seen it only weeks before in the McDougall collection. The connoisseurs' verdict is still out, but the majority seem to think that *The Physician* is one of three signed and dated versions of this work; a fourth is by Jan Adriaensz van Staveren, one of Dou's students. The painting in Vienna, believed to be the original, is painted on oak; the others, including that owned by the McDougall, on copper. Dou was Rembrandt's first student, training with him in Leiden while in his teens, and for a significant period he eclipsed his master's reputation.

Taking the train to Hungary and on to Budapest was intimidating. At the Hungarian border, fast asleep in my bunk, I was woken at 2 a.m. by a soldier in full uniform with a gun slung over his shoulder, shining a torch into my eyes. He stared at me for a few moments, examined my passport and then moved on. Budapest was crowded with tourists but I found a bed for the night in a house of a deaf geriatric with no English, who kindly vacated her large sitting room for my stay. I shared with the owner a bathroom and a toilet behind a curtain. It was de rigueur in Europe to see bullet holes in large public buildings and in Budapest there were many that were reminders of the 1956 revolution. I had distant but fond thoughts of my first fiancé, Tibor.

And then the glorious art and architecture of Venice completely seduced me. I have one vivid memory that has not been blurred by seeing endless architectural gems since: the arcade awnings in St Mark's Square. Their beauty and grace captivated me, as they had Doris Lusk, when she was in the city in 1975. As she noted, 'I was so attracted by the texture, variety and mobility of the light canvas awnings that I recorded them on the spot with sketches and slides'. The resulting outstanding series of watercolours is now housed in the Auckland Art Gallery Toi o Tāmaki.

Siena, the terracotta town, a UNESCO World Heritage Site and living masterpiece to 'the ideal embodiment of a medieval city' was everything I could have wished for, especially the zebra-striped Duomo, meticulously crafted and beautiful. Serendipitously, during the first night of my stay, hundreds of people gathered to watch an outdoor classical concert in the Piazza del Campo. I made my way there, found a seat at a table, ordered a wine and sat back, as if in a dream, to people-watch. Later the spectacular fireworks show against the architecture of the square and the campanile conjured up emotions and words in my head well beyond my capability to articulate.

I spent Dorian's twenty-second birthday in Florence. My art history courses had not prepared me for seeing the originals. The visual feast went on and on. But the days were moving by quickly and soon it was time to move on. I was desperate to get to France and Vincent van Gogh country, around Arles. Trains took me via Nice and Marseilles. Once I was on French soil I was content. It felt right. After Arles, and day trips to Avignon and Pont de Gard, it was on to the glories of Paris. One of the musts for me there was a visit to the cemetery at Père-Lachaise to pay homage at Oscar Wilde's tomb, designed by Jacob Epstein. (No, I did not add a stamp of my red lips to the plethora of others already there.) I found a memorial to a Monsieur Dorian, Minister of the Interior during the 1870–71 Siege of Paris. Also memorable was the site of the Bastille (now the Opéra Bastille), where, according to family lore, my supposed ancestor, Bernard René Jourdan, Marquis de Launay, was the French governor when the fortress was stormed on 14 July 1789. His head was separated from his body, attached to a pike and paraded through the streets. I picked up a bright red rental car in Tours and was stopped by a gendarme just once for speeding on a country road. I was let off with a warning. After three days exploring the Loire Valley and its chateaux, picturesque villages and limestone cave houses, while navigating a left-hand drive vehicle on narrow streets and over gutters, it was on to Brittany and my last fling in mainland Europe before making my way across to England.

As registrar, I had been corresponding with Annette Thompson, the daughter of Christchurch painter Sydney Thompson, about the proposed retrospective exhibition of her father's work, *At Home and Abroad*, to be held at the McDougall from December 1990 to the beginning of February 1991. Annette had invited me to stay with her and her partner, Mimi Tallec, if I was ever in Concarneau. They lived in the house named Kost Ar Pin, on the Allée des Sauges, where Thompson had died in 1973. I gratefully took up their offer and felt privileged to find I was to sleep in Thompson's stand-alone studio in the garden, where he had painted for the last years of his life.

Annette was a superb guide. She introduced me to delicious crêpes in the local crêperie – blé noir (black wheat flour) for savoury crêpes and froment (white flour) for sweet ones. And we saw all the places that had meaning for Thompson and revealed the great respect in which he was held. There is a street, albeit a dead-end one, named after him, and I viewed five of his paintings in the Concarneau Town Hall. We visited Locronan and the Chapel of Notre Dame de Bonne Nouvelle and next to it the laver – a good laundering system with rocks, soapy water and rinsing water, all from the well. We visited the Gallerie Gloux, the green house with the balcony where Thompson would sit painting scenes of the harbour. Annette took me to where he was represented at the Musée de Pont-Aven and the Musée de Quimper, and I stood at his simple tomb in the Concarneau cemetery. By the time I left, I had a renewed appreciation for Thompson's French work, and for him personally. It was not difficult to understand why there was such a continuing and powerful appeal for these beautiful essays in colour.

I had been away for two months – time to go home.

For the 1975–76 Christmas holidays I was lent an old caravan,
which I had towed down to the South Brighton camping ground.
I enjoyed the camaraderie of the other adults, Dorian had plenty
of children to play with and the beach was just across the road.

The H. B. Bower & Co. Ltd premises in Tuam Street, Christchurch.
My office was to the right through the front door. Upstairs were
the rattan weaving looms. The extrusion plant was on the ground floor
in the Venetian Gothic building, glimpsed at the left. - *Bower family archives*

Picton Avenue, 1980.

The Armagh Street cottage.

My mother and Tom Burtt, with his dog Abigail, inspecting my new purchase.

Conal McCarthy and Anne, caught up in the moment, dancing on the
table while trying to avoid the hanging light. Conal went on to become a
world authority on museum studies, though his destiny, like mine,
is far from obvious here.

This ad, which appeared in *Art New Zealand*, shows the
Robert McDougall Art Gallery staff in 1985. Left to right: education officer
Ann Betts, technician Les Fibbens, director John Coley, conservator
Lynn Campbell, registrar Anne Crighton, cleaner Walter Holmes,
custodian Gordon Ducker, shop manager Merilynne Evans,
exhibitions officer Roger Smith, administrator Jenny Barber,
curator Neil Roberts and exhibitions technician Hubert Klaassens.
– *Christchurch City Council*

Ralph in happier days with Latiesha (left) and Vicki-Anne.

Over Christmas 1989 I took on the Routeburn Track – solo.
The 39 kilometres took me four days as I was not physically fit but I
relished the challenge, especially on the graded climbs.

Ralph and Daniel, on 17 December 1989, with their home-built
Starling and sailing trophies won by Daniel. Ralph died suddenly,
aged 49, on 5 January 1990.

Mother and daughter on Norfolk Island – Anson Bay (left) and the
summit of Mount Pitt, May 1990.

Anna at the opening of *A Canterbury Perspective*,
Robert McDougall Art Gallery, Christchurch, 1990.

In February 1992, with exhibitions officer Hubert Klaassens, I drove north
to collect *The Gorse King* by Denis O'Connor, a very heavy sculpture of
33 pieces of Maheno limestone which had to be collected from the artist's
studio on Waiheke Island.

An artist's protest against the commercialisation of Mozart partly obscures Ludwig Schwanthaler's statue of the composer: referring to Austria's largest newspaper, the label reads, 'Is its opportunistic reporting supposed to bring new readers?' 11 September, 1991.

The arcade awnings in St Mark's Square,
Venice, captivated me in 1991, as they had Doris Lusk in 1975.

Doris Lusk, *Arcade Awning, St Mark's Square,
Venice (6)*, 1976, Pencil and watercolour, 510 x 636 mm.

– Auckland Art Gallery Toi o Tāmaki, purchased 1980

Anna and Jude Ritchie with their longhouse hosts,
during a visit to Sarawak, 1992.

Sculptor Margriet Windhausen putting the finishing touches on the bronze
relief for the Kate Sheppard National Memorial, which had just been returned
from the foundry, 1993.

The upstairs bathroom and the kitchen of
86 Chester Street East as they were in 1993.

The front door and porch of 86 Chester Street East, before and after.

For the International Gnome Convention hosted by the McDougall in 1995,
Merilynne Evans and I each commissioned a gnome from Colin Bryce:
Vera and Jack Duckworth from *Coronation Street*. Note the signature sticking
plaster holding Jack's glasses together and Vera's hoop earrings.

When Kevin Kennedy (Curly Watts) came to Christchurch in June 2001,
regular members of the dinner group held a *Coronation Street* Celebrity Tour
Down Under lunch at the town hall. From left: Sue James, Merilynne Evans,
Pat Unger (front), Anna, Kevin Kennedy, Jenny May, Alister James, Julie King.

My father had inscribed the Lord's Prayer on paper stuck to
one side of this silver threepenny piece.

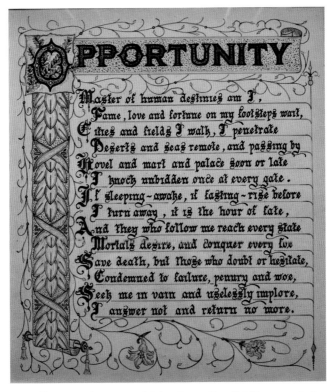

OPPORTUNITY

Master of human destinies am I,
Fame, love and fortune on my footsteps wait,
Cities and fields I walk, I penetrate
Deserts and seas remote, and passing by
Hovel and mart and palace soon or late
I knock unbidden once at every gate.
If sleeping~awake, if feasting~rise before
I turn away, it is the hour of fate,
And they who follow me reach every state
Mortals desire, and conquer every foe
Save death, but those who doubt or hesitate,
Condemned to failure, penury and woe,
Seek me in vain and uselessly implore,
I answer not and return no more.

An illuminated version of John James Ingalls' 'Opportunity',
crafted by my father.

Anna and Barbara Davies with the statue of Tame Horomona Rehe, Tommy Solomon, at Manukau, Chatham Islands, 1998.

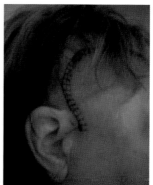

Anna with a very inadequate comb-over! Note the perfect blanket stitch by neurosurgeon Martin MacFarlane.

Anna with the mayoral Daimler in the Botanic Gardens, 1996.

A council meeting in the Provincial Government Buildings, February 1996. Anna is seated third from bottom left (in green jacket), between Denis O'Rourke and David Close. Vicki Buck presides and, on the far right, council secretary Max Robertson takes the minutes. – *Christchurch City Council*

I was canonised by the often acerbic, caustic and formidably talented printmaker Barry Cleavin, whose inscription on a laser print read: 'Dear Saint Anna of Chester St, the residents of 53 Proctor Street are much reassured that you are crusading once again on the cities behalf – congratulations and best wishes. Wonderful! Barry.' – *With permission of the artist*

Paul Hartigan's *Nebula Orion*, 2001.

But I found myself travelling again the following year. In 1992 Christchurch experienced a long, cold miserable winter and there seemed no better time to visit Jude Ritchie, a colleague from the McDougall who, with her partner Neil Carmody, was living in the coastal settlement of Lumut, some 30 kilometres from Kuala Belait, the second biggest town in Brunei. When I arrived in the capital, Bandar Seri Begawan, on 12 July, I contentedly compared the 29°C heat with the 2° frost I had left. At the local restaurant the waitress had whispered to Jude, 'Would you like our special tea?' When Jude nodded, the woman placed a large teapot and three glasses on the table, then demurely bowed her head and left. 'Special tea, Anna?' enquired Neil, as he poured a bubbly golden briskly chilled liquid into my glass. Ah, beer. This clandestine practice was, of course, because we were in a devout Muslim country where alcohol was prohibited. During my stay a quick flight from Brunei to Kuching in Sarawak was a must for two reasons: I was fascinated by the ethnology of the indigenous people of Borneo, the Dayaks and Ibans, and I was desperate to visit an orangutan reserve.

Just 20 kilometres south of Kuching we found these fabulous creatures at the Semenggoh Forest Reserve. It is an unforgettable experience to walk through the rainforest where this endangered rare species roams free, protected, cared for and fed. As I was walking along the track I felt a soft, furry little hand reach up to take mine and looked down to see an adorable baby orangutan happily trotting alongside me. My heart melted, but then guide Maryann Teo sternly told me to let go. We could look but not touch. These beautiful creatures are being threatened by the culling of the rainforests: the sound of chainsaws and bulldozers roaring in the distance was very disturbing.

In Kuching we met guide Edwin Mindod, a Land Dayak and father of seven children. He agreed to take us to a traditional longhouse and before we left instructed us to purchase cigarettes and lollies and to take a packed lunch. Given that there were no means of tracing where we were going, we really did trust our lives to Edwin and the two Iban boatmen. After a 100-kilometre bus trip to Gedong village, at the junction of Gedong and Badang Sadong rivers, we transferred to a dugout canoe. We eventually came to a small jetty, from which we walked to the longhouse. Of simple construction, it was built with natural forest materials and raised off the ground on stilts. Twenty-one private rooms sat next to each other along the back wall for the Iban families living there, with a wide communal area running along the front. Dogs, pigs and chickens roamed everywhere. The Iban were steeped in ancient animism rituals and there were fruit offerings at the entrance to the house.

We were welcomed like royalty with gongs and dancing and offered cracker biscuits and watery sweet black coffee. In return, we shared our lunch of chicken sandwiches, cake, oranges and bananas with the children, after handing over our gifts of cigarettes and lollies. Ibans were famed head hunters until the government made the practice illegal. There was evidence of this past history in a collection of hanging circles of human skulls placed intermittently along the length of the communal area.

Once back in Brunei I contacted Dr Morni Othman, whom I had met through my friends well-known Christchurch psychologist Ralf Unger and his wife, artist and reviewer Pat. He had studied for his PhD at Lincoln University and was director-general of the Forestry Department for Brunei. Dr Othman arranged a chauffeur-driven car with an English-speaking guide to drive me around for a day. My guide, Dayang Anny Arbi, as a member of the project committee for Sustainable Integrated Rural Development, had spoken at an open forum at Lincoln University just weeks before my visit to Brunei. We saw Prince Jefri's private beachside palace, Brunei Museum, with its ornate engravings and patterns, and many mosques. While drinking tea with Dr Othman at the end of the day I learnt that 61 per cent of Brunei was in virgin forest compared to 1 per cent in New Zealand. The country was, however, highly, even comically, over-bureaucratic and the workforce underemployed. For example, when you presented your passport at the airport, one woman would take it and remove a staple, then pass it to a second woman, who wrote something on a new piece of paper, which she passed to the next woman, who stapled that to the passport. Finally, the passport would be hand-delivered to the boss, a male who had his own office, who stamped it. Once the whole lengthy procedure was completed, the women would go back to reading their comic books or doing crosswords until the next customer arrived.

I was sorry to leave Brunei and Sarawak but I am glad to have seen this remarkable area before it became popular with tourists.

CHAPTER 11
More Sadness and Joy

Nineteen ninety-three marked the centenary of women's suffrage in New Zealand and as a member of the Christchurch City Council's Women's Suffrage Sub-Committee I was heavily involved in planning the celebrations. These included the creation of a 9-metre-long wall hanging for the town hall designed by Dunedin artist Di Ffrench and stitched by members of the Canterbury Embroiderers' Guild, naming a meeting room at the civic offices the Camellia Room – the suffrage campaigners had worn white camellias – and adding to its walls portraits of all women Christchurch city councillors past and present, assisting with the *White Camellias* exhibition at the McDougall, and the making and unveiling of the Kate Sheppard National Memorial. Pat Unger and I made several trips to the Timaru home of Dutch-born New Zealand sculptor Margriet Windhausen, who had been selected to fashion the memorial. Placed in a landscaped area on the banks of the Avon River in Oxford Terrace, this was unveiled on 19 September by Governor-General Dame Catherine Tizard – a significant monument to a noble cause.

But 1993 was a remarkable year for me in another quite unexpected and significant way. It all began in 1992 after I returned from Brunei. I was in the gallery basement storage area retrieving works for an exhibition when Merilynne called me upstairs. A young woman had introduced herself as Vera and explained that she was on holiday from Melbourne and had traced me on behalf of her sister, Jeanette – my daughter. Jeanette, who lived in Munich, was reluctant to contact me herself but happy for her sister to be her envoy. After a brief conversation I discovered that they had been adopted by the same couple and raised together as sisters. My immediate reaction was that I did not wish my daughter to feel abandoned for a second time. I asked her sister to tell Jeanette that I would be very happy to start a relationship, initially through correspondence. This would give us both the opportunity to learn about each other's lives.

Then, of course, I needed to inform Dorian that he had a half-sister. The time had never seemed right until now. I asked him to meet me at Pedro's, one of my favourite eating places, as I had something important to tell him. He pestered me to say immediately what it was but I refused. When, over dinner, I relayed the whole story, his reaction was unexpected. He looked me in the eye and said, 'Is that all, Mum? I thought you were going to tell me you had cancer.' He heaved a sigh of relief and took the news well. In fact, he seemed quite pleased that he had a sister.

In March, accompanied by her considerably older partner Michael, Jeanette came to Christchurch. My 28-year-old daughter was tall, very slim, elegant and beautiful. Michael said later he could see the likeness between us: we even walked the same way. I was terrified, quite unsure what to say. I wanted everything to be perfect for her but bridging the years between her birth and our meeting was difficult. I had to explain that, when she was born, New Zealand followed a policy of closed stranger adoption, in which all contact between the child and its natural mother was severed. This had not stopped me from wondering about her – where she was and if she was happy with her adopted family. Then the Adult Information Adoption Act, passed in 1986, allowed adopted adults and birth parents to contact each other, if they wished, providing an opportunity to bring years of denial and secrecy to a happier conclusion. And a happy conclusion was something I earnestly desired, though I had been reluctant to go down the path myself. How could I explain my feelings at the time of the adoption? It was so long ago. How could I explain that if it had been now, I would have had the determination and courage to make a different decision? Would saying that help either of us? So many questions with no adequate answers.

My little Armagh Street cottage thankfully had three bedrooms, the third used by Dorian, who took leave to come home and meet his sister. Michael did not speak English and my German was not very good, so it fell to Jeanette to talk to him and translate for us, which I am sure she found extremely tiring. I spent the short time they had in Christchurch showing them around and enjoying getting to know Jeanette. Dorian and I did the best we could to make them feel welcome and the visit was a success. Pat and Ralf Unger hosted a lunch at their house in Gleneagles Terrace for the new arrivals, together with my friends and immediate family. This delightful occasion gave Jeanette a chance to meet everyone and allowed Michael to talk with Ralf, who spoke German well. In her nineties, Pat remembered how 'you could feel the emotion swimming around the room'. Everyone agreed that it was a remarkable mother-daughter reunion.

I commissioned Margaret Hudson-Ware to paint a double portrait of me and Jeanette. She took photos of us seated in the garden and these images became both a treasured reminder of our first meeting and a useful reference for Margaret. Almost a year later she wrote to me, apologising for the length of time it was taking to finish the portrait. She did say, however, that, 'This is not a sad painting ... This is revealing itself to be a soft-strong-graceful work with overtones and undertones, but mostly a lovely work of you both.' It was titled *I Hereby Consent* – the first words of the legal document I signed to complete the adoption. When Jeanette saw the painting on a subsequent visit she did not like the portrayal of herself. I think it convincingly recaptures a sense of mutual wariness and reserve, with an attempt at affection felt, probably by both parties, but not quite succeeding.

Six months later, in late September, I landed at Munich International Airport, where I was met by Jeanette, Michael and Georgie, their old English sheepdog. Their house was in Puchheim, a town of some 20,000 residents located 18 kilometres from Munich. It was obvious, from the beautifully furnished house with its art, specialist lighting and exotic indoor plants, that Michael was wealthy. As I wrote in my journal, 'I feel so strange and mixed up. Also met Helga, Jeanette's adopted mother – she is so sweet and tiny and I immediately liked her. She told me she was mother 1 and I could be mother 2!' The next day, after attending Oktoberfest, we visited Michael's leather fashion business in downtown Munich, where he generously gave me several beautiful leather and suede jackets. I could feel myself loosening up a bit and two-hour walks with Georgie through the nearby forest were an ideal way for Jeanette and me to chat. She told me about her sister, her upbringing, her father and Helga, the parents' marriage split and the ultimate decision to move to Germany with her mother. She had known, intuitively, that she was adopted, which inevitably made her feel that she had been unwanted. I learnt that she loved to draw and she was excellent at fashion design, a skill she used working for

Michael. As the days passed and we discovered more about each other, I became more relaxed. When Jeanette was at work, I stayed in Puchheim, walking Georgie and exploring the area, either on the excellent bike lanes or walking. Sometimes, I would take Georgie into the city on the S-Bahn to meet Jeanette and Michael after work. Dogs were allowed everywhere.

At weekends, road trips were planned with no expense spared. We travelled in style, stayed at the best hotels, a lot of alcohol was consumed and meals seemed to take priority over sightseeing. The autobahns, with their notorious lack of a speed limit, took some getting used to. The police drove Porsches and Michael cruised along at 180 kilometres per hour in his Mercedes. On Tuesday 19 October I noted in my journal, 'I did a lot of thinking in the night. I have a lot of shit to get rid of somehow. I still feel guilty about Jeanette and having buried memories for nearly 30 years it takes some facing up to. If there had ever been a doubt if she was my daughter it was immediately dispelled when I discovered yesterday Jeanette has a red patch on the nape of her neck. My mother, Dorian and I all have one the same.' My 32 days with my daughter were certainly memorable and I was sad. But I was happy to witness her evident sense of contentment in the close bond with Helga. I could return home comforted with that knowledge.

When I returned to Germany two years later, the highlight of the visit was time away with Helga – Mother No. 1 and Mother No. 2 getting to know each other on a journey of discovery while visiting the Tyrol to view the Dolomites. I was distressed to discover that the knitting and sewing I had done for the baby all those years ago was not sent with her when she was flown to Invercargill: Helga said the baby arrived in a singlet and nappy only. When I was due to depart, Jeanette wanted to see Buckingham Palace and other highlights, so we flew to London. The irony of the visit to England, where she had never been, was not lost on us. We drank a toast to be returning to the country together, 30 years after her conception there.

When I had been in Brunei, Kathy had contacted me to say that she had seen an advertisement for the sale of my favourite Christchurch house, a grand Victorian pile on the corner of Chester Street East and Madras Street. When passing it I would think, 'I will buy that house one day and restore it.'

So, on my return, Kathy and I inspected it and I decided there and then I wanted it. It was an impulsive buy but one that I have never regretted.

It had been a satisfying achievement to take a run-down central city worker's cottage and make it into a lovely home. But it was time to move on. The completion of the restoration was much admired and word soon leaked out that it was for sale. When esteemed children's author Margaret Mahy came to view the cottage with her daughter Penny, she loved its eccentricity and cosiness and promptly purchased it. I could not think of a more suitable owner.

Numbers 86–100 Chester Street East, four pairs of kauri timbered semi-detached Victorian townhouses, were designed and built in 1892 for William Widdowson, who purchased the land in 1890. An architect, surveyor, builder and landowner, Widdowson had arrived in Christchurch from Nottingham in 1858. After he died in his home at No. 102 in 1915, 86–100, which had been built for family members, were not sold until his last surviving descendant died in 1961. The houses then went on the market and were converted into flats and offices during the 1960s rental boom. When Madras Street was widened in 1982, the Chester Street East Residents' Association saved Nos 86 and 88 from demolition. It was only later that I learnt more of the history of Widdowson and his extensive family and descendants. It did not surprise me that, despite a century of change, the 'genius of the place' was still palpable. The Widdowson name cropped up in two distinctive areas that connected me indirectly with the family. First, he was a deacon of the Trinity Congregational Church, which I would later be directly involved in saving and restoring after the 2010–11 earthquakes. Second, as a member of the Canterbury District Health Board for 12 years, on my way to meetings I would pass the portrait of his granddaughter, the formidable Grace Widdowson, OBE, who was 'lady superintendent' in charge of all North Canterbury's hospitals from 1935 until 1952.

The Victorian architectural style of the eight houses, which were designed to mirror one another, is somewhat reminiscent of the San Francisco's famous 'painted ladies', yet well-heeled residents of West Hampstead, London, would certainly feel at ease in them too. Some detailing also echoes the influence of the Arts and Crafts movement. The façades at 86 were distinguished by their side-by-side double bay windows facing Madras Street and the double bays at the front. The framing and weatherboards for the houses was kauri and the party walls between them triple brick. The decorative iron work and bull-nosed roofs of the front porches were supported by turned pilasters. By 1992 Youth for Christ owned Nos 86 and 88, which were in a shabby state: 86 had been turned into offices and its bathrooms removed for storage; 88 had been converted into two flats. Because I could not afford to buy both houses – they were on one title – Kathy and I decided to jointly purchase the property, which we did on 5 October 1992.

As Kathy remembers, 'This was in the days when banks just threw money at you. I don't think either of us had any paperwork such as evidence of income, savings etc. We just appeared with only our enthusiasm and, in my case, an overexposure of cleavage which I thought at the time might distract from my lack of funds. When we were asked about how much deposit we had, I blithely said, "Nothing", and Anna said, "Oh, don't worry. I'll lend you the deposit."' Surprisingly unfazed, and in fact very entertained, the bank manager continued, asking how much we wanted to borrow. 'We hadn't even worked that out, so we asked to use his calculator and sat there in the meeting trying to work out how much we needed.' Somehow the required funds were approved. 'How we walked out of that bank with a mortgage I will never know. I put it down to my cleavage but Anna put it down to the fact that she actually did have some funds.' Youth for Christ leased back both 86 and 88 for one year. This gave me time to plan ahead and I was then able to purchase Kathy's share.

On possession day, I organised a bring your own picnic lunch for my friends and family. As soon as I had entered 86, it had embraced me but my visitors did not see it through my eyes and were aghast. I looked past the fact that the houses sat on a site with low picket fencing and no garden or even a shed or garage. I saw beyond the fact that everything was blue, my least favourite colour for houses. The exterior was painted blue and white, with a blue colour-steel roof. Inside there was blue and white paintwork and trims, blue carpet, blue lino, blue curtains, blue ceiling roses and even blue wallpaper. Subsidence had caused the party wall to settle to such a degree that you stumbled slightly when walking down the hallway. Walls had been removed and others built where they should not have been. The beautiful coloured leadlight windows had been painted over in black but at least they had not been removed. The upstairs bathroom had been filled with shelving for sports equipment and storage. There was an apology for a kitchen and no bathroom downstairs, though there was a toilet. The back door led onto asphalt.

But the rooms were light and airy and many period features remained. The original ceiling roses were intact, as were the mullioned windows. The rimu staircase was untouched, although painted, and the kauri doors were still there, though they, too, had been painted. The original rimu flooring emerged from beneath archaeological layers of carpet and linoleum. There were four rooms upstairs and a bathroom, while downstairs there were what should have been a drawing room, a formal dining room, a kitchen, sitting area, a cloakroom and toilet. (I would later add a garage and laundry with internal access to the back of the house.)

I spent the next 17 years, as budget allowed, methodically removing all the blue, returning the walls to where they should have been and, room by room, restoring the features and decorating. I lived upstairs with a basic kitchen while the downstairs one was upgraded. Every Saturday I would laboriously remove the black paint from one of the 10 leadlight windows until they were all taken back to their original colours. I have an aversion to white painted ceilings so when it came to choosing the colours for the rooms, the ceilings and walls were done in the same colour. With the plaster cornicing, ceiling roses and deep skirtings painted a light putty colour, the result was pleasing. My creative DNA was exercised for the choice of interior colours: dramatic mauve for the drawing room and the main bedroom upstairs, deep sea-green for the TV/library room, a luscious custard yellow for the downstairs and upstairs hallways and a pōhutukawa red for the cloakroom. Imported wallpaper friezes put up in most rooms suited the age of the house.

Gradually both the exterior and roof were painted, again removing all evidence of blue. The five different shades of green and cream selected for the exterior highlighted the detailing of the original design. I installed a 1.8-metre picket fence along Madras Street and built a brick wall around the front courtyard, where a garden slowly evolved, improving each season with perennials coaxed out of the difficult soil. In these happy but busy years the house became my release from the pressures of work.

In 1994 I spent my fiftieth birthday quietly at home. Dorian presented me with personalised car plates that said '4 ANNA'. He told me he wanted 'ANNA 1' but it was already taken. He was offered 'ANNA 2' but perceptively said, 'No thanks. My mother is to feel special, not coming in second.' That touched me even more. We ceremoniously attached the plates to Rhonda Honda and they have been transferred to all my subsequent vehicles. To celebrate my half-century I secretly had an understated yellow rose tattooed on my shoulder, just above my burn scar. This remained unnoticed until I took my five-year-old granddaughter swimming some 10 years later. 'Gran's got a tattoo,' Olivia proudly announced to her parents.

My stepmother Joan, from whom my father had parted, walked a fair distance from her home to give me a gift on the day. In my happy mood I did not detect any sign of forlornness within her but a week later I was informed that she had committed suicide on 19 January. She was 69. I felt so sad and only wished I had been aware of her desolate plight. Her death notice stated that she was the 'dearly loved nana of Dorian, and the late Vicki-Anne', her beloved grandchildren. Three days after my birthday, family and friends celebrated Dorian's engagement to Helen Morgan. I held a party for them at home at Armagh Street.

That year, too, at the age of 77, my father had his gangrenous left leg amputated above the knee. His third wife, Kathleen, was asked to sign the permission for the surgeon to operate but because his heart condition meant he might not make it through the operation, she did not feel capable of doing so and asked me to make the decision. It was made clear to me that without the amputation he would not live long anyway and so there was no choice. Though wheelchair bound, he lived for another three years. During his post-operative recovery in a Christchurch Public Hospital ward he found himself next to my friend, artist Barry Cleavin. They enjoyed each other's Goonish company as they shared a bizarre and quirky sense of humour. Barry wrote a poem, 'Noel', which was later published in *takahē*:

> Noel, when asked what he would like,
> > Tonight,
> > Friday
> From a prescribed possibility
> Of charted medicines
> Replied,
> 'Morphine would be good thank you ...
> with a curl of lemon and an umbrella.'

The Mercy Angel returned with
a 25ml plastic measure of Alkaloid Cocktail.
above it a large, unfurled black crow umbrella.

That night Noel dreamed his remaining
upper leg – saved from gangrene –
was sharpened to a point,
polished to high Kauri hue,
embellished with Koru and such like

I heard him struggling with his dream.

During a weekend in March 1995, a very different kind of exhibition was
hosted by the McDougall – the International Gnome Convention, curated by
art teacher and gnomologist, Henry Sunderland. It is possible that gnomes
as we know them can be attributed to English landowner and gardener
Sir Charles Isham who, in 1848, imported terracotta character figurines from
Nuremberg in Germany to populate a mammoth rockery garden he was
creating on his estate at Lamport Hall, Northampton. This began a fashion
for such garden ornamentation in Victorian England. The last survivor from
the original group is the Lamport Hall gnome, believed to be the oldest in
the world and an undoubted, and extremely valuable, celebrity. 'Lampy', as
he is known, was couriered to Christchurch by the executive director of the
Lamport Hall Trust, George Drye and his wife Fiona. The loan conditions
were strict. On arrival it was placed in an alarmed case. During opening
hours four security guards were on duty and when the gallery was closed full
security was also required. Just 15 centimetres tall, the Lamport Gnome was
insured for £1million.

Other representatives of the international gnome community made
an appearance. Five gnomes travelled from the South Pole and others
came from Japan, Fiji, the United States, Germany, Australia and Korea.
Terry Major, half-brother of British Prime Minister John Major, personally
accompanied his gnome from London. Prime Minister Jim Bolger sent
Beaumont (which had been presented to him at the opening of the
Clyde Dam), author Keri Hulme sent her 'invisible' gnome, the Mayor

of Christchurch, Vicki Buck, sent the mayoral gnome and the Wizard of New Zealand sent Lares. In all, 145 gnomes registered for the convention and as registrar I was personally responsible for issuing loan documentation for each. The exhibits were kept behind a picket fence and only so many people could enter at any one time because of the crowds: queues stretched from the gallery entrance, down the path alongside the Canterbury Museum and out to Rolleston Avenue. It was mad, it was fun and it was popular: the show attracted over 8500 smiling spectators.

Not to be outdone, Merilynne and I each commissioned a gnome from Colin Bryce: Vera and Jack Duckworth from *Coronation Street*. I was an avid *Coronation Street* fan until most of the traditional characters had died and TV1 decided to skip the 18-month lag from Britain and lurch straight into current episodes. Many of my friends and colleagues also devotedly watched this beloved television saga. When Kathy gave me a *Coronation Street* cookbook for Christmas in 1993, I had the idea of organising *Coronation Street* dinners, which became a mini Christchurch cult. There was a set format. Since my table accommodated eight, we had seven core members and room for one invited guest. Invitations were sought after and we even had people on a waiting list. For the three-course meal each member was given a recipe from the book. It had to include the exact ingredients stated – otherwise the offending chef would be blackballed. It was great fun hunting down particular ingredients: Johnson's Grocery in Colombo Street was a favourite source of British stock. A dinner might consist of such favourites as Deidre's Pea Soup as a starter followed by Alec Gilroy's Beef in Beer (his recipes always had to include booze) or Jack and Vera Duckworth's Meat and Potato Pie. Desserts were easy: Percy Sugden's Paradise Trifle, Rita's Summer Pudding or Mike Baldwin's Spotted Dick. Appropriate table decoration was provided by gnomes Vera and Jack. After dinner there was a quiz, with a *Coronation Street* teapot trophy awarded to the winner.

The year 1997 began with a wedding and ended with a funeral. Dorian and Helen's marriage on 25 January turned out to be the only time my blood family were ever together, as Jeanette came from Munich. Merilynne made the wedding cake and the ceremony and reception were held in my home and garden. The officiating minister was Jonathan Kirkpatrick, the Anglican Dean of Dunedin. It was a special day with friends clustered in the courtyard, in perfect weather, listening to the music of the Belgillith Trio and enjoying good food and wine.

Having silently sought my father's approval for most of my life, I received it unprompted just three days before he died. When we celebrated his eightieth birthday on 7 September, he had looked awful and after a short time was put to bed. He had been in and out of hospital for most of the year and was extremely frail and gaunt.

In late October, when he was back in Princess Margaret Hospital, he asked me to take him in his wheelchair to the chapel, where we sat in silence together. When we were back in his room he whispered, 'I believe you can do things better than me.' I understood, then, that he had seen me as in competition with him. I found this painful and unfair, and yet it was well meant, his way of paying me a compliment. But it came as little comfort. I would rather have had some sign of affection. Looking back, I can see that, in a way, our lives followed similar trajectories, from seemingly nothing to experiencing satisfying personal achievement.

His death, on 28 October, was long and tortuous. Although 'do not resuscitate' was written in his notes, the hospital staff did exactly that. Kathleen, Dorian and Helen and I sat by his bedside for hours, listening to his uneven breathing – moments of uncertain inhalation followed by pauses until, eventually, there was silence. He had been impatient, eccentric, perfectionist, artistic and an authoritarian. He had alienated Ralph, and me to a lesser degree, through hurtful and thoughtless behaviour. As we sat there, though, faced with the finality of death, it all seemed irrelevant.

His brother Ray inserted his own poignant message in the death notice in the *Press*: 'To Busy, who had the proud duty of ringing the school bell when a pupil at Normal School.' Dorian inherited his watch and I received three items as a legacy from my father. The first was *Rumpty Dudget's Tower*, a book that his sister Vera had given him for Christmas 1926 when he was nine years old. He used to read it to Ralph and me when we were children and it was always kept in his bedside cabinet drawer. The second was a silver threepenny piece with a piece of paper glued to one side. On that tiny surface my father had written beautifully, in black ink, the Lord's Prayer. He had told me, with justifiable pride, that he had done it with the naked eye. The third item was a lovely illuminated version of the poem 'Opportunity' by John James Ingalls. I remember him spending hours crafting this. It always hung on the wall in his study and now hangs in mine.

Once the funeral was over, Kathleen went home to Scotland and I was left with my father's ashes. After they had sat on my desk for over a year,

I carried them down to the Avon River on the south side of the Colombo Street bridge, opposite where he had lived. There I cast them into the water where I imagined him, as a boy, playing among the bulrushes and flaxes. The ashes did not, as I expected, waft through the air on the gentle breeze but lay in a mound on the riverbed as the water washed gently over them. I revisited that spot many times after that, watching the mound slowly lessening until it was no more. I did not return.

My father's death was not the end of the sadness for our small family. In March 1998 Nova rang to tell me that her son, my nephew Daniel, had been in a car accident and was in hospital in Auckland. Two days later, he died. Nova's grief at losing her beloved Ralph eight years before had been indescribable; again, her fortitude and emotions were tested to the limit. My mother and I flew to Auckland to find Daniel lying in his bedroom with a heavily sedated Nova next to him. It was a tragic sight. Daniel, who had been deeply affected by his father's death, had insisted that, when he died, he wanted his ashes to be taken to Spirits Bay, the last place he had gone with Ralph. Nova had said it was too far away and too lonely, but Daniel had replied, 'All oceans meet.' Nova and Latiesha fulfilled his wish, taking Daniel's ashes to Spirits Bay on 23 July, his birthday. Nova gallantly carried on with her life, devoted to Latiesha and, later, to her grandchildren Sacha, Jessie and Jozef. A note in my 1998 diary says, 'I have buried three generations of male Hichens in eight years, my father, my brother and my nephew – Dad, Ralph and Daniel. The name for that branch of the family has now died out. I feel a great pit of sadness and loss.'

There was more travel in the late 1990s: I went to Hong Kong and Macau in 1997 with my friend Barbara Davies and in January of the following year, inspired by the current exhibition of the works of Margaret Stoddart at the McDougall, I decided to visit the Chatham Islands; Barbara went with me. Stoddart, one of New Zealand's best-known flower painters and landscape artists, had made two trips to the Chathams – in 1886–87 and again in 1891 – to paint and visit friends. Because of her travels, we have an extraordinary visual record of that time, not only of the flora, but glimpses of Moriori, Māori and colonial history. By retracing her steps, I wanted to absorb the fascinating history and culture of the island, though where she walked or went on horseback Barbara and I went by four-wheel drive.

Stoddart's first visit to the Chathams took her to Wharekauri, on the northern coast, where she stayed with her friend Mabel Potts, formerly of Governors Bay. (Stoddart's family lived not far away in Diamond Harbour.) Mabel had gone to the Chathams in 1881 with her husband, Edward Chudleigh, who had established a sheep run there. The old house was well documented and photographed but I was disappointed to learn that it had been accidentally burnt down by shearers staying there only five years earlier. Still standing nearby is a ponga house, known to the locals as Te Kooti's whare – the Rongowhakaata leader and prophet had been exiled from the mainland to the Chathams in 1866, along with a number of Hauhau prisoners, who had erected the building. The Chudleighs had used it for storing apples. Stoddart was also a frequent visitor at the Shand homestead at Te Whakaru on the north-east coast, near Kaiangaroa. The house, built by German Moravian missionaries, was enlarged by Archibald Shand when he and his wife Elizabeth settled there with their family in the 1860s. All that is left are a chimney and a stone outhouse.

South of Te Whakaru are the famous Hapupu National Historic Reserve Moriori dendroglyphs, carvings of human figures in the bark of living kopi trees. Stoddart painted these and the ancient rock carvings, petroglyphs, further down the coast on the west side of Te Whanga Lagoon. A page from Stoddart's album, in Canterbury Museum, shows a photograph of the house at Te Whakaru taken by Alfred Martin in 1877, surrounded by watercolour paintings of the petroglyphs and dendroglyphs. Also in the museum is a harrowing 1887 watercolour by Stoddart of massacred Moriori remains and skulls lying openly on the beach at the main port of Waitangi. Her second visit to the island was with the party accompanying Christchurch Bishop Churchill Julius for the consecration of the St Augustine's Church at Te One. The small wooden church is still there.

By the time Barbara and I visited it, the house of Tame Horomona Rehe, Tommy Solomon, the last full-blooded Moriori, who died on the island in 1933, had disintegrated into a heap of timber boards, doors and window frames, with only the brick chimney still standing. Nearby were his grave, and a memorial statue unveiled in 1986. The unrelenting Chathams wind and rain had taken their toll on the statue's cement fondu, which showed major cracking.

The raw, tortured and powerful scenery, from the basalt column formations to the white beaches, the lagoon teeming with whitebait, the rolling expanses of rusty red fern, the historic stone cottages and old homesteads, the forests – all have remained vivid in my memory. Michael King titled the book he wrote about the Chathams, with photographs by Robin Morrison, *A Land Apart*, and it truly is that.

My mother died on 16 October 1999. She had not been well when I spent the previous Christmas with her in Queenstown and had moved to Christchurch to stay with me while she had treatment for acute myeloid leukaemia. Still hopeful of a positive outcome, I had prepared a room so that I could care for her when she left the bone marrow unit at Christchurch Public Hospital, where she spent many weeks. This did not happen. Sam, Mum's partner of 20 years, stubbornly refused to travel from Queenstown to visit her, despite many offers of transport. It was heartbreaking to witness my mother waiting for him. Then she was too sick and too frail to come home with me. When the hospital could do no more for her, I eventually found a garden room at a brand-new retirement complex that also provided medical care. She was there for only two months. When I visited with Merilynne one Saturday I intuitively felt the end was near and the doctor confirmed this. I lay holding her in my arms all night, listening to her quiet breathing until, just before midnight, it stopped. I involuntarily gave a heart-wrenching howl. For all our differences, there was, as there is between all mothers and daughters, a kind of blood-hyphen, that is, finally, indissoluble.

Mum's funeral service, at St Michael's and All Angels, was held during Heritage Week and Jenny May, who was in attendance, quickly and thoughtfully removed the sign at the church entrance that read 'Another Heritage Week Event'. The church was full of family, friends and colleagues: I was so grateful. Sam was not there.

As a solo parent, I had often turned to Mum for practical help, especially once Dorian had turned five and I could work full time. She and Dorian became very close over the years and forged a special and enduring relationship. I could not, however, forgive or forget what she did to me, especially the abandonment when I was a teenager. She may not have shown affection for me in an obvious way but she did finally reveal her pride in my achievements. Nevertheless I could not bring myself to give a eulogy and quoted instead some words written by Charles Kingsley: 'What is the commonest, and yet the least remembered form of heroism? The heroism of an average mother. Ah! when I think of that broad fact I gather hope again for poor humanity, and this dark world looks bright, this diseased world looks wholesome to me once more, because, whatever else it is or is not full of, it is at least full of mothers.' I had hoped that my mother would be interred in the family plot with her parents, but she requested her ashes be thrown from the same spot as her beloved son Ralph's, from Cave Rock at Sumner. My mother and my father had now gone their different ways, in death as they had in life.

PART

THREE

Public Life

CHAPTER 12
Politics

Public life crept up on me. In the early 1990s, sitting in my basement office at the McDougall, I asked myself, 'Do I really want to keep doing this job for the rest of my life?' The answer was 'No'. I loved my position as registrar and enjoyed the camaraderie of the staff, but change was in the air and I needed a challenge. The move to a new art gallery was imminent and I decided to move on. But to what?

I had flirted with the idea of entering politics back in the 1960s but was not settled or experienced enough to pursue that path then. However, living east of the inner city, I became concerned at the decline of services to that area. I was also affronted by the argument that because those living in the more affluent areas of the city paid more rates, more money should be spent in their suburbs. This argument had some substance but it should not mean that others were deprived of an aesthetically pleasing environment and access to good roads, footpaths, street trees and parks. I was also concerned about the destruction of the city's built heritage, and the aberration of modernity blighting its character and identity.

Local politics appealed to me because it brought people closer to the decision-making that would directly affect their everyday lives. That was how I could make a difference and bring about change. As the Dalai Lama once said, 'If you think you are too small to make a difference, try sleeping with a mosquito.' The timing was serendipitous. An ideal start would be standing for a local community board as a political 'apprentice'; this would give me valuable grounding should I wish, later, to be a city councillor. For my central city board, Hagley, I attended a candidate selection meeting for Labour, and was particularly lucky in the character and quality of my selectors, city councillor Alister James and Banks Peninsula MP Peter

Simpson. I was duly selected and after my first campaign in 1992, I was elected to the Hagley Community Board. I stayed for 15 years, becoming chair after only 18 months. My very first public event was at the time of the women's suffrage centenary in 1993, when I was asked to dedicate a seat in Richmond Green. I was both touched and taken aback when an elderly woman came forward, curtsied and presented me with some flowers from her garden. I smiled shyly and said, 'Thank you.'

Active politics did not come naturally to me but I was comfortable with my slightly left of centre social democratic philosophy and my broad approach to local government politics. That said, I never regarded myself as a strongly partisan political animal. For the next Christchurch City Council election, in 1995, I was fortunate to be endorsed and supported by retiring councillor Linda Constable as her replacement for the Hagley Ward. When the results came through, and I learnt that I had been elected, together with Denis O'Rourke, I was overwhelmed with excitement. Vicki Buck, the mayor for my first term, ranks as one of the city's most popular and effective civic leaders. She was young, and a delight to work with and she preferred informality. Vicki was Vicki and that's how she liked it. What you saw was what you got. It was nothing for her to wear jeans or casual trousers and a cardigan when officially greeting VIPs, as though she was about to pop down to the shops.

Among other things, the wearing of the mayoral chain disappeared from council meetings and other formal events. One disappointment for me, and a matter over which we disagreed, was the classic 1970 Daimler that former mayor Sir Hamish Hay had used for formal occasions. Vicki wanted to be rid of the proverbial gas guzzler, which tended to break down, and in 1996 put a recommendation before the council to sell the Daimler by tender. I rose to my feet and exploded. The car was, I argued, part of Christchurch's civic history. As the city's last mayoral car, it should be preserved. I moved an amendment that the Daimler should instead be permanently loaned to a suitable museum and, wonderfully, other councillors rallied behind me and the motion to sell was defeated. Soon after the car found a home at the Air Force Museum in Wigram, the mayor received a letter of thanks from the director, stating that the 'magnificent Daimler' had been one of the most popular displays at the museum's open day. Vicki forwarded this to me: she had written across it the words 'Special for Anna!'.

Also refreshing was Vicki's accessibility. Her door was always open and she was ever welcoming. There were no cliques and she treated everyone without fear or favour. For both elected members and staff, the council was a happy place. The 1990s in Christchurch are inseparable from Vicki's mayoralty: for nine years, our first woman mayor was a dynamic and positive civic leader whose broad smile and infectious laugh conveyed the message that life was to be enjoyed and Christchurch was a great place in which to enjoy it. What an encouraging environment in which to launch my public life.

I had not long been a city councillor when, for several months in 1996, council meetings were held in the Stone Chamber of the heritage-listed Provincial Government Buildings, while the ground floor of the civic offices in Tuam Street (formerly Millers department store) was being completely rebuilt. Designed by architect Benjamin Woolfield Mountfort, and built in timber and stone in the Gothic Revival style, Christchurch's provincial government buildings were the only ones left in New Zealand (though they were, sadly, significantly damaged in the Canterbury earthquakes). When I took my seat at the table, I joyously felt the weight of history upon me. The chairs were roomy and I found them comfortable, though many councillors did not.

Though the cold seeped into our bones during winter meetings, I was very upset when the custodian tried to warm things up with an enormous furnace type blast heater. As I pointed out, this would adversely affect the fabric of the chamber's interior and was a potential fire hazard. The heater was removed and replaced with more appropriate electric ones. When the council moved back to the revamped chamber in Tuam Street, the chairs and U-shaped table went too. I continued to enjoy my historic chair until it, like the others, was replaced by modern ergonomic swivellers in 2005.

Local political life was not always serious. A memorable, light-hearted occasion was the Politicians v Sponsors hockey game held at Porritt Park in October 2001. I had never played hockey in my life but gave it a go. It was a bit daunting, however, when I found I was defending against Lesley Murdoch, a former New Zealand representative cricketer and field hockey player. Then, part way through the game, I was struck on the head by a ball.

As the *Press* noted next day, 'Christchurch City Councillor Anna Crighton finds hockey, like politics, is not a game for the faint-hearted.'

But there were hair-raising moments too. In 2001, I was stalked and received threatening phone calls and messages that I was being watched every time I came home at night: 'I can get you when you leave your car to open the garage door.' The police put a tap on my phone, I had an automatic garage door opener installed and Dorian, comfortingly, came to stay at night. By then he was too tall for his old bed and I had to put the mattress on the floor so he could stretch out. When taking him a cup of tea in the morning, I would, endearingly, find him reading his old Asterix and Tintin books. I was extremely relieved when the stalker was caught.

Beneath the surface, all was not quite as harmonious within the dominant 2021 Labour group as it appeared. I found that I had the greatest difficulties with some colleagues who were supposedly on the same team. Those in the conservative 'opposition' were very rarely adversaries, and more often than not pragmatic and pleasant. There was an unhappy episode for me in 2002. On 14 March, a front-page *Press* headline read 'Therapy for "bullied' councillor"'. Denis O'Rourke's confrontational style – vilification, bullying and intimidation – had left me emotionally distressed, but my days of feeling victimised were well and truly gone and so I took counselling advice about how to handle the situation. My frank admission, which came amid growing unease around the council table about the behaviour of some councillors, was reported by the journalist present. Gail Sheriff's own slanging match with O'Rourke at a meeting the week before had been prompted by the latter's continual bullying of his colleagues, particularly female councillors. Paddy Austin described O'Rourke's behaviour as unacceptable, while long-serving councillor Pat Harrow said that I had been 'particularly poorly treated by Cr O'Rourke whose interpersonal style had to be reined in. The unacceptable bullying had to stop.' Subsequently the Christchurch 2021 caucus asked me to publicly withdraw my claim that I had been forced to seek counselling, but I refused.

Inter-councillor relations deteriorated over the 2001–04 term. A *Press* feature article referred to dramatic tantrums, snide allegations and counter-allegations, and vicious name-calling. Political groupings splintered. The atmosphere became so fiery, and sparked such public derision, that Local Government New Zealand felt forced to protest on behalf of its members among the council staff.

During the latter part of my 12 years as a city councillor, there were two loosely aligned cliques within the council ranks: an A team, mostly acolytes of Garry Moore, who had been elected mayor in 1998 and remained in the role until 2007, and a B team, who were the others. I was never part of Garry's A team. I was aware of the frequent practice of logrolling – 'I'll support you if you support me' – but was not prepared to support it. I believed that decisions should be made on their merits, for more rational and objective reasons, regardless of personalities or party lines. This did not, of course, preclude lobbying. It was general knowledge that the B team was known as 'The Mushrooms' – i.e., kept in the dark. As a result, some information to which all city councillors had a right was not always being shared. When this happened to me I would call on Peter Mitchell, the city solicitor, put my case and stipulate that if I did not have the information I required by 4 p.m. that day, I was going to the *Press*. 'I don't think withholding information from an elected city councillor would pass the page 1 test,' I would tell him. This worked, but sometimes the information was only available to be read in the office and you were not allowed to take notes. Councillors Linda Rutland and Oscar Alpers also laid complaints regarding the withholding of information.

Nevertheless, I had a good working relationship with most of the other councillors, with their extraordinarily varied personalities. I preferred the kind of professional relationship whereby we could debate an issue yet happily enjoy a glass of wine together afterwards in the councillors' lounge. But because I found trust and reliability from others a rare commodity in my life, I kept fairly well to myself and did not encourage after-hours social activities with council colleagues. I considered my own home sacrosanct from politics. Alister James, in my team, proved to be an exception. Though we could certainly lock horns at work, he and his wife Sue became good friends and later neighbours when they moved in only two doors away. He is currently my bridge partner. Also on our team, I enjoyed the advice and support of David Close and Charles Manning, who brought gravitas, experience and decorum to the council table when some started to meander off piste. Barbara Stewart, a member of the 'opposition' and later a valuable and supportive member of the Arts Culture and Heritage Committee which I chaired, grew wonderful radishes and because she knew I loved them, hung a bag of them on my gate each season. Barbara and I lobbied for the Town Hall auditorium to be renamed the Douglas Lilburn Auditorium in 2006. And when Garry Moore and his wife Pam entertained councillors and senior staff at their home, I was always struck by her friendliness and graciousness.

I also enjoyed good working relationships with the staff. Max Robertson ruled supreme over the committee secretaries; I had worked with him in the Department of Statistics back in 1962 and we would often reminisce over those days. Warren Brixton, who was a first-rate committee secretary for the committees I chaired, is now company secretary for the Christchurch Heritage Trust; we have enjoyed a good working relationship for almost 30 years. The same applies to Jenny May, who combines personal style with an incisive mind. From the moment in 1997 when I met Jenny, who had been employed by the council to research heritage information, we became a formidable and very successful team. It was inevitable that our paths would cross, with my advocacy for heritage retention and protection. Our strategy? Jenny would make the bullets and I would fire them.

For the 1998–2001 council term, I was chair of the Environment Committee, which included heritage in its terms of reference, and there was plenty going on. On 11 February 1999, for example, our agenda items included reports that MP Nick Smith had mooted the demolition of Addington Prison when its current usage ceased, Leinster House was signalled as being in danger for demolition, the octagonal units of the Jubilee Hospital were being dismantled and removed to be rebuilt on another site and staff had been involved in discussion with the Wizard and sculptor Mark Whyte regarding a plaque in Cathedral Square. The former brick saddlery building at 355 Riccarton Road, built about 1889, was on the verge of demolition but working with the owner proved fruitful and its restoration assured. Significantly, this was when the earthquake strengthening of the Arts Centre was being reported and progressed. This proved to be a beneficial platform from which to launch my campaign for heritage retention.

I had always admired Helen Clark, who retained the arts, culture and heritage portfolio for the three terms when she was prime minister, from 1999 to 2008. By doing this, she shone the light on this vital but often underfunded area. Until then, money for the arts always seemed to be cut or even scrapped when budgets were tight and yet, in times of hardship, it is to the arts that we turn. When we, as mayor and councillors, discussed what council committees should be included in the next three-year term, 2001–04, I was the driving force behind one embracing arts, culture and heritage, and I am proud to say that this came to pass. It was the first council standing committee of its kind in New Zealand and I became its first chair. Oscar Alpers, Paddy Austin, Sally Buck, Pat Harrow, Alister James, Gail Sheriff and Barbara Stewart put up their hands to be members. Previously the arts had been dealt with by two separate committees and culture and heritage were hardly recognised at all. Now all three areas took centre stage.

The key areas of responsibility were libraries and information, heritage, festivals and events, arts promotion and planning, art in public places, the Christchurch Art Gallery and multiculturalism. Our major priorities for 2002 included reopening the old Municipal Chambers on the corner of Worcester Boulevard and Oxford Terrace to house Our City Ōtautahi, a venue where issues and information about the city's environment and physical development, past, present and future could be displayed, explained and debated. We also established an 'Intercultural Assembly' of key people involved in ethnic relations to improve the way the city was approaching refugee and immigrant matters. The new Christchurch Art Gallery was soon to open, and we also launched a strategy for Art in Public Places. Libraries were an integral part of our programme. Sadly, though, the committee lasted for only one term. After the 2004 election, thanks to the Local Government Commission, the number of councillors was slashed from 24 to 12 and standing committees ceased to exist.

I regretted the drastic reduction of numbers – going from 24 to 18 would have proved more efficient in the long term. The slashing to 12 provided the impetus for Mayor Garry Moore's relentless drive towards his vision for the city to be run like a corporation with a board. I felt this was inappropriate. In my view, councillors were representatives, not directors. I felt, too, that the switch from committees to portfolios was undemocratic: committee meetings had been open to the public but portfolio meetings were to be closed. It seemed to me that this change, prompted by the mayor to streamline procedures, reduced public access to information and opportunities for citizens to attend council deliberations. However, following complaints not only from me but also other councillors, Garry allowed the public to attend most portfolio meetings.

Councillors quickly found that, though their pay rates had increased with the smaller council, they were confronted with a greater workload and less time in which to carry it out. This situation was made worse by complex staff reports and supplementary papers being delivered without warning and too late for proper consideration before two-weekly council meetings. This sort of pressure could lead to elected members merely rubber-stamping council officials' recommendations. When I complained, Garry snapped that if I could not read a document in two days, I should not be on the council. I pointed out that I *had* read, in a day, the document under consideration, but council staff had been working on it for a month and it was much too complex to absorb and analyse in such a short time.

Thanks to amalgamation and some boundary changes, my ward became Hagley–Ferrymead Ward and my running mate for 2004 was Linda Rutland, who was a Ferrymead councillor. The election was strongly contested with the other two incumbents, David Cox and Denis O'Rourke. Seven others were also throwing their hats in the ring, making a total of 11 hopefuls contesting two seats. It was a colourful race but one I decided, at the outset, would be my last, should I be successful. The stakes were high.

It was to be a tough fight. To exacerbate the challenge, I was diagnosed with an aneurysm and admitted to Christchurch Public Hospital on 2 August, just two months before the election, for a craniotomy to clip an unruptured right middle cerebral artery. While I was sitting up in bed after the surgery, out came the laptop and I got on with catching up on my emails, that is, in between long periods of dozing. What a sight I must have looked, with a half-shaved and bandaged head complete with the tube for the drip emerging from the top. When I complimented the surgeon on his sewing skills he smiled wryly and said, 'The younger ones don't do blanket stitch.' When I got home, my very understanding hairdresser came around and cleverly cut and thoughtfully rearranged what hair I had left to disguise the wound.

With no sign of a potential stroke or epileptic fits after the successful operation, though still on morphine, I worked from home. I kept very much off the radar, pamphleting letterboxes with covered head at 6 a.m. when few people were about. However, because wherever I went I wore hats or scarves, the rumours were rife that I had had a face lift (my face was swollen) or, even worse, cancer. I let the gossip drift around me.

There were a couple of skirmishes from two of my rivals in an attempt to derail me. David Cox sniped at me mildly over a Christchurch City Council heritage grant I had received to paint my houses at 86 and 88. He believed I should set a good example by paying part of the grant back. In fact, I had paid back the $2500 loan, which was received before I became a councillor, 12 years earlier. Denis O'Rourke, however, displayed some ferocity. He included a few unhelpful words about me in his campaign circular, but they did me no harm. He, not I, became an election casualty, polling fifth out of the 11 candidates. I was unashamedly proud of my win, given the challenging circumstances under which I had campaigned. The hard work over the last nine years had paid off.

In my first term as a city councillor, I continued to work at the gallery – I had applied for and received special dispensation from the auditor-general to retain both roles – though only part time. However, once the council workload increased, and because I was chairing the Arts, Heritage and Culture Committee, which included the art gallery, I resigned to avoid a conflict of interest. I earned less as a councillor than I did at the gallery, but for me it was not about money, it was about service. I was reluctant to let go of my position at the McDougall: it seemed like cutting an umbilical cord. I had been there, as a temporary and a permanent employee, for over 20 years, and like to think I served it loyally, but there was really no alternative.

I look back with pride on my 15 years as a community board member and 12 as a city councillor. They were exhilarating and rewarding. I worked hard and calculated that for around the 10 per cent of time spent in the spotlight I put in 90 per cent, under the radar, that was sheer bloody-mindedness, determination and hard work. The calibre of the staff I worked with was impressive and because there was trust on both sides we got things done. In 1995 heritage was barely mentioned on the council agenda; by the time I retired in 2007, the budget for the retention and restoration of heritage buildings was healthy and a heritage staff team well established. I am proud of that.

The words of the British politician Denis Healey, 'Fortunately, personal ambition has never been my consuming passion. I have always wanted to do something rather than to be something', ring true for my own career. As I said in my valedictory speech, I stood for the council 'to make a difference and I believe I have'. I was overwhelmed by the many accolades I received, especially the words of a press statement from David Close, who chaired the Labour Local Government Committee. Until I appeared, Christchurch had not, he said, seen a councillor so committed to arts and heritage, 'and is unlikely to see her like again. Anna will be remembered for her passionate advocacy for heritage buildings, but she was more than an advocate. She was skilled at working with others to devise practical plans to save heritage buildings, to strengthen, restore and refurbish them, and to find an ongoing use compatible with the historic character of the building.' David also kindly highlighted my strong interest in urban design and my support for the arts and artists, working to secure funding for projects that enabled artists not only to produce their work but also to display it for public enjoyment'. He stressed, too, my social justice work: 'She believed in free entry and free use of libraries, the art gallery, the museum and other cultural facilities, arguing that user charges were a barrier for low-income people who had already contributed via their rates.' They were touching words from a thoroughly decent colleague.

But retire? Me? Certainly not. It was time to make another move, which I did partly at the behest of my good friend, art historian Mark Stocker. As he told me, 'The council chapter in your life is almost over. And I'm very glad I discouraged you once from heading for Parliament, which at one stage looked like a real possibility – would you really have relished the intellectual and emotional company of Rodney Hide or John Banks? No, it's time for a PhD chapter or twelve. Your status should change from Councillor Crighton to Dr Crighton but it can't be both.' I did follow this advice but I knew leaving the council would leave a gaping hole in my life. To cover that gap I served on public and private boards, including the University of Canterbury Council for four years and the Canterbury District Health Board for a dozen. I retained my board roles on the New Zealand Historic Places Trust, Christchurch and Canterbury Tourism Limited and the Theatre Royal Charitable Foundation, among others.

CHAPTER 13
Debacles, Debates and Decisions

Although I took special interest in art, culture and heritage, I never held back from expressing my views on all kinds of issues. I enjoyed a good difference of opinion, even a battle, provided it did not become ad hominem, which lowers the tone of the argument and helps nobody. It took me a while, as a relatively new councillor, to find my way around pushing issues I felt strongly about. I cut my teeth on the 1999 Avebury House debate, when calls to demolish the 115-year-old house in the eastern suburb of Richmond split the council.

I argued that the house was of historical and social significance, because of its association with the early development of Richmond and with prominent settler, Dr John Seager Gundry, the original owner of the land on which William Flesher, also a significant city figure, built the homestead for his family in 1882. A turreted and gabled essay in picturesque colonial carpentry, the house was a good, and rare, example of the domestic architecture of local architect James Glanville, who designed buildings in Christchurch and Canterbury in the late nineteenth and early twentieth centuries. The house's expansive lawns, planted borders and established trees had been used as a public park in council ownership for 56 years.

But the council wanted to pull it down. It was, said some, too costly to restore and then maintain, and besides it was not listed and therefore not significant. Someone else suggested it was in the wrong area. My counter-argument was that the west of the city had Riccarton House and Mona Vale, both of which were in similar condition to Avebury House before restoration. The 'wrong' kind of people in Richmond deserved an equal opportunity. I lobbied for support from fellow councillors and was overjoyed when the decision was made to keep and restore the building.

Once neglected, Avebury House is now maintained in Christchurch City Council ownership, and administered by a trust, as a great community asset.

My appointment as a council representative on the Canterbury Museum Trust Board in 2001 came at a vital time: the revelation of architect Ian Athfield's concept designs for the update of the New Zealand Historic Places Trust Category 1 and the Christchurch City Council Group 1 buildings. When I was given the privilege of a private viewing of these plans, with just museum director Anthony Wright and Athfield, I voiced my disquiet about suggested major changes to Benjamin Mountfort's façade on Rolleston Avenue. I could not agree with the windows being cut down to ground level so that diners could look down Worcester Boulevard from the proposed restaurant – Mountfort had designed the building as a museum, not a café. Nor could I agree that the museum's present entrance should become a toilet, rubbish store and kitchen entrance. This would also mean bastardising the façade of the 1958 Centennial Wing for a main entrance, thus downgrading both original heritage entrances.

I am not some kind of reactionary who opposes any serious architectural challenges and changes to heritage buildings on principle. Changes are needed, and nowhere more so than in a living, breathing entity such as Canterbury Museum. But it was a question of how much the changes affected significant heritage values. Just because they were the brainchild of an outstanding architect like Ian Athfield did not mean that we should cave in to his genius, especially where listed heritage structures were at stake. Then there was the plan to elevate the whare whakairo on and overhanging the roof facing the McDougall Art Gallery, which I considered culturally and architecturally inappropriate.

At a subsequent board meeting, the plans were put forward without consideration of any of my concerns and with a budget and timeline that overlooked the cost of gaining a resource consent for the alterations. Dumbfounded, I advised the board that the alterations must be subject to a publicly notified application for a resource consent. After that and subsequent meetings, I felt that I had been deemed an impediment to the plans, because I had consistently – but selectively – disagreed with aspects of them and spoken my mind. And indeed I was not replaced at the end of my three-year term when other council appointments were. There was a maelstrom of emotion swirling around the museum redevelopment, with passionately divergent views. The label 'wanton vandal', reported in the

Press, clearly hurt Anthony Wright but he responded by saying, 'A small but vocal group of short-sighted people is indulging in "misinformation bleating".' A group of concerned residents, including the Christchurch Civic Trust, forged an alliance to fund a challenge to the alterations. A protracted and extremely expensive legal process ensued as the Museum Board attempted to drive its plans through.

In November 2003, the city council appointed commissioner David Collins to hear the museum's application for resource consent but because of his supposed sympathy for heritage, he suggested that another commissioner should sit with him. Nelson barrister Bill Rainey was chosen. After a lengthy hearing, the commissioners approved more than half of the elements of the application, with a detailed set of restraint options. After various appeals, in May 2006 the Environment Court cancelled the consents issued in 2005 and the High Court disallowed the museum's application for its redevelopment plan. It was a win for heritage.

I felt totally vindicated. I often wondered how different things would have been if, back in 2001, I had had the majority support of other Museum Board members for my argument that the revitalisation project was compromising the integrity of the historic buildings. It would have saved many people a lot of money and grief.

My fellow board member Alan McRobie, representing Waimakariri District Council, and I were appalled by the process. Barbara Stewart, like me a Christchurch City Council representative, originally agreed to the concept, but later courageously withdrew her support, stating publicly that 'it was an error of judgement. I got it wrong.' Fast forward to the present. Anthony Wright has been a long-serving director, devoted to the cause of the museum. Plans for its redevelopment, to bring it into the twenty-first century and provide much-needed display space, were redrawn for full public consultation over a long period of time and changed to address concerns that were raised. The mistakes of the past were not repeated and resource consent was granted with acceptable conditions.

The differences of opinion between Garry Moore and me became legendary. They were highlighted during the lengthy saga surrounding Leinster House in Merivale. Moves to demolish the Edwardian structure began in

1998. When I led the charge to save this grand house first from demolition, then removal from its site, I received backing from a significant number of councillors, heritage organisations and many in the general public: more than 3000 Merivale residents signed a petition supporting its retention. By voting against it, Garry scuppered my plan for council involvement to keep the building where it was. What really riled me was that he had used his casting vote as mayor, when councillors were evenly split on the issue. When I asked him later why he had done so, he replied, 'Because you voted against an issue that I wanted.' I was not prepared to accept this and moved a notice of motion for another vote on the matter at the following council meeting. This time it failed by 14 votes to nine. It took eight years of tenacious battling for Leinster House to remain where it had stood for more than a century, but finally the battle was lost and in 2006 the house was moved to North Canterbury.

Few heritage issues gained as many column inches in the *Press* and the *Star* as my 1998 proposal to resite the statue of James Edward FitzGerald from Rolleston Avenue at the western end of Cashel Street to Latimer Square. A leading colonist and the first man ashore from the first four ships that brought the founding settlers to Lyttelton in 1850, FitzGerald was a larger than life Irishman, a close friend of John Robert Godley, the founder of the *Press* and the first superintendent of Canterbury, before entering national politics in Wellington. The many, many writers to the newspapers, who included artists, historians, intellectuals and comics, focused on where the statue should have been erected. Some said Cathedral Square, in front of the *Press* building. Others said in Latimer Square, looking towards Cathedral Square. A few were happy to let it stay where it was. I had an ally in renowned artist Bill Sutton. We both pointed out that sculptor Francis Shurrock and eccentric donor R. E. Green had wished the statue to be in the open area, under a clear sky – not in front of the *Press* where FitzGerald's back would be to the public, nor where he ended up in Rolleston Avenue. The storm raged on until the early 2000s, then abated – and nothing changed. FitzGerald, with the Botanic Gardens behind him, still gazes down Cashel Street, with which he had no association at all. And most passers-by neither know nor, I fear, care.

In 2003, I was approached by Earle Crutchley, No. 237644, 25 Battery, 4th Field Artillery Regiment, 2NZEF. He was battling for a plaque on the Citizens' War Memorial in Cathedral Square to recognise the role of the 'forgotten force', the Merchant Navy, which faced great danger and the loss of many lives, to deliver equipment, food, fuel and troops in both world wars. As he said, 'Without their participation the war would have been lost. Surely they deserved a total recognition equal to other forces.' Sympathetic to his cause, I suggested that he present his case to my next Arts, Culture and Heritage meeting. This he did. Then bureaucracy took over. Because it was a heritage-listed item, both the New Zealand Historic Places Trust and the Christchurch City Council had to approve attaching another plaque to the memorial. Historic Places agreed, as did the Christchurch RSA, but the council's heritage planners did not – a plaque was 'not compatible'. 'With what?' I asked; compatible with honouring heroism it certainly was. The matter was thoroughly investigated over two months of reports, meetings, consultations and more meetings, but I successfully shepherded the matter through to a successful conclusion. A plaque was installed on 22 April 2003 and dedicated the following day.

The same impulse lay behind my desire to save a gun. Canterbury men fighting in the 1899–1902 Anglo-Boer War had seized a large machine gun mounted on iron-clad wooden dray wheels and brought it back from South Africa to Christchurch as a memento. It stood near Queen Victoria's statue in Victoria Square until, in 1912, a group of pacifists dragged it to the Avon River and shoved it in. Council workers retrieved it and placed it more securely in front of the old Magistrates' Court building, opposite Victoria Square. There it remained until 1973, when Vietnam War protesters urged that this image of war be removed from the inner city. So it was banished to Ripapa Island in Lyttelton Harbour, where few would ever see it. How could such a relic be ignored? After a year of negotiations the gun was placed permanently at the historic military site on Godley Head – not to glorify war but, as I explained, as a symbol of sacrifice and loss.

A proposed high-rise residential building overlooking the estuary at Ferrymead became, as I predicted, 'a towering inferno' for the council. Community outrage greeted the news, in 2004, that consent had been granted for a 14-storey building without public notification. Although this was one of many matters over which Garry and I managed not to clash, my motion that the council should debate the issue of public notification of consent applications for contentious sites was lost. This did not necessarily reflect councillors' feelings. They, like me, all knew that such decisions were made by independent commissioners without political influence, which made the debate pointless. The motion did, however, highlight the situation. Many Christchurch people expressed anger at having been unable to have their say about the Ferrymead tower; many agreed with my statement that the proposal 'would scar the environment' and was 'unacceptable'. The building eventually went ahead but at a much reduced height. It was demolished after the Canterbury earthquakes of 2010–11.

I also became embroiled in the proposed $800,000 refurbishment of the council chamber in 2005, to include a smaller chamber and the removal of the public seating gallery. In March of the previous year the council had resolved to do only 'essential maintenance' on the civic offices because of the imminent move to the converted NZ Post premises on Worcester Boulevard. In my opinion spending council funds on major refurbishment so close to the move was wantonly wasteful. The work went ahead anyway.

I had several reasons for my opposition. I believed Lesley McTurk stepped well outside the boundaries of her chief executive's role when she claimed she could proceed with the refurbishment under her powers of delegated authority even if the mayor agreed with it; the refurbishment cost disappeared from the council agenda; ratepayers' money was being wasted; there was no budget allowance for the work; and the building, the former Millers department store, was a registered Category 2 historic place. This meant that major changes would require prior consultation with the New Zealand Historic Places Trust. This did not take place.

Most councillors shared some but not all of my views. Linda Rutland, who was against the plan, helpfully sought an opinion on the refurbishment from the auditor-general. His report supported opposition to the refurbishment. My request for a formal council debate was declined, but the mayor belatedly apologised: 'I made a mistake, thinking I got it right.' The next day he discussed the letter on National Radio, saying, 'I see this as maintenance because we actually need a good working space.' But it was all too late: the work had already been carried out and the refurbished chamber was officially opened in March 2005. All I could do to register my protest was refuse to attend.

The year 2006 certainly threw a few curve balls. This was my last term as a Christchurch city councillor and I felt that, by then, my debating skills were the best they had ever been. There were some tricky issues to navigate. Garry, supported by the majority of the council, wished to sell the Christchurch City Council/Christchurch City Holdings Limited shares in the Lyttelton Port Company to a Chinese company. I and a few others opposed the proposed deal. Only two of the original Labour members on council remained, Garry and me; my position put me squarely in the minority. The Chinese company would have a total 49 per cent shareholding plus management rights. It was effectively a joint venture: Christchurch City Council would retain control of the physical assets while Hutchison Whampoa, owned by Li Ka-shing, the world's tenth wealthiest man, would assume control of the port operations. This was serious stuff and the debate was heated and protracted. It was the thin end of the wedge for a foreign exploratory intrusion into New Zealand's port sector. When critics argued that such a valuable strategic asset should not pass into foreign control, Garry said that such worries seemed to come from 'conspiracy theorists'. Port Otago proceeded to buy 10.1 per cent ($20 million of ratepayers' money) of Lyttelton Port holding. Contrary to some opinions, I believed that Otago intentionally disrupted the impending sale as it did not wish to have a well-resourced competitor so close to its own operations. This brought another player into the mix and with other complicating factors, including a vociferous backlash from the public, the deal did not proceed.

Around the same time yet another difference of opinion arose between Garry and me. In April 2006, cracks were appearing in Lesley McTurk's tight regime. A council survey showed staff morale was in a serious, even destructive state, and a copy was leaked to the *Press*. David Cox had also written to the mayor, fellow councillors and McTurk, expressing concern about her aloofness to councillors and her 'unprofessional manner'. The *Press* wanted answers too. On the front page of the Saturday 1 April 2006 issue the headline read 'Councillors "forced" to sign pledge'. This was no April Fool's joke. Garry had called all councillors to an urgent meeting late on the Friday afternoon to tell us that the survey had been leaked, that the reporter wanted answers and that we must sign a pledge of loyalty in support of McTurk. If we did not sign, she could bring personal grievance proceedings against individual councillors. Thirteen councillors and the mayor signed, but Helen Broughton and I held out; Helen requested further information regarding the legality of this move. When it was obvious that we were not going to sign, we were taken into an adjacent office where Garry waved the pledge and demanded we sign. He persisted, and after heated exchanges Helen finally broke and signed, leaving only me. I was, to put it mildly, uncomfortable about being bullied into signing such a document, but I, too, was finally worn down. Mine was the last signature on the page but above my name I wrote 'under duress'. When the pledge was published on the front page of the *Press*, I was appalled to see that those words had been struck out.

On 5 April 2006 I wrote Garry a letter in which I explained that, after independent legal advice, I was retracting my endorsement of the pledge, which had been given as a result of what I believed was a misrepresentation of my duties and responsibilities as a city councillor. I also requested that, to save any future embarrassment or conflict, I should not be asked to sign any such document regarding the CEO's performance unless it was legally required. Being forced to sign such a risible document was anathema for me – was I in North Korea, I wondered?

I could be flexible when I needed to be. When, in 2006, the council was trying to avoid a rates rise, suburban libraries were seen as a cost-cutting target. Six other councillors, the mayor and I argued in favour of closing some suburban libraries and the mobile library service but, following public consultation, I made an about-turn. I had been reminded that a library is not just a place to borrow books, but an integral part of its community. Also in the gun that year were the council's suburban service centres: the proposal was to remove from them a range of financial transaction services, in order to save $423,000 a year. A lone voice, I suggested that the council should instead consider stopping its $400,000 sponsorship funding of the New Zealand PGA Golf Tournament. I appreciate the elegance of the game and the pleasure it gives to many, but, as I said at the time, 'I think our service centres are more important than a game of golf!' One lunchtime I even bravely showed my support and joined the picket line standing at the entrance to the civic offices. Though my motion failed, it must have stirred some consciences as a large majority of councillors voted to look elsewhere for cost cuts.

But council politics were often not as grim and adversarial as this. For the Women's Suffrage Day celebrations in 2006 I combined my love of history and local body politics by initiating and coordinating an exhibition of photos of Christchurch female councillors, past and present, called *Women in the Council Chamber*. The first ever city council meeting had been held in Christchurch in 1862 but it was 55 years until the first woman councillor, Ada Wells, was elected in 1917. After her came such luminaries as Elizabeth McCombs, the first woman elected to the New Zealand Parliament and the second woman, after Theresa Green, to be elected to the Christchurch City Council. The formidable Mabel Howard, who was a councillor intermittently for almost 20 years from 1933, brought a much-needed splash of colour and flamboyance to an increasingly tired-looking council. She could be manipulative, prone to rages and excessively jealous of her own prerogatives, and I can only despair at her limited capacity to understand modern art when she said of Frances Hodgkins' *Pleasure Garden*, 'You've got it the wrong way up.' But her abilities and achievements in local government, while also serving as an MP and becoming the country's first woman Cabinet minister, were undeniable.

Then there were the stories of recent councillors: Helen Garrett, Linda Constable and Mollie Clark, who recalled, during a particular feisty debate, the male councillor who rose to say, 'Councillor Clark, you should be home in the kitchen getting the tea.' Mollie quietly smiled: 'I knew then that I was winning.' All current six sitting women councillors, out of a total of 13, and Vicki Buck, were interviewed by Liz Grant, creating an oral archive that is available on line through Christchurch City Libraries.

Christchurch may appear to be conservative but it has a strong radical tradition of women city councillors who were part of the crusade for equality. And their diverse backgrounds lent colour, reality, pragmatism and common sense to the role. Women really *are* better at multi-tasking. As a former city councillor, a proponent for the arts and a very vocal, unapologetic promoter of our cultural heritage, I am constantly mindful of the tradition I have inherited, and am extraordinarily grateful for the achievements of my predecessors.

When I went to university I did not take, or contemplate taking, a paper in political theory, though now that I am totally out of the game, I could well find it fascinating. I do not believe, however, that this gap in my education was an impediment during my years as an active local politician. Indeed I have never seriously agonised over the evils of capitalism or the role of the state. What I am concerned about – and I think this is a very Kiwi thing – is to have a society at ease with itself, where everyone feels they have a stake, where there are no widespread and extreme differences in wealth, with decent and affordable education and health care and with a high voter turnout in elections. Probably I feel most strongly about everybody having a fair go, and when I see injustice, I speak out. It is not a case of being particularly left-wing or right-wing. Both have their faults – the former is often permanently angry and disaffected, the latter permanently complacent and often selfish. But my values generally accord with the centre left and I remain proud of New Zealand's record as a liberal democracy, particularly with the governments of Clark and Ardern at a national level. If I am looking for intellectual credence in all this, I find it in American historian David Hackett Fischer's brilliant *Fairness and Freedom*, a comparative study of New Zealand and the US, and I'm glad I'm part of the former.

As former *Press* journalist and local government reporter Mike Crean noted, I tried always to be available to the media, whether newspapers, radio or television: 'coverage of any issue, major or minor, relating to Christchurch heritage, art or culture was likely to include at least a comment from Anna, and often something of greater substance … Her responsiveness, awareness, knowledge, trustworthiness and common sense always made the effort worthwhile.' Mike was also generous enough to say that my opinion pieces for the *Press* were 'well researched, stylishly worded and thought-provoking', and spurred readers to write countless letters to the paper, usually supporting my stance. 'I doubt if any other councillor has figured more often, or more positively, in the pages of the *Press* than Anna Crighton.'

CHAPTER 14
Art Explosion

Old Christchurch's collection of art in public places had consisted mainly of stern statues of city fathers – no mothers apart from an unamused Queen. Then there was a famous Antarctic explorer, a few quaint memorials and the over-the-top Peacock Fountain. There was certainly a noticeable dearth of Māori art. An outstanding exception was master carver Riki Manuel's 6-metre tōtara pou whenua, standing beside the Avon River in Victoria Square, which had been commissioned by Ngāi Tahu as part of the 1990 commemorations of the Treaty of Waitangi. But from around 2000 an explosion of public art illuminated the city. This not only marked the new millennium, but also the 150th anniversary of organised Pākehā settlement in Canterbury. As an art and architectural historian and advocate, city councillor, chairperson of the council's Environmental Committee and the inaugural spokesperson for the Art and Industry Biennial Trust formed in 1999, I became the go-to person to sanction any art or heritage initiative. I was also appointed to the board of Turning Point 2000, established in 1996 to foster closer relationships within the community as it looked back over our past, celebrated our present and looked to the future, and on Art 2000, set up to showcase the visual arts in Canterbury to celebrate the new millennium. In turn I chaired the Year 2000 Project and the Art Committee of NCC (NZ) Ltd, a Thailand-based national convention centre management company that administered the town hall and the convention centre.

My vision was to revitalise the central city with contemporary works of public art which people could see and enjoy, and which would show future generations what we were all about. I weathered attacks from all quarters, even including some prominent artists and architects, and convinced fellow councillors that art should be included in annual council budgets.

The council was happy to splash money around on promotion events like Cup and Show Week but kept the purse tight for festivals of art and culture. As I pointed out, many people would not necessarily want to go to Addington for the trotting cup, but they would read books and visit art galleries. I stuck to my guns. Council budgets for art rose from $40,000 to $250,000 a year, plus operational expenditure for cleaning and maintenance of works. By 2005 veteran *Press* art critic Christopher Moore ranked me in the city's top five people of influence in the arts and the following year an editorial in the paper described Christchurch as 'the hotbed of contemporary art'. The arts scene, it said, had begun to change, 'thanks to the enthusiasm of a few individuals, like Cr Anna Crighton, who braved braying philistines and persuaded the city council to sponsor art'. This was very gratifying. I was prepared to actively campaign, facilitate, lobby, cajole and publicly crusade for art projects, but there were many others involved too. Usually gaining funding was the result of sound argument. During the first decade of the new millennium, a variety of eye-catching art appeared in Christchurch's public spaces. So that locals and visitors could navigate their way around these installations and sculptures, a handy souvenir 'passport' was produced, which provided maps and details of each work.

The establishment in 2001 of the city council's Arts, Culture and Heritage Committee made a huge difference. Subsequent projects included Paul Hartigan's neon art work, *Nebula Orion*, on the power distributor Orion's new Armagh Street substation building in the central city. As I explained to the Orion board, when seeking their sponsorship, a neon art work on an electricity substation made sense. *Nebula Orion* survived the 2010–11 earthquakes.

There was also Graham Bennett's kinetic sculpture, *Reasons for Voyaging*, which stands outside the new Christchurch Art Gallery Te Puna o Waiwhetū. Its scale and size in its context are perfect. Surely all New Zealanders, Māori and Pākehā, must feel the pull of this work, for we all came here as voyagers, or are descendants of voyagers. And of course there was David Marshall's trio of mischievous bronze corgis on a High Street intersection. (In 2022 they were moved to a new location.) I found it astonishing that three pieces of bronze, four counting the ice cream cone, could have taken up so much newspaper and air space in 2003, the year of celebration for the fiftieth anniversary of Queen Elizabeth II's coronation. I just wanted people to enjoy this cute and playful example of street art but an avalanche of letters to the *Press* and the *Star* could see no good or joy in such frivolity. Have a laugh, have some fun, was my riposte. And most people did, as far away as England: I was even interviewed live about the corgis on the BBC London breakfast show.

Sadly, while the corgis survived, sculptor Michael Parekōwhai's bunnies, Cosmo and James, an initiative of the Art and Industry Biennial Trust, never made it past conception. The idea of huge fibreglass rabbits cavorting in Cathedral Square, albeit only for three months and at no cost to Christchurch, was too much for many. I still feel angry that, in spite of my constant explanations, many opponents totally misunderstood the meaning of temporary and nil expense to ratepayers. I remain riled by the ferocious and insulting comments that riddled the media and the general unwillingness to recognise Parekōwhai's conception of the rabbits as a metaphor for colonialism. There was a light moment, though, when two very large plastic bags of carrots arrived at Civic Offices from Ohakune, home to the giant quirky carrot sculpture – one for the mayor and one for me. It was hardly a consolation but the gift did make me smile.

My relationship with the Art and Industry Biennial Trust, which became the Scape Public Art Biennial Trust in 2002, went back to early 1998, when Deborah McCormick and Warren Pringle approached me with their proposal to establish such an organisation. I immediately saw the merits in promoting art in public places using industry contacts instead of relying on the public purse. When the trust was launched in August 1999, Sir Kerry Burke became chair, I was vice-chair and the trustees were Mike Kelly, Dorenda Britten, Adrienne, Lady Stewart (now Dame) and Gillie Deans. I nurtured the first major project to launch Art & Industry onto the public art scene in the year 2000, using my influence from the various relevant committees but especially as honorary curator of NCC Ltd. The result, a large neon sculpture of 100 metres of glass tubing pumped with an argon gas/mercury vapour mix by expatriate artist Bill Culbert, was commissioned for the façade of the Christchurch Convention Centre. With its twisting and spiralling bright blue neon tubing attached to and piercing through the large windows of the façade facing Kilmore Street, *Blue* was the largest neon work produced by Culbert in New Zealand. The artist's significant relationship with Signtech the Signmasters established a precedent for working on art projects with local industry. This show-stopping reflection of the Canterbury landscape was lost when the February 2011 earthquake condemned the building.

So the central city became a gallery of installations, many of them alfresco. Then, in the post-earthquake recovery era, Christchurch picked up the broken pieces and put further new works on display. In every case, the art was contemporary.

CHAPTER 15
Heritage Matters

In any city proud of its architecture, as Christchurch is, the dividing line between art and heritage can be difficult to discern. As both an art lover and a heritage guardian, this did not trouble me. While on the council I battled continually with colleagues who begrudged the spending of public money on buildings they did not consider worth keeping. You can imagine my seething rage when hearing that the Minister for Canterbury Earthquake Recovery, Gerry Brownlee, had dismissed many of Christchurch's quake-damaged historic buildings as 'old dungers' fit only for demolition. There were many such conflicts, though seldom as bellicose as that one. Most often my campaigns succeeded.

My heritage crusade began with the impending demolition, in 1996, of the Kaiapoi Woollen Mills building on Manchester Street. The loss of such a significant building sparked my sense of outrage and proved to be a watershed moment for me as a first-term city councillor. Such needless destruction of a stately piece of industrial history showed that politicians could not be trusted to preserve heritage. On the advice of lawyer Charles Levin, we established the Christchurch Heritage Charitable Trust, plus a limited liability company to act as its trading arm. Also on Levin's recommendation, we approached former city councillor Derek Anderson to be its first chair. He jumped at the opportunity and became a key figure as chair of both the trust and the company from its beginning in 1996 until 2014. The other inaugural members were Ian Clark, Hamish Doig and me.

I differed philosophically and politically from the more conservative Derek on many issues, but he had useful experience in property development and restoration and a reputation for positivity and getting things done. He also had strong influence in Christchurch business circles. The trust's plan was to buy at-risk heritage buildings, find potential commercial uses for them, make the necessary renovations and then on-sell them with a protective covenant. The profits would then be available to fund further projects. The Canterbury Trust granted $600,000 as a start-up fund. Arrangements were made for bank loans and council grants to assist with our first project – the restoration of the 1881 Excelsior Hotel, on the corner of High and Manchester streets. Most notable among the later buildings the trust saved from demolition was the former home of the city's first newspaper, the *Lyttelton Times*, in Cathedral Square, which backed onto and included the *Star Sun* building in Gloucester Street.

Sceptics complained that the trust was little more than a covert arm of the city council, set up to secretly divert public money into projects that would fail to stand up to basic council scrutiny. But the public thought otherwise. Newspaper reports and editorials of the time revealed the growing wave of popular opinion in favour of protecting the city's built heritage. I was part of this. I argued at council meetings and public forums, wrote newspaper features, did interviews and responded to every objection that was lodged. The trust even brought me national recognition. As early as June 2000, I was interviewed for *North and South* magazine, which described me as 'a highly vocal heritage campaigner [who] has been instrumental in saving some of the city's most significant old buildings'. The article also recounted my infamous run-in with David Carter, a local MP and owner of the inner-city Coachman Hotel.

It was the sound of a chainsaw snarling from inside the Coachman Inn on Gloucester Street that caught my attention as I was walking past in July 1997. Knowing the heritage building was at risk of demolition, I burst through the door to see what was happening. A demolition worker brandishing a chainsaw was about to remove a large and intricately beautiful stained glass window from the stairwell. Standing nearby was David Carter. 'Don't do this,' I said. 'Please stop this vandalism of a beautiful old building.' A heated discussion followed and Carter finally conceded. He had been trying unsuccessfully to restore or sell the 1902 Joseph Maddison-designed building but he agreed to halt all further demolition. I then had to convince the council to buy the Coachman and resell it with protection for its heritage status. The $1.025 million asking price was excessive for the time and controversy over the purchase raged for months, but at last the council did purchase the building. This, my first activist attempt to protect part of the city's heritage, also marked the beginning of getting heritage issues seriously considered on council agendas.

To draw attention to the importance of protecting the city's built heritage, I proposed that the Hagley-Ferrymead Community Board, which I chaired, should hold annual heritage awards to incentivise and recognise owners of historic properties. The board was keen and the awards, a first for Christchurch, were established in 1997. They celebrated those in the community who had worked hard to save or restore heritage structures, be they cottages, houses, shops or commercial buildings. The awards attracted sponsorship from the *Star* and proved popular from the start, with many people nominating entries each year. I was convinced that the awards gave the local community a sense of place, pride in and awareness of the historic character of their environment, but when I retired in 2007, the scheme was dropped. It was a great disappointment to me but I refused to be thwarted. In 2010 I initiated the city-wide Christchurch Heritage Awards, which were later expanded to become the popular Canterbury Heritage Awards.

My next case was very different: seeking to rescue the historic Addington Prison, just off Lincoln Road, which was slated for demolition. I set about cajoling and coercing local government, central government, Ngāi Tahu, neighbouring businesses and other agencies to preserve the Victorian-era jail. The issue divided the community, drawing emotional responses both for and against preservation. Built in 1872, the prison was designed by the pre-eminent Gothic Revival architect, Benjamin Mountfort, who also designed, among other buildings, the Canterbury Provincial Council Buildings, Canterbury Museum and much of Canterbury College, now the Arts Centre. Addington Prison was considered to be of 'national or regional importance, the protection of which is seen as important'. After the government closed the jail in late 1999, Ngāi Tahu bought it in early 2000 and showed some support for the idea of turning the main building into a museum. National Party MPs, in opposition at the time, wanted the buildings demolished and the land cleared for development.

While I was ratcheting up a public campaign, there was a change of government and deputy prime minister and local MP Jim Anderton weighed in behind me. His support was crucial. Saving at least the main prison building, the cell block, an important example of Mountfort's work, was critical. Further, very few New Zealand jails of that era had survived. Cities worldwide had turned old prisons into museums that continued to attract many interested viewers, so commercial viability should not be a problem. But those in favour of demolition referred to the building's brutal ugliness and its harking back to 'a darker side of our colonial past'. Catholic priest and human rights activist Father Jim Consedine offered to knock the first block of stone from the wall; Mayor Garry Moore said he would knock out the second.

I believed that recognising the truth in history would cast light on the social conditions of that time and increase our respect and understanding. History should not be sanitised but honestly reflect all aspects of the past so that we can learn for the future. Being chair of the council's Environment Committee did enhance my influence on heritage preservation. With the support of historic architecture experts, notably Jenny May and Dr Ian Lochhead, I lobbied widely and swung popular opinion successfully. Late in 2006, the building became a popular backpackers' hostel called Jailhouse Accommodation, which imaginatively uses the original cells as bedrooms and bunkrooms.

When the former Sydenham Methodist (and later Samoan) Church on the corner of Brougham and Colombo streets faced the wrecker's ball in 2001, I was there. Wearing my Environment Committee hat, I recommended the establishment of a local trust to save the 1878 building. I could see, however, that a lack of funds would probably defeat the trust's efforts. I therefore persuaded the building's owner to withhold demolition and give the trust a chance to present proposals to fund it. Negotiations dragged on and on. It was a close-run event, with several missed deadlines, until the council finally brokered a deal with the developer at the eleventh hour. The church was not particularly attractive and unlikely ever to be economically functional, but it was one half of the southern entrance to the commercial precinct of the historic 'model suburb' of Sydenham. The other was the old stone post office that stood opposite, on the other side of Colombo Street, and housed a popular restaurant. The land next to the old church could be used for low-cost housing and the building itself could be converted into a community centre for local residents. A new trust saved the church but it became another victim of earthquake damage, and then of wreckers with dubious motives.

A pleasant duty in 2001, as chairperson of the Arts Centre Trust, was to welcome a $500,000 grant from the Canterbury Community Trust to help the Arts Centre buy and renovate the former Christchurch Girls' High

School at the southern end of Cranmer Square. I was thrilled that the grant would ensure the building was returned to its former glory and allow it to be a part of the city's heritage precinct, which included the Canterbury Club, the Arts Centre, Canterbury Museum and the Christchurch Art Gallery, based along or near Worcester Boulevard. Later, not on my watch, the Arts Centre sold the building, which was subsequently severely damaged in the earthquakes and demolished. At the time of writing, the site remains barren.

Certainly unusual was the informal heritage listing of a jacket. Charles Manning, a former Canterbury University senior lecturer in classics, wore the same sports jacket to meetings and functions for all his 21 years as a city councillor. The garment, in a faded oatmeal shade of brown, blotted with egg stains, was a 1977 Donegal tweed hacking jacket, created by English tailors Hirsts of Harrogate. It featured such minor modifications as leather elbow patches and acknowledged its age and use by rips and tears to the interior lining. Manning, a popular figure among all his peers, retired from the council in 2001 to become an environment commissioner. In a memorable farewell, I ambushed him and declared the jacket to be a heritage item of artistic, cultural and historical significance, one of only six of its kind extant in the world and the last in New Zealand. I moved successfully at a council meeting to slap a heritage covenant on the jacket, forcing Manning to retain it in its original condition. 'Research has shown,' I declared, 'that it has been cleaned very minimally so its originality is without question.' Manning smiled in a professorial sort of way as he was served with the certificate, which he accepted with typically good grace.

It was in 2001, too, that I lost an election poster. It was presumably torn from a fence somewhere in the city. So how did it end up neatly packed behind an old Italian marble altar in the Rose Historic Chapel, formerly the chapel of St Mary's Convent, on Colombo Street? I had previously visited Paddy Snowdon's Linwood salvage yard to check on an altar that he had bought from the chapel in 1995. Six years later, after much encouragement from me, Paddy returned the altar to the chapel, all spick and span, plus the poster. Paddy told me that since I had convinced him to restore the altar and return it to its original home, he decided to fix the poster to the back of the altar, like an unseen time capsule, in recognition of my contribution to preserving elements of the city's past.

Heritage is not, of course, only embedded in the preservation of historic structures. High-profile debates of this sort tend to catch the greatest publicity and enflame the fiercest arguments, but one of my favourite success stories was gaining an exemption for heritage buildings from the ban on open fires imposed by the Canterbury Regional Council in 1998. Christchurch smog was a major health problem, but the city-wide ban was met with considerable public resentment by the many people who loved their open fires and coal burners. That resentment was eased somewhat by measures taken to help homeowners install electric and clean-burning wood heaters. I, however, sought an exception for heritage buildings listed in the city plan because in such places open fires were 'integral heritage features' that should be retained. Thirty-two exempt heritage buildings, some of them with multiple fireplaces, were allowed to keep their home fires burning. They ranged from public buildings, such as the Great Hall at the Arts Centre, to historic homes, like the Deans family's Riccarton House, to humble domestic villas. Many on the list did not survive the earthquakes, but the Great Hall and Riccarton House did and, after painstaking restoration efforts, present glorious testaments to important themes in Canterbury history.

I have described just a few of the dozens of heritage causes I fought during my time as a councillor. There were many more, including several churches and chapels, cinemas and theatres, stores, hotels and post offices. Most sites were within Christchurch, with a couple in Lyttelton (then part of Banks Peninsula District). Not content with handling only single buildings, the Environment Committee launched into attempts to enhance whole streets by restoring and highlighting their heritage features, notably New Regent Street and Lower High Street in the central city. And there were also historic trees, particularly the row of poplars beside the Avon between Manchester and Madras streets, which were threatened at one time. Few people realise that they are part of the Edmonds story. Thomas Edmonds came from humble beginnings in Poplar in the East End of London. The trees link the Edmonds Band Rotunda and the Edmonds

Clock Tower, which he gave to the city in 1929 to mark his 50 years in Christchurch.

Heritage matters also took me further afield. In June 2005, it was a great privilege to be a cultural ambassador representing the New Zealand UNESCO National Commission in Gangneung, South Korea, at an international local government workshop titled Sustainable Development: Safeguarding the Intangible Cultural Heritage and Promoting Inter City Networks. Gangneung is a beautiful city on the eastern coast, just south of the border with North Korea. I could see the guards in towers policing the no man's land between the north and south. Smaller than Christchurch, Gangneung has 128 cultural properties, 34 of which are state designated heritage. I presented a paper called 'Pūharakekenui: The Styx – Safeguarding our Cultural Heritage'. For this I worked closely with Christine Heremaia of the Greenspace Unit of the Christchurch City Council, who was the main driver behind the successful Styx Vision 2000–2040, and architect Pere Royal. The Styx Mill Conservation Reserve, from source to sea, embodies all the necessary ingredients to form a case study of intangible heritage – ecology, recreation, landscape, heritage, arts and culture. The source of the Pūharakekenui/Styx River, in Nunweek Park, was home to freshwater lobster. The Kaputone Stream and Smacks Creek no longer run entirely through open swamp but mostly through urban development in Northwood and Belfast. This fragile ecosystem, which has been restored and protected from further urban encroachment, is of great cultural value to Māori and a living laboratory for educational purposes as the river flows to the sea.

Over nine days in 2007, the 31st UNESCO World Heritage Committee was held in Christchurch, attended by hundreds of participants and observers from the 178 state parties to the World Heritage Convention. I had advocated strongly for the conference to be held in Christchurch, and was thrilled when it was chosen ahead of Auckland and Wellington. The head of New Zealand's delegation was Tumu Te Heuheu Tūkino VII, paramount chief of Ngāti Tūwharetoa and a fellow board member of the New Zealand Historic Places Trust. (I had become the trust's South Island representative in 2003.) I helped to develop an accompanying programme of events, talks and activities, which Tumu had requested, and, with observer status, attended as many of the meetings as I could. Witnessing the complex procedures for historic heritage listing on an international scale was inspiring. It certainly put into perspective my own experience of assessing cultural registration as a member of the New Zealand Historic Places Trust Registration Committee. The whole stimulating experience helped to explain my compulsion to visit UNESCO World Heritage Sites and confirmed my views of the pros and cons of heritage in New Zealand. On the one hand, we are a liberal democracy and our 'can do' ethos is a massive plus. On the other hand, our heritage protection legislation is pathetically weak and ineffective.

The story of First World War soldier Henry Nicholas was once little known. The bones of this highly decorated Canterbury man lie in a French graveyard, but he needed to be acknowledged and honoured in his home province. A carpenter who hailed from nearby Lincoln, Nicholas received the British Empire's highest military medal, the Victoria Cross, for conspicuous bravery at Polderhoek in Belgium in December 1917 before he was killed, at the age of 27, on 23 October 1918, just three weeks before the Armistice. He was posthumously awarded the Military Medal for his courage in action in France only a few days before his death. B. J. Clark, a leading figure in the local RSA, read about Nicholas and decided something must be done to honour him. I wholeheartedly agreed. When I requested information, via the *Press*, the responses included a letter that Nicholas had written to his sweetheart during the war, sent to me by her niece. Another response was a telephone call from retired city manager, John Gray. As brigadier in the Territorials, and a war historian interested in the New Zealanders' campaign on the Western Front, John noted the sad irony of Canterbury's only First World War VC winner being largely overlooked. We collaborated in producing a monograph about Nicholas. Around my long hours on council business, I researched and wrote his pre-war life story, and John used his military background, and knowledge gained from visits to the Belgian and French battlefields, to write of Nicholas's wartime exploits. The resulting volume was valuable in enlisting support and raising funds for a memorial. For months I lived and breathed Henry Nicholas.

After establishing a Nicholas Memorial Project Committee, with B. J. Clark as chair and me as his deputy, and with the guidance of Deborah

McCormick from Scape, we commissioned Mark Whyte to produce a statue, which would stand next to the Bridge of Remembrance. It would be the city's first public statue since that of Robert Falcon Scott was erected eight decades earlier. A major promotion for the project was the accompanying exhibition, *Nicholas, Under Three Flags,* held in Our City Ōtautahi, curated by me and designed by Mark Gerrard. It drew 6000 visitors.

Mark Whyte's larger-than-life statue ensures Henry Nicholas's spirit has returned to Christchurch, but that spirit is not bellicose. He carries no weapon but gazes in contemplation towards the bridge over which he and other Canterbury soldiers had marched on their way to Lyttelton before sailing away to fight at Gallipoli, in Belgium and France, and in the Middle East. Many never returned. Enclosed in the statue's plinth are bricks from the wall of Le Quesnoy, the French town that Kiwi soldiers stormed and from which they drove the German occupiers in their last battle of the war. The men had been inspired by the courage of their comrade, Henry Nicholas, who had died only days earlier.

After many meetings, phone calls and emails, after seeking finance from all quarters, after organising and writing the content for the monograph and the exhibition, collecting loaned memorabilia, after overseeing the progress of the sculpture, and arranging the unveiling of the statue, I was overwhelmed with excitement as the project neared its successful ending. The unveiling on 7 March 2007 was a triumph. I was proud to be acting mayor, in Garry's absence, and lead the service. The military band, the guard of honour (which I inspected) and the catafalque party all came from Burnham Military Camp and included Territorial Force Members of 2 Battalion Group, the successor unit to the Canterbury Regiment in which Henry Nicholas served. Along with a 23-strong party from Le Quesnoy, there were the Chief of Army, Major General Lou Gardiner, the French ambassador, Jean-Michel Marlaud, and Nicholas's nieces and other descendants. After the speeches, the grey army blankets that appropriately swathed the impressive bronze figure were removed, followed by the resonant familiar words of Laurence Binyon's 'For the Fallen', the haunting notes of the Last Post and the blessing of the memorial by the dean of Christchurch. I could not hold back my tears. We did not forget.

PART

FOUR

A New Millennium

CHAPTER 16
Triumphs, Tragedies and a Big Party

I witnessed the opening of the new millennium atop the tower of the 1876 Timeball Station, standing high above the port of Lyttelton. It was a glorious evening and it was magical to be standing on the roof, looking over the wall towards the harbour and the Port Hills. The wine flowed and the food was plentiful for the 60 people invited by Heritage New Zealand Pouhere Taonga, as the Historic Places Trust is now known, to witness such a significant moment. Three minutes before midnight the red ball was hoisted to the top of the mast and, on the signal, dropped at exactly 0000 hours on 1 January 2000. It was the first in a worldwide wave of timeball drops that circled the globe, finishing in Washington DC. As the ball fell, every ship in the harbour sounded its klaxon in a deafening burst of noise that sent shivers up my spine. Jenny May drove me home, where I watched the rest of the world expending collective billions on spectacular fireworks, all celebrating in their own way. And, like millions of others I had saved everything on my computer and stocked the pantry – for what? The planes did not even fall from the skies.

The council's Turning Point 2000 Trust had organised a year of significant celebrations and commemorations. At noon on 14 December 1998, a large digital clock on the façade of the Millennium Hotel in Cathedral Square had been unveiled to announce the days, hours, minutes and seconds left until 1 January 2000. The millennium year had additional historical significance for many in Christchurch and Canterbury, since the weekend of 15–17 December marked the 150th anniversary of the arrival of the Canterbury Association settlers. For the gala costume ball held in

Victoria Square, a grand affair with dancing under the stars on a glorious balmy evening, I commissioned a replica 1850 gown with bone bodice and frills and furbelows created for me by Vivian Kirby, a student from the Technology Design School at Christchurch Polytechnic. My partner for the evening was my friend Tim Barnett, MP for Christchurch Central. The day after the ball, I and Dr Terry Ryan, representing Te Rūnanga o Ngāi Tahu, deposited a time capsule, arranged by Jenny May, in Four Ships Court in Cathedral Square.

For me, the new millennium re-emphasised the need for contemporary public art works, for the current generation to stamp itself on our history. While I was chair of the Art 2000 group we initiated three major public art works – *Chalice 2000*, *Bridge 2000* and *Tapestry 2000*.

For the first, Art 2000 prepared a brief and invited Christchurch born-and-bred and internationally acclaimed sculptor Neil Dawson, to submit a proposal for a large piece for Cathedral Square. His concept was assessed by a sub-committee of Art 2000 members, painter Don Peebles, and architects Sir Miles Warren and David Sheppard. This art-conscious panel gave a resounding yes to the 18-metre cone of coloured steel. When the maquette of *Chalice* was unveiled to the full council there was applause and it was readily accepted. However, a strong sense of déjà vu ensued as we noted that there could well be another great public Christchurch row about the sculpture. And there was. As Dawson said, 'You have to expect some comment when you are rearranging Christchurch's front room!' The resource consent notification drew eight public submissions – four for and four against – before the decision came in *Chalice*'s favour.

I often walked down to the Square in the early hours of the morning and again late in the evening to view *Chalice* being assembled. I might have driven the project through, but the feeling of nervousness about whether people would accept the sculpture was always there. There were many anxious months of waiting as delays continued, perhaps inevitable given a project of this scale. It was finally unveiled at a public ceremony on 7 September 2001. When delivering my welcome speech I looked up from the specially erected stage in Cathedral Square to see a sea of faces. It was overwhelming. And even more so when the cathedral bells rang

at 8.30 p.m. and the blue lights within *Chalice* flicked on. After stirring
uncertainly at first, the crowd erupted into loud applause when the lights
reached their full brightness. I could feel the power of *Chalice* answering
its critics. Dawson said it was a surreal moment to see his 'crazy idea' reach
its final destination.

I had prophesied that the people of Christchurch would become
very fond, protective and then proud of *Chalice*, and they did. When the
September 11 attacks on the Twin Towers in New York happened just four
days after the unveiling, it was to *Chalice* that people were drawn, strewing
it with flowers and messages of sympathy. As Mark Stocker told the *Press*,
'*Chalice* has style and elegance' and 'a spirituality suited to our secularised
age'. Now it would be hard to imagine Cathedral Square without *Chalice*.
Is there any better argument for public art than that?

Plans to commemorate the new millennium with a strikingly modern
footbridge across the Avon opposite Dorset Street sparked unfortunate
division within the community. I had seen many contemporary footbridges
in my travels and was excited by the idea of marking the new millennium
with a strikingly modern example – something challenging, functional and
quirky. The idea of the bridge was acceptable but the chosen site, and the
design by Andrew Drummond, was not. Drummond's design, 'From Here
to There', was selected from 47 entries by judges Don Peebles, Sir Miles
Warren, Paddy Austin, John Coley and me. It became a case of bridge over
troubled waters. The design drew opposition and condemnation and the
resource consent hearings about the process thinly disguised the fact that
Andrew Drummond is not an easy artist and his stylish and original design
had a divisive effect: some people simply did not like it. I supported the
project through all stages but negativity by a few scuppered it in the end.
The whole scenario was a nightmare; as chair of Art 2000 I had to take the
heat, and I did.

The concept for a tapestry for Christchurch was first mooted by Will
Cumming, a mixed media artist, tutor at the Christchurch Polytechnic and
a member of the Art 2000 Advisory Group, who would die, too early, in
2002. The committee embraced the idea and *Tapestry 2000* made the cut,
but with several conditions. It had to be big, it had to capture the spirit of
the millennium and it had to include community input. Measuring 3 by 5
metres, it became the largest tapestry ever made in New Zealand. Master
weaver Marilyn Rea-Menzies from the Christchurch Tapestry Workshop

was selected to supervise its creation. The making of the tapestry followed the ancient tradition of weaving on a vertical loom, where the coloured weft threads making up the design are laid into the vertical warp threads. The open competition held for the design was won by Philip Trusttum, whose abstract design featured the word 'Christchurch' written in a schoolboy script across a work described by the judging panel as a 'huge message of celebration, visually uplifting and effervescent'. It was also a mirror of Phil's engaging personality.

Over the following 16 months it certainly became the 'people's tapestry' as a steady stream of adults and children, locals and tourists, appeared at Marilyn's Arts Centre studio to observe or to weave: anyone was welcome to make a piece of the tapestry and many found it addictive. In total over 2750 people carried out some weaving, including Chelsea Clinton, in New Zealand with her father in 1999 for the APEC summit in Auckland. I was a constant visitor to the loom to feed my weaving addiction and to inspect progress. After being cut off in August, the tapestry was officially unveiled on 28 November in its new home in the Christchurch Town Hall.

As well as the three major projects championed and funded by Art 2000, the NCC (NZ) Art Committee, which I chaired, commissioned a mural called *Passport to the New Millennium*. Also designed by Philip Trusttum, it was installed along the west wall of the Christchurch Convention Centre from the Kilmore Street entrance in the south to the Peterborough entrance in the north – 84.18 metres long, 2.44 metres high and consisting of 138 panels. The sum of $250,000 was needed for its purchase and CoCA director Warren Feeney spearheaded the fundraising campaign. The council contributed $50,000 and the rest came from a lottery grant and public subscription. Not everyone approved however. In a stinging attack, Councillor Barry Corbett said it reminded him of a 99c roll of gift wrapping he had used that morning. For those who enjoy detail, the mural was the largest ever painted in New Zealand, took six months and used 120 litres of paint. It had been intended to sell the panels after the celebrations were over but there was a public outcry demanding it be kept as one art work. The mural remained in situ until the convention centre building had to be demolished after the earthquakes. The panels were saved and placed in storage, awaiting a new home.

Turning Point 2000's Advisory Groups included three projects that were a lasting legacy and a reminder of the first people of Canterbury/

Waitaha. A pre-1850 heritage trail recognising sites of significance to early Māori; the millennium Harakeke Medicinal Garden on the lower slopes of Whakaraupo Park as a resource for flax weavers and practitioners of the ancient knowledge of rongoā (traditional Māori medicine); and Waka 2000. Riki Manuel designed and, with the assistance of local craftsmen, built and carved an impressive 20-metre waka. The hull was created at Rehua Marae in Springfield Road and the decorative side panels (representing ancestors of local iwi), prow and stern carved at Te Toi Mana Art Gallery in the Arts Centre. The waka was intended to lead a flotilla at New Brighton beach early on New Year's Day but, sadly, was not finished in time, though it was launched later that year at Kerrs Reach. And Christchurch composer Joe Tamaira was the winner of the Year 2000 song competition with his 'A New Sunrise', which celebrated the province's diverse cultural community and achievements and the arrival of the new millennium. Five thousand copies were given to the crowds who thronged New Brighton at first light on 1 January 2000.

My first grandchild, Olivia Grace was born on 1 September 2000. Our joyous and lasting relationship started the first moment I saw her; I took one look and was immediately besotted. An irreverent friend said I reminded him of Margaret Thatcher. 'How come?' I demanded, somewhat indignantly. 'Well, when her first arrived, she told the media, "We are a grandmother!"' 'Yes, we are,' I agreed.

But on 21 February 2002, I received a tearful phone call from Dorian. His and Helen's expected second child, Emma, had been stillborn. I rushed to Christchurch Women's Hospital to see Dorian waiting for me at the end of the corridor with this wee bundle in his arms. Emma looked perfect and beautiful but impossibly still. We wept together, then went to console a distraught and heartbroken Helen. As a family we endured the funeral service with the tiny coffin. I wore the double load of my own grief and the suffering of my son. No explanation from the medical professionals was ever provided for this tragic anomaly. A year later the family attended a Christmas Memorial Service organised by Sands (Stillbirth and Neonatal Death Support Group), at the Ferrymead Historic Chapel. Each family was given a helium balloon on which to write the baby's name and our messages and these were released at the end of the ceremony. All the others flew in a group to the north, but Emma's went solo to the south. I could not help but think, That's my girl, independent and different.

Happily, a year later, Alice Louisa was born on 5 March 2003 and we all fell in love with her. Then I minded Olivia and Alice when Harriet Claire appeared on 18 May 2005. My beloved granddaughters, my girlies, who call me Gran, brought immeasurable delight into my life and continue to do so. They provided me with constant pleasure as I kept in touch with their thoughts, fun and inquisitiveness. Bath time was a special favourite for me: just to sit there and watch their creativity from seemingly nothing was always a source of amusement and admiration. In their younger years I ensured that each one could swim proficiently. Over several consecutive years, as each came to her fourth birthday, we spent every Saturday morning in the Centennial Pool for swimming lessons, followed by playtime. And I encouraged all three to learn music. Alice continued with her lessons well into her teens, playing clarinet, saxophone, penny whistle, guitar and composing music. Taking Alice to music lessons and orchestra was such a joy and her special love of musicals meant that I was able to attend productions with her in Christchurch and in Melbourne. And Olivia, conscientious, thoughtful and loving, became a wonderful role model for her two younger sisters. Harriet, full of personality, was a great conversationalist from a very early age. Oh, how enjoyable were our chats as we went off weekly to whatever activity prevailed at the time – gymnastics, music, tap, musical theatre, soccer. Harriet tried them all. I spent as much time as I could in their happy company. I like to think I was good for the girls as they grew up – and I have no doubt at all that they were wonderful for me.

Before the sesquicentennial festivities at the end of 2000, in July the Christchurch City Council sent Pat Harrow and me to represent the city at the Urban 21 Conference held in Berlin. I decided to go via London and spend a few days beforehand with my friend, Maggie Hillock who, only hours after I landed, took me to Shakespeare's Globe, where we saw Vanessa Redgrave as Prospero in *The Tempest*. Standing right at the front of the pit, we had an excellent view. To see Redgrave, so close, striding around the stage wearing a long leather coat, was mesmerising. Her performance was powerful and extraordinary.

After the conference in Berlin, where I was able to visit the rebuilt Reichstag, I had a special task to perform. Not wanting to trust the postal system, Ralf Unger had asked if I would courier precious Unger family documents to the new Jewish Museum, designed by Daniel Libeskind, which had recently been completed but was not yet open. The documents from his grandfather, Enkel von Leopold Brinnitzer, included lithograph and watercolour certificates of appointment dating from 1913 to 1942 and a greatly loved family treasure, a Shabbat doily from about 1890. I had willingly agreed to do this and so when I had a spare day took the U-Bahn to Lindenstrasse. I had arranged to meet the director, New Zealander Ken Gorbey, whom I knew; his wife Susan had been a colleague at the McDougall. As I approached, I could see the museum's massive and spectacular titanium-zinc façade bearing the distinctive symbolic iconography of Libeskind. His extraordinary new building stood next to the baroque 1737 Kollegienhaus, which had formerly housed the Berlin City Museum. Ken met me at the entrance of the old building and from there we took an underground passageway into the recently completed and empty museum.

I was not prepared for the emotional impact of the interior. If the underground entry was confusing, then the underground axes, the angled walls and bare concrete voids, and the oblique slashes of windows, appeared unsystematic. The empty space was strange and frightening. Flights of steps leading nowhere; passageways – narrow, steep and constricting; voids clearly discernible from bridges. One staircase I approached led up to a blank wall that made me stop, stand still and contemplate. Libeskind had used the voids to address the physical emptiness resulting from the expulsion, destruction and annihilation of Jewish life in the Shoah. But the 'room' that had the greatest impact on me was the Holocaust tower. Alone, I heaved open the heavy door to enter a not large but cold bunker-like concrete silo. Once I was inside, the door clanged shut behind me. Looking skyward I could only see a sliver of light through a narrow slit and on the wall leading upwards was a ladder, just out of reach. The symbolism was clear and I fell for it, feeling hopelessly trapped and anxious. The power of the architecture was truly overwhelming and I told Ken that I thought the building should stay empty and be allowed to speak, without being cluttered by exhibitions.

It was not far to rail down to Munich to visit Jeanette, who was sharing a flat with her new partner, for 10 days before returning to New Zealand. The visit did not work out and we parted with unresolved issues. I genuinely wished to atone for the deep hurt she felt at my perceived abandonment, but the gap that had grown between us was too wide to bridge. It was bitterly disappointing, as in our previous meetings I felt we had both really tried to come together. Jeanette and I barely spoke for the last few days of my stay and, miserable, I kept mainly to my room, where she would bring me my meals. On the last day we drove in silence to the railway station, where she put me on the train to Frankfurt to catch my flight home. She walked away without a backward glance and we did not see each other again.

Since leaving my marriage in 1970 I had enjoyed the occasional affair but I was seldom tempted into making a serious commitment. I made the deliberate decision to focus on Dorian, my girlies, my education and my work rather than personal love and fulfilment. Then I met Mark Gerrard. He had been delivering pamphlets in my area for the Hagley Labour Electorate Committee of which he was secretary. As I became more involved in the same committee, I saw him regularly at different meetings. We became friendly and he regularly called in for a chat, the occasional meal and regular late-night walks which were great for counteracting council stress. Months after our first meeting, I invited him for dinner. It was 1 November 2001. The evening was balmy, we dined outside in the courtyard, drank copious amounts of wine and listened to music. He stayed the night and never went home. As someone who did not encourage relationship commitments, this was a momentous achievement for me and, as it turned out, for him too.

Mark was the absolute antithesis of most of the men I had known. He was extremely knowledgeable and entertaining, which lent our discussions an intelligent edge, and, more importantly, he taught me how to live and enjoy life and not just work. Our relationship brought me through bad memories of the painful entanglements of the past and promised a brighter future. It was a revelation to find such a companion. He was 16 years younger than me, distrusted emotions, which he kept in check, and was totally loyal. For me, trust rated higher than love: Mark gave me the confidence to trust. Ours was a relationship built on understanding and empathy without complicated emotional bonds, which suited us both. As a councillor and a public figure, the minute I walked out the door my partner assumed the role of a 'political spouse'. All my colleagues, whatever their political persuasion, relied on a real and very necessary inner supportive network, and Mark was readily accepted into this. I emerged a more rounded person from our relationship, which lasted for 19 years before we went our separate ways. We continue to be the best of friends.

In 2003 I became the South Island representative for the New Zealand Historic Places Trust Board. My area, which comprised 10 branches, included the whole of the South Island, except for Nelson/Tasman (which was included in central), Stewart Island and the Chathams. The most northerly branch was Blenheim, the most southerly in Invercargill. I took every opportunity to visit each mainland branch at least once every two years. This entailed a lot of road travel, with Mark driving, which I had to schedule into my other board and council commitments. In addition, when John Acland chaired the trust, he appointed me as the board representative to accompany the chief executive to annual meetings held in Australia. In terms of identifying, conserving and protecting heritage, Australia's strategy was similar to New Zealand's – both countries recognised that natural and cultural heritage underpins sense of place and identity. Where they differed was that Australia's natural, historic and indigenous heritage came under one umbrella.

There were Māori representatives on the board, two of them with high status, and they had their own Heritage Council. I was honoured to be asked to become the board's representative on that council, because of my knowledge of and interest in all things Māori, but the appointment had to be okayed by Cabinet and my name was not approved by the National government, who chose Ian Athfield instead. I did, though, chair the Registration Committee, which met bi-monthly in Auckland to make recommendations on which items should be listed. All those put forward by the Māori Heritage Council came to us for consideration and after that they would go to the full board for sign-off. I attended many official Māori occasions, such as unveilings, throughout New Zealand.

When I discovered that the Kate Sheppard House in Christchurch, a nationally and internationally significant building, had not yet been listed by Historic Places, I was appalled. Sheppard, the major figure in the campaign for women's suffrage in New Zealand, had been largely forgotten until not long before 1993, when the centenary of the enfranchising Electoral Act was celebrated. The house at 83 Clyde Road was her home from 1888 to 1902, 14 crucial years during which she undertook her notable work. It was there that she met important national and local figures, planned activities, prepared speeches and wrote letters, pamphlets and numerous articles, all aimed at asserting women's right to vote and to have greater equality within society. It gave me much pleasure to shepherd the property through the registration process and finally see it listed in 2010.

There are thousands of heritage advocates spread throughout New Zealand, all with a similar philosophy to mine and all with an interest in the ongoing protection of our historic places and buildings. But, like me, they are up against those in power who make policies without considering heritage retention. People often asked me, and still do, why heritage protection is important. The bigger picture, and one that I have spent many decades painting, is glaringly obvious to me as a historian. Heritage matters because it provides tangible milestones and reminders of our nation's journey. Built heritage tells the story of our towns and cities' past and progress, of our settlers of many origins, and of the homes, businesses and public buildings they erected and created. All these provide inspiration for artistic creativity, a foundation for tourism and economic development. Such places help us to remember, to learn, to belong and to share our stories with others. They are sentinels of living memory. Unlike the heritage of foreign soils, their uniqueness lies in the immediacy of the connection between us as descendants, and our ancestors. They are about people, they are about place and they are about time. New developments presage the flattening effects of globalisation, the spreading of a sameness that threatens to weaken and destroy all sense of place. You can be immune to the historical and aesthetic appeal of heritage, and you can live by bread alone, but you would miss so much.

In April 2004 Mark and I flew to Britain for a much-needed break. I was to attend a Creative Clusters conference in Brighton, so we planned to tack on some visits afterwards. I chose Bath, Mark chose Edinburgh and Sheena Dickson, my stepmother Kathleen's cousin, had invited us to stay with her in Oxford. Of all the adventures we had on that trip, visiting Oxford, where I had never been, was the most intriguing. (And of course there was the connection with Christchurch, named for John Robert Godley's college.) Sheena was sharing a house with her friend Lynda Patterson, from Dromore, in Ireland's County Down. Lynda lectured, and Sheena studied at Mansfield College. Sheena had been to New Zealand several times and in 2003 Lynda had accompanied her. Sheena had already decided that she wished to move to New Zealand, preferably Christchurch, and I had assisted her with some introductions to help with this. As Lynda flew over the Southern Alps, the clouds parted and she immediately fell in love with New Zealand. An avid tramper, she was passionate about the outdoors and often ventured to Iceland and Scotland, camping whenever she could. There was a large poster of the Southern Alps on Lynda's Oxford bedroom wall.

After visiting Bath and Edinburgh we returned to Oxford and the day before we were to leave for home Lynda asked me if I would help her with introductions and contacts as she, too, was seriously considering a move to Christchurch. As the city's representative on the Christ Church Cathedral Foundation, I was in a position to do so. Back home I discussed Lynda's ambition with Dean Peter Beck, and presented him with her excellent CV and references. The result, after a successful phone interview, was that Lynda emigrated to New Zealand in 2005. She had been instructed to first attend St John's Theological College in Auckland for a year to study for the ministry, absorb the culture and learn te reo. She also undertook research for her PhD on biblical hermeneutics. Because I was often in Auckland for Historic Places Trust registration meetings, we were able to catch up and plan her move to Christchurch. Thanks to her fantastic sense of humour, our times together were always fun. In November 2005 she flew down from Auckland for her ordination as deacon at Christ Church Cathedral. Former Mansfield College colleague and friend, the Reverend Dr John Muddiman, travelled from Britain to celebrate the occasion with her. He spent most of his time, when not with Lynda, hunting for excellent New Zealand wines to add to the famed Mansfield College cellar. The shared dinners with these two brilliant theological scholars, who wore their learning so lightly, were memorable.

Christchurch had become New Zealand's first city in 1856; it required a bishop to achieve this status. On 30 July a special civic service, full of pomp and tradition, was held in the cathedral to mark the signing of the letters

David Marshall's bronze corgis, installed on a High Street intersection in 2003, didn't please everyone. The fuss was all beyond my eldest granddaughter, Olivia, who, at four, laughed delightedly as she sat on each one in turn.

Bill Culbert's *Blue*, Christchurch Convention Centre, Kilmore Street, 2000.

Anna supporting the
picket outside the
Kaiapoi Woollen Mills
building, 1996.
- *Jenny May*

Unveiling ceremony for
the statue of
Henry Nicholas,
VC, MM, 7 March 2007.
- *Christchurch City Council*

Anna dressed for the gala costume ball, 15 December 2000, celebrating the 150th anniversary of the arrival of the Canterbury Association settlers.

Neil Dawson's *Chalice*, with messages and flowers placed in sympathy after the September 11 attacks on the Twin Towers in New York.

Anna and Philip Trusttum with the winning design for *Tapestry 2000*.
– *Christchurch Star, 10 March 1999*

The cutting off of the tapestry is always an occasion for celebration and the first time it can be viewed in its entirety. I was there on 22 August 2000 when Prime Minister Helen Clark was given the honour of tying the last knots and cutting the threads to release the work from the loom. Philip Trusttum at rear.

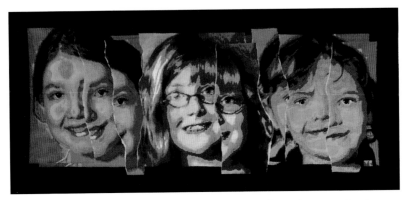

In June 2012, after the earthquakes, I commissioned Marilyn Rea-Menzies to weave a tapestry, on her high warp loom in the Gobelin tradition, of my 'girlies', representing hope for the future. From individual photos of Olivia, Alice and Harriet, Marilyn drew up three concepts from which my granddaughters chose the symbolic fractured version. Marilyn achieved, in nearly two years of work, a special artwork that would become a family heirloom.

Mansfield is not a famous Oxford college, and is one of the smallest. But it is significant when it comes to wining and dining, and those in the know will almost certainly pass up an opportunity to eat at, say, St John's or Magdalen if there is a conflicting invitation from Mansfield. From left: Dr Tony Lemon, Anna, Mark Gerrard, Lynda Patterson, The Reverend Dr John Muddiman (partly obscured), others unidentified.

Outside Christ Church Cathedral after the July 2006 civic service.
From left: Councillor Graham Condon, Mayoress Pam Sharpe,
Councillor David Cox, Mayor Garry Moore, Dean Peter Beck,
Councillor Norman Withers, Anna, Christopher Lewis (Dean of Christ Church,
Oxford), Councillors Pat Harrow and Barry Corbett, Bishop John Gray
and Dr David Coles Bishop of Christchurch.
– *Anglican Action, September 2006*

Anna at her 'super' party with
granddaughters, Harriet, Olivia
and Alice, 12 January 2009.

The giant spider sculpture, *Maman*, by Louise Bourgeois
heralds a grand entrance to the Guggenheim.

My kitchen at 12.51 p.m. on 22 February 2011. In the foreground is the water
tank, which landed in front of my kitchen bench where I was standing.

Anna and conservator Carolina Izzo inspecting the plasterwork rescued from the Isaac Theatre Royal, April 2013. – *Theatre Royal Charitable Foundation*

The former Trinity Congregational Church before the earthquakes.
– CC BY-SA 2.0 Taken by Robert Cutts, 2007, Wikimedia Commons

The former Trinity Congregational Church after the earthquakes.

Anna and Richard Lloyd, project manager,
outside Trinity in 2015 and the interior in
2018, showing the magnificent double-barrel
vault timber ceiling.

Shand's in Hereford Street in May 2013.

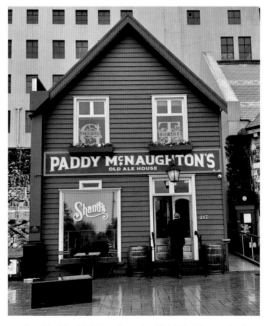

Shand's restored as Paddy McNaughton's Old Ale House, in December 2020.

Anna speaking at the launch of Historic Places
Aotearoa at Government House, Wellington, in 2012.

Anna, seated right, crossing the Yellow River at Lanzhou on an inflated
sheepskin raft traditionally used by the locals. Such transport was not usually
offered to tourists but I had to try it.

After attending Cousin Lesley's seventieth birthday celebration in
San Francisco in 2017, Dorian and I decided to tick off another dream of mine:
watching the All Blacks play France in the electric atmosphere of the
Stade de France in Paris, which we did on 11 November.
The final score in a feisty game was All Blacks 38, France 18.

Family lunch before Dorian and I escaped to France in April 2019.
From left: Alice, Harriet, Mark, Anna, Dorian and Olivia.

Dorian relaxing outside the cottage at 12 Rue de Pont Neuf, Céret, April 2019.

Dorian and Anna by the Pablo Picasso fountain in Place Picasso, Céret.

Entry doors to the off-site storage vaults, St Petersburg.

Jeannette, Dorian and Anna celebrating the end of our road trip
from Céret to Paris, 15 May 2019.

I had to stand in the middle of the street to get my shot of the Volkov Theatre.
I have my umbrella; the city's bear symbol has his axe, Yaroslavl.

Dame Patsy Reddy presenting Anna with her insignia
as a Dame Companion of the New Zealand Order of Merit.
– *Government House, Wellington*

Always in step – Dorian and Anna in the cloisters of
Abbaye de Fontfroide, Narbonne, France, 2019.

patent from London that cleared the way for the appointment of the first bishop, Henry Harper. Dr Christopher Lewis, the Dean of Christ Church, Oxford, attended and The Oxfords male quartet sang with the cathedral choir. Lynda, by this time part-time priest assistant at the cathedral, kindly asked me to lead the prayers of intercession. It was a privilege to be asked but I felt a little anxious about the request. There had been an absence of 'faith' in our family, a tradition I inherited and followed. The only times we went to church was for a wedding, funeral or christening. Lynda knew this, as this topic was often discussed, but she felt it was right for me to take this role because of my commitment to community. I do recall that, when I had finished the prayers and returned to my seat, I felt an overwhelming sense of purpose.

There was a 150th birthday bash on 29 July in Cathedral Square and all of Christchurch was invited and celebrated in style. Seven hours of live performances, a 150-metre-long carrot birthday cake, over 200 'crazy Cantabrians' dressed as their favourite things about the city, buskers, clowns, candy floss and stilt walkers. The main heritage icons, including both the Anglican and Catholic cathedrals, were wrapped for the occasion in red and black ribbon, as were the statues, flagpoles, the *Press* building, the Victoria Street clock tower and the trees in the Four Avenues, to name a few. The *Press* marked the occasion with a souvenir liftout and a request for readers to nominate their favourite things about living in Christchurch. The final list of 150 included the museum, the art gallery, Sumner beach, Cathedral Square, the Peacock Fountain, *Chalice*, the Botanic Gardens, the town hall, its flatness, the cultural mix and so on. Only a few individuals were named: the Wizard, Vicki Buck, Norman Kirk, Philip Burdon and as 'examples to keep local citizens well informed of what they do on the citizens' behalf', Ruth Dyson, MP for Banks Peninsula, Tim Barnett MP for Christchurch Central and, the only city councillor mentioned, Anna Crighton. I took that as a badge of honour.

It was in 2006, too, that Lynda, having completed her ministerial training in Auckland, moved permanently to Christchurch. On Sunday 29 January she was invited to preach at the cathedral for the first time. I was immediately captivated by her rhetoric, enhanced by her lilting Northern Irish accent, and the accessibility of her message. She spoke in a way that was both thought-provoking and made you laugh – and cry. Peter Beck, always very supportive of Lynda, recommended her for the position as Director of Theology House, Merivale, when Dr Ken Booth retired. She took up her duties there on 1 December and the next day was ordained at Christ Church Cathedral by Bishop David Coles. I arranged a reception of celebration for her afterwards in the Timber Chamber of the Provincial Council Buildings.

Having already announced my retirement from the council in 2007, I planned my exit strategy very carefully. Other retired councillors had found it difficult to go from a high-profile life to seemingly nothing, with all invitations and networks suddenly cut off. My first move to avoid such a fate was taking my whole family, and Mark, to visit cousin Lesley in Las Vegas, with, of course, a trip to Disneyland on the way. The bus driver for the trip from Los Angeles to Las Vegas told us he would love to go to New Zealand but did not think he could drive there – not enough straight roads and too many corners.

I was determined to have one momentous celebration in my life and my sixty-fifth birthday in January 2009 was the time to do it and so I threw myself a 'super' party. My first birthday was spent in hospital with burns, turning thirteen and beginning my first year at Otago Girls' High passed without ceremony, as did my not especially sweet sixteenth. I had passed my twenty-first in a bedsit in Chichester, pregnant and waiting to come home, and my half-century quietly at home. Other milestones, too, had come and gone without fanfare. This once in a lifetime celebration needed to have it all: great food (three-course buffet menu) and wine, live music and dancing set in a unique venue. And so it was: on the stage of the Theatre Royal with music by the outstanding Stu Buchanan and his Garden City Big Band. The stage set looked spectacular: a dozen tables of 10, each representing a special year in my life, with the sparkly curtain backdrop and specialist lighting. An invitation went out to 120 special family members, friends and colleagues. Of my many 'parents', HB was the only one left to attend. The seating was carefully planned with like-minded people for each table: family, close friends, neighbours, former McDougall colleagues, city councillors, Labour and heritage colleagues, council staff, travel companions, artists and so on. The band played songs made famous by Glenn Miller, Count Basie and Harry Connick Jr while we dined, then ramped up the volume with foot-tapping boogie and rock'n'roll that got everyone on their feet. Mark and I had spent a few weeks practising in the garage and we led the dancing onto the floor. I had a ball.

During the last year of the decade, in May 2010, I took myself off to Spain and Portugal to feed my appetite for Spanish art and architecture, both contemporary and historical. In Barcelona, I had my fill of Gaudi marvels. I went north to Bilbao specifically to visit Frank Gehry's spectacular Guggenheim Museum. I lucked onto a major solo exhibition devoted to the art of Anish Kapoor, the highlight of which was his mixed media, *Shooting into the Corner*.

From Bilbao I boarded the El Transcantábrico, a luxury private train with original 1923 Pullman saloon cars. This was my hotel for the next six days as it took me along the famous Pilgrims' Way across northern Spain and through a less-visited part of Europe to Santiago de Compostela. One of the outstanding buildings I visited along the way was the San Julián de los Prados, also known as Santullano, in the city of Oviedo. It always strengthens my resolve when defending the retention of historic heritage in New Zealand when I see such a gem as this pre-Romanesque church, which has been protected for centuries. I could feel the history emanating from the hand-hewn stonework. In Portugal, visiting Porto, once an outpost of the Roman Empire, gave me the opportunity to walk over the Maria Pia railway bridge, built in 1877 and attributed to Gustave Eiffel.

I experienced some remarkable and memorable times during the first decade of the new millennium and was optimistic about the future. The next decade would be challenging in the most unexpected ways.

CHAPTER 17

I Hit the Wall

When I was re-elected to the council in 2004, for what I had already vowed would be my last term, I had received a phone call from Dr Mark Stocker, who had been at Canterbury University but by then was Associate Professor of History and Art History at Otago. He congratulated me but added that he was sorry too, as he was keen for me to study at Otago for my PhD under his supervision. I held that thought and after pondering it further, early in 2008 I submitted a seven-page proposal for a thesis which, to my delight, was accepted.

I had no bones to pick with my alma mater, the University of Canterbury, but I was an elected member of the university's council, which meant a potential conflict of interest, and Mark Stocker's encouragement and the hospitable Department of History and Art History at Otago beckoned. I knew I wanted to focus on the Robert McDougall Gallery but Mark, for whom I had great admiration as a supervisor, made it clear that a straightforward blow-by-blow history just would not do: a thesis had to have a thesis. But what? Then an idea came to me, immediately encouraged by Mark. Public art galleries tend to publish information on works in their collection – title, date, image, provenance and so on – but almost none of it relates to why that particular work was chosen and how: the culture behind the selection. The McDougall had conformed to a 'British World' model, but its history and identity also raised distinctive and fascinating cultural issues with Canterbury and of Aotearoa New Zealand. And so from 2008, based in Christchurch, I spent four years researching and preparing my thesis: 'The selection and presentation culture of the Robert McDougall Art Gallery, Christchurch, New Zealand, 1932–2002'.

I had the advantage of my lengthy experience as registrar/collections manager at the Robert McDougall Art Gallery and through that had enjoyed the back stories about the art works – the stories the public did not get to know about. My institutional knowledge was matched by a dedication to the rigours of archival research and the pleasures of interviewing past directors, colleagues and art world players. Particularly enjoyable were the one-on-one interviews with past directors, Dr Rodney Wilson and John Coley, as well as former staff member and later kaitiaki, Jonathan Mane-Wheoki. Both Rodney and Jonathan died soon after I completed the thesis – this was vital oral history gathered just in time.

The challenges of doing my PhD at a distance were few. I visited Otago regularly to meet with my supervisors and discuss progress, review work done to date and complete quarterly checks. But writing sustained research close on 30 years after my MA was scary at first. At the sessions my two supervisors – Mark and Dr Alex Trapeznik, affectionately nicknamed 'the Commissar' – were, to mix my metaphors, akin to getting my teeth pulled by the bad cop and the worse cop. But all three of us, especially me, were committed to producing a credible and sustained body of scholarship. The university was extremely helpful in providing me with technology and information. I also received notices of PhD courses about how to start, what to expect along the way, how to finish and to learn that 'hitting the wall' at some stage was quite normal. I prolonged these visits south to enjoy a touch of campus life, fossick through the Otago University Bookshop and absorb the intact Dunedin heritage cityscape.

After a year or two, I was required to give a seminar presentation on my research. I felt trepidation, especially as Mark Stocker was overseas at the time, but it went fine, and I felt a genuine sense of interest from everyone present. Such seminars produce suggestions – the most valuable in this case coming from visiting Australian professor Timothy Rouse, who told me kindly but in no uncertain terms, 'Bone up on your Bourdieu!' I did.

But as I reached the final stages of my research and writing, a 7.1 magnitude earthquake hit Christchurch on 4 September 2010. My house was severely damaged but still habitable and I continued as best as I could with my thesis, though without access to two important areas for research information: the Christchurch City Council archives and the University of Canterbury Library and archives. Then, on Boxing Day that year, there was a large aftershock and my house was much more seriously affected. This inevitably resulted in a further lull in my work. I was back into a good writing routine when a 6.3 magnitude earthquake devastated Christchurch on 22 February 2011, causing death, injury and widespread destruction. I had to immediately evacuate my extensively damaged house. My computer and research material and notes for the main text, plus those for the introduction, conclusion and epilogue, had to be retrieved from my red-stickered home. Christchurch City Libraries, which had been an invaluable source of information to that point, was now closed, as were the *Press* archives. However, the library and archives of the Christchurch Art Gallery Te Puna o Waiwhetū remained open and I made good use of them over the next months. I will always be so grateful to the ever helpful and cheerful Tim Jones, who immediately appreciated the value of my research. But then another 6.3 magnitude earthquake on 13 June meant I lost access to that source as well.

I hit the wall.

I sought and was given a six-month break from the university. Despite this official time off, I could not settle and continued to work sporadically until the first complete draft of my thesis was completed. The encouragement I received from all staff, from my supervisors to the head of department, Professor Barbara Brookes, and the Director of Graduate Research, Dr Charles Tustin, was hugely important at a time when I had little energy and motivation. The final bound copies were submitted almost a year later, in September 2012. To celebrate this milestone, my family and I went to Fiji to soak in some sunshine and rest and relax. It was a necessary venture for all of us. Olivia had been spooked by the earthquakes and was very nervy, Dorian was stressed at work and from holding things together for the family and Helen had been coping in a badly damaged house sitting on a section mired in liquefaction. It was a tonic to get away and play, swim, laugh and experience a casual and relaxed way of island life alien to us all.

In December that year I received the gratifying news that I had been awarded my PhD. Mark Stocker told me that the examiners 'were unanimous in acknowledging the significance and quality of Anna Crighton's research, and accordingly awarded the thesis with distinction'. I punched the air. I was capped later that month. The walk down the main street in Dunedin to the Regent Theatre, led by a piper, was a thrilling occasion that was shared by Dorian and partner Mark as they sat at a bar table en route, enjoying a celebratory drink. The whole day was extraordinary, from the presentation of a corsage and a large specialty chocolate fish (yes, a Cadbury's chocolate fish – a tradition for Otago graduands), donning the gown, the procession, the capping ceremony, the celebratory drinks and nibbles on the lawn of First Church and a celebratory dinner to end all dinners with Dorian, Mark and Mark Stocker at a whisky bar restaurant. I somehow got through the day in a daze.

The terrifying memories of the February 2011 earthquake have dimmed somewhat but the intensity of the fear is forever seared on my mind. I had been standing at my kitchen bench, preparing my lunch and making a cup of tea. When I felt the shaking, I looked up through the skylight above and saw the original 1892 cast-iron riveted water tank falling towards me from where it had sat on the parapet, anchored by gravity, for the last 119 years. I was frozen to the spot, but something had made me move. All I can recall is running down the hall in slow motion. If I had dropped, covered and held, as per the rule book, I would have been crushed beneath the water tank, which crashed through the roof and planted itself firmly through the floor. I suffered deep bruising down the right side of my body where it must have caught me as I moved. It was some time before I could enter the kitchen again.

My diary simply states '1pm house abandoned'. My house in Chester Street East is situated in the central city, one block north from Latimer Square and the CTV building, which pancaked and killed 115 people, and one block east of the Pyne Gould Guinness building, in which 18 died. As I stood outside, traumatised and in shock, not quite knowing what to do, a steady stream of injured and crying people hobbled past me down Madras Street, their pale faces tense and fearful. The street was running with silt and water. It looked like a scene from a war zone and these were the refugees. I turned away in despair and retreated to my front courtyard to wait, though for what, I cannot remember. Dorian, on his bike, was the first to appear to make sure I was okay. He had been at lunch at the Bealey pub and rushed home to Avonside to check on his wife and children. Once he knew that they were alright, he cycled over to me. Mark, who had been in Ballantynes, came home as fast as he could, making his way through

Cathedral Square and the rubble and aftershocks. He, too, was uninjured.

My house was munted, as we said in those days, and uninhabitable. Mark dug the liquefaction silt away from the garage door to enable us to get the car out. He also had the foresight, and risked entry to the upstairs of the house, to retrieve the computer on which I had been writing my PhD. He went back a second time and carried down the safe from my study in which I had Chapters 1–6 in revised draft form, but not yet entered onto the computer. Then we fled to his sister's place in Northwood. That was surreal: it was so different on that side of the city. The suburb was untouched. A man was mowing his berm and others were going about their normal lives while across town people were trapped and dying in collapsed buildings. Christchurch became a city of two halves. I existed on auto pilot for some months before I was much use to anyone. There are thousands of horrifying, harrowing and painful stories out there and this very brief account of mine is just one of them. Millions of words have been written about the disaster and the bravery and courage of so many people.

The earthquakes and the thousands of aftershocks took more out of me than I cared to admit. I struggled inwardly for some time with the 'new normal', which dented my usual resolve and sapped my energy. But somewhere in the back of my mind I knew I had to keep going. Mark, as a contractor for the central city venues of the Provincial Government Buildings and Our City Ōtautahi, lost all his work within minutes. Dorian, too, was finding life difficult. He and the family left their house and went to stay with Peter Somerville and Margaret Foyle in Balcairn, North Canterbury. It was a very generous offer to accommodate two adults, three children, a dog and a guinea pig. After things settled down a bit, the family returned to live in their Avonside house, though it, too, was munted and had no working toilet. The Christchurch City Council provided a huge receptacle on the road into which families emptied their effluent. The section was silted and many of the floor piles had collapsed, giving an uneven floor. Ten-year-old Olivia was traumatised but Alice and Harriet seemed to tackle the new way of living with high spirits. Dorian's office in Oxford Terrace had to be abandoned and the firm moved to temporary premises at Heller's factory in Kaiapoi.

It was to be some time before I rallied again to complete my PhD, resolve the restoration of my house and once again take up the heritage cause. At my lowest ebb, as I lay really depressed in the small bedroom of our temporary accommodation in Melrose Street, Dorian came to visit. 'This is what my life has come to,' I said. 'Mark comes in with a bucket of hot water and a cloth and wipes the mould from the walls while I lie here.' Dorian quietly left but in a sombre mood. A week later he returned with a solution. I could put a deposit on a house using part of my mother's legacy, and since my income was such that I could not get a mortgage, he would arrange that and the rental would pay the outgoings. And so it was. Properties to rent or buy were at a premium but we managed to purchase one in Westminster Street, Mairehau. Mark and I moved in.

But there is more. After the earthquakes came the deluge. We had been in our new residence only a few weeks when, in a bone-chilling June, the city was inundated by persistent rain and storms. We were living in one of the worst affected parts of the city. Civil Defence set up a welfare centre at Mairehau Primary School in case residents had nowhere to go. At 11 p.m. one night, there was a knock at the front door and a man was there advising us to evacuate. The Flockton Basin area was under water and it was lapping at the top step of our front entrance. I was in bed at the time and said to Mark, 'I'm not going anywhere. I've had enough. If I have to make my bed on the table, so be it.' We stayed. The aftermath of that experience was a wardrobe containing mouldy shoes, while broken drains under the floor hardly helped and the front lawn was permanently flooded. Once things settled down again, living at Westminster Street proved to be a perfect solution and it certainly helped me to regain my health and my spirits.

In December 2010, after the first earthquake, Heritage New Zealand appointed me to the Canterbury Earthquake Heritage Buildings Fund Trust (CEHBF), which I chaired. This was a government initiative with a multi-million-dollar budget that would match dollar for fundraised dollar so that grants could be made to save and restore heritage buildings. At first the governing legislation was the Canterbury Earthquake Response and Recovery Act 2010, but after the February 2011 earthquake, and the passing of the Canterbury Earthquake Recovery Act the following April, I called meetings weekly because of the urgency to support owners of salvageable heritage buildings that were immediately threatened because of section 38 notices. This section of the 2011 act gave the chief executive of the Canterbury Earthquake Recovery Authority (CERA) the power to carry out or commission demolition almost at will. The timely decisions of the CEHBF saved many heritage buildings.

Trustees, representatives from the Christchurch, Selwyn and Waimakariri councils plus independents, received no remuneration and gave their time voluntarily. Staff members from the three councils received applications, assessed their eligibility and, along with the designated heritage adviser from Heritage New Zealand, presented them to the trust with recommendations. The two largest donations we received were $5 million from a benefactor, which went to the Arts Centre of Christchurch, and $1 million from Fletchers. For the latter I met with CEO Mark Binns to discuss which high-profile building would benefit from their donation. After a tour of several candidates, we decided to save and restore the landmark McKenzie & Willis façade on the corner site where High Street faced Tuam Street. Ensuring preservation of this 1911 historic three-storey façade, designed by the England Brothers for furnishing store A. J. White, would obviously enhance the area. Between 2010 and 2014 trust members collectively gave many hundreds of hours and made a significant, largely unseen contribution towards retaining remnants of other heritage buildings as reminders of Canterbury's historical past.

Hands-on projects helped to salve my wounds as I witnessed the destruction of so much in the city that I had fought for. The recreation of the Isaac Theatre Royal and the saving and restoring of the Shand's and Trinity buildings were overwhelmingly challenging projects.

The Theatre Royal Foundation, of which I had been a director since 2001, met soon after the February earthquake, when the most damage to the building had occurred. We needed to assess whether to repair or rebuild the theatre. The board, under chair Ray Eddington, had decided some years earlier to change the insurance cover from indemnity to replacement, but even this amount would not be enough. The board discussions were weighty. There was no question as to what option I vehemently supported. My role on the board had always been as watchdog over the heritage values and fabric of the building. After lengthy discussions and consultations with professionals, the board started to turn from a new build to rescue. Eventually, the decision was driven by heart, not by rational commercial thinking. We announced, in late January 2012, that the existing theatre would be deconstructed carefully and recreated and improved. It was a huge risk and a mighty challenge but the board took a leap of faith.

Before the deconstruction of the auditorium, the theatre had to be stabilised. Also vital was the taking of 3-D scans before the salvage of much of the heritage fabric, so that we could eventually reconstruct the original features. The doors and their hardware, the two round 1908 Art Nouveau poppy windows from the side walls of the auditorium, the original Art Nouveau windows from the first-floor façade and undamaged plasterwork taken for mouldings were all recovered and placed in storage. Also retrieved were the plaster reliefs of William Shakespeare and Sir Henry Irving, which had looked down from above the royal boxes, and the only original crystal 18-branch chandelier to survive. The marble staircase, which could not be moved, was built into a rather large box to protect it during the major construction work around and over it. We were also able to save the poster collection, both framed and archival, so valuable as a visual history of most of the shows held at the Theatre Royal since 1866. (The 1908 building we know today replaced two earlier theatres of the same name that stood on the opposite side of Gloucester Street.)

One of the defining and much-loved features of the theatre is the signature dome, with its enchanting, softly coloured painted panels of scenes from Shakespeare's *A Midsummer Night's Dream*. The process of rescuing and restoring the dome was both an engineering and conservation challenge. We were blessed that Italian conservator and restoration expert Carolina Izzo, trained in Florence, accepted the assignment to do exactly that, along with Emanuele Vitulli and his son, Luigi, and their dedicated assistants. Carolina had worked on the restoration of the famous San Carlo Theatre and other historic buildings in Naples, and her experience and considerable knowledge were invaluable. The dome was returned in as good a condition as when it was first installed. The other miraculous tale was that of the plasterwork. Working with Carolina and her people, Gary Watson and his team were able to make patterns from the salvaged pieces and recreate the elaborate profiles that were everywhere in the theatre. My special request was for some gilding of the plasterwork, which had long disappeared. To my delight, Carolina acted on that wish.

If the save or rebuild debate had been intense, the wrangling over the future of the exuberant Edwardian façade was even more so. Over the decades it had been painted several times. The architects for the project, Warren and

Mahoney, submitted a concept of the theatre repainted completely in white. This may have made the theatre look more contemporary but it would have drowned the effects of its historic detailing. Conservation architect Tony Ussher had completed a heritage conservation plan that supported the restoration and strengthening of architects Alfred and Sydney Luttrell's original design. After much discussion, and with supporting evidence from me, the board finally and unanimously agreed to leave the façade unpainted and to restore its initial appearance.

On Friday 22 August 2014 Mayor Lianne Dalziel and I placed a time capsule, which I had packed in a special conservation board box that was in turn inserted in a fireproof and waterproof container, in a roof cavity of the theatre. The contents? That is confidential. We planned to raise the curtain again on 17 November, before a sold-out Russian dance spectacular for the grand opening. But would the theatre be ready? Activities behind the scenes on the day were frenetic as board members joined staff and contractors in feverish excitement to work on last-minute tasks. Andrew Logan cleaned the arms of all 1290 chairs and carted boxes of beer and wine to the bar fridges. I laid carpet tiles and assembled lockers. Chair Joy Simpson, who had been scrubbing floors, was still vacuuming as people were walking in for the show. We only received our certificate of public use three hours before the opening. But everything was very alright on the night.

The saving of the theatre became one of the most significant success stories of Christchurch's post-quake recovery. The full story of the restoration is told in the 2016 book, *Recreating the Magic*, which the board asked me to produce, with chapters written by Dr Ian Lochhead, Liz Grant and me. It is not just a narrative about bricks and mortar but about the amazing team of hundreds who all, in significant and minor ways, contributed to the extraordinary final result because they were determined to ensure the survival of a vital piece of architectural heritage.

For 25 years the trustees of the Christchurch Heritage Trust worked diligently to safeguard Christchurch's built heritage through a dramatic period of change and it was dispiriting and depressing to learn that every building we had fought to retain and restore had fallen victim to the 2010

and 2011 earthquakes. And they were not small structures: the Excelsior Hotel in High Street, the *Lyttelton Times* building in Cathedral Square, the *Canterbury Star Times* in Gloucester Street and, more recently, Smith's Bookshop in Manchester Street. They were all an integral part of the city's story, all highly recognisable landmarks and all heritage listed. Statistics as at June 2015 stated that Canterbury lost around 40 per cent of its 922 heritage buildings. In the central city alone, demolition equated to 48 per cent of 309 such properties. That is an extraordinary number. The ongoing pre-earthquake conflict between heritage protection and development pressures was exacerbated afterwards, especially in light of the scorched earth policy practised in the central city by CERA. Central Christchurch has been rebuilt almost out of recognition, and largely with the soullessness of internationalism. Fortunately, the remaining heritage buildings that were not demolished by nature or by humans have been rescued.

Undaunted, however, the trust regrouped and was determined to rescue whatever it could. It was fitting that our focus should be the former Trinity Congregational Church, on the corner of Worcester and Manchester streets, the oldest masonry structure in the central city – and only weeks away from the bulldozer. A late example of the early French Gothic style, it was an innovative and challenging design and the first example of its type in stone in New Zealand. Especially interesting was the combination of timber and stone in the church's interior. And then there was Shand's in Hereford Street, Christchurch's oldest surviving commercial timber building, which was slowly being destroyed through neglect. The pair dated back to 1875 and 1860 respectively and both enjoyed Category 1 listings with Heritage New Zealand. Both needed saving and time was running out.

Enter Richard Lloyd. Richard, a former captain in the Royal New Zealand Engineers, received a call from an old army mate, Greg Wilson, with whom he had trained overseas. The pair's general role was military construction and demolition, building and destroying everything from bridges and roads to minefields and runways. Greg, who was working for CERA, had just signed the demolition order for Trinity Church's owner Alan Slade. Greg asked Richard if he was interested in saving the building. If so, he would have to move fast as its survival could only be guaranteed for a matter of weeks. Richard was indeed interested and he did move fast. He connected with Philip Barrett, from the Christchurch City Council Heritage Unit, whose sentiments were similar. Richard was also keen to apply injection grouting to strengthen the walls – a method commonly used in Italy – instead of applying unseemly and intrusive concrete and steel for strengthening. Concurrently, he started negotiating with Slade to purchase the building. He also approached the CEHBF for a grant of $250,000 for 'make-safe' work, to which we agreed. (Because I was chair of CEHBF and on the board of the Christchurch Heritage Trust I declared a conflict of interest and stood back from discussions and voting.) The council approved a $1 million grant for restoration work. But the clock was ticking and Richard, unable to raise the necessary funds to complete the purchase, approached the trust to take over the purchase and the restoration, including the grants already approved.

It was not a difficult decision to make. The background history of Trinity was compelling, its corner landmark site outstanding, the early French Gothic style innovative and the only damage to the timber interior was from pigeon droppings. The double-barrel vault ceiling was described by Dr Ian Lochhead, Mountfort's biographer, as one of his 'most impressive and original inventions'. It would have been a travesty if such intricate craftsmanship had been destroyed and dumped. Kate Sheppard taught Sunday school at Trinity in the 1880s and worshipped there, as did Henry Nicholas VC. Richard was not only passionate about the project; he also had the required knowledge for the trust to engage him as the project manager. At the time of writing, the restoration is not completed but it is on track to be finished soon, with a tenant ready to move in. The trust did not have the funds to restore the tower but instead a porch was extended along the northern façade.

Erected just 10 years after the first Canterbury Association settlers arrived, on land owned by John Shand, Shand's was a charming, quirky and historically significant reminder of Christchurch's pioneering past. By the time of the earthquakes, it was an oddity at 88 Hereford Street, a small two-storey wooden building that once fronted a dirt road now wedged precariously between its much larger and sturdier neighbours on a thriving and busy thoroughfare.

Though damaged, Shand's Emporium, as it had been known since the late 1970s, withstood the 2010 and 2011 earthquakes, but was left isolated on its site. Subsequent years of neglect prompted the Christchurch Heritage Trust to step in to rescue it. There was a special fondness among Christchurch people for this little building and repairing and restoring its heritage fabric would keep that legacy alive. I contacted architect William Fulton to measure up the piece of land at the back of Trinity to see if it would fit there and was delighted to learn that it would. By planning a covered atrium between the two buildings, and a new annex at the back to house toilets, offices and commercial kitchen, the two heritage buildings could be restored to their original envelopes and stand alone. In June 2015 the trust purchased Shand's from its owner, Anthony Gough, for $1. It was then moved to its new position on Manchester Street, next to Trinity, where it stands proudly in its revived livery of green and red, a tribute to its strong and indomitable character and a reminder of its role as a portal to the past.

As for my own house, red-stickered and cordoned off in the Red Zone, like thousands of others I endured the grief and anxiety of years of entanglement with the insurers as I battled for a payout that would enable me to restore my house. Early on, I made several illegal trips to the house, using, like many others, helpful contacts and some smooth talking to pass through the red-zone barrier, controlled by army personnel. The first was to rescue my art collection. Then I hired a truck so that I could remove all my furniture. Their men were not allowed to enter the house so Dorian rounded up his mates to bring everything out onto the street for loading. They worked at great speed – there were still horrendous aftershocks – and my house was emptied in no time. From there everything was taken to Peter and Margaret's at Balcairn and eventually loaded into a container. While it was in the Red Zone, my house became a place for unwanted guests. On one illegal trip, I found the garage full of small items of furniture, garden ornaments and a lot of rubbish: it appeared to be a collection point for stolen goods from neighbouring houses. I also found empty beer cans littered around a wing-back chair in an upstairs room, where the occupant had been comfortably seated while reading Dorian's collection of war comics (which, sadly, disappeared). But this was not so bad when compared with the overflow of excrement in the toilet, which would not flush as the water had been turned off. The police called several times to take finger-prints but the intruders were never found.

The insurance claim was finally resolved after years of lengthy correspondence and meetings – I lost count of the number of so-called 'assessors', who inspected the damage – but only because my solicitor threatened High Court action if the matter was not settled within 10 days. Settlement was promptly made. I requested that the payout come directly to me, as it was important that I was the project manager for the restoration. I engaged Maiden Construction; Greg Bridge was the foreman in charge. He and they did an amazing job.

The house was repositioned on its foundation with new piles, the party wall was rebuilt, the interior was stripped of 10 tonnes of lath and plaster before compliant linings were installed with every possible area insulated, all trims and doors removed were restored and reinstalled and rimu flooring was replaced where required. As a 'betterment', the architect even managed to squeeze an en suite into the main bedroom. The original colours were retained and the only difference between before and after was a warmer house and level floors. The whole restoration took over a year to complete. It took a little longer to tame the garden. After more than five years of neglect, most things had been strangled by weeds and I had to start again. On 3 September 2016, the house was officially reopened by Mayor Lianne Dalziel, and blessed by the Reverend Sheena Dickson, after which Mark and I moved back in.

The day we moved in provokes special memories, not all of them good. I was so happy to be back in my home again, but the first evening turned out to be a disaster. The weather was abysmal – driving rain, wind and bitterly cold. All I wanted was to wallow in my bath, which I did. When it was emptied, however, the water went straight out of the plug-hole and through to the room below, ruining floor, ceilings and walls. It was a scene straight out of a sitcom, but I was not particularly amused. The connection between bath and outlet had been left untethered. At the same time the radiator in the kitchen leaked when turned on and water poured onto my new rimu floorboards. And that was not all. The same night a tree on the neighbour's boundary fell onto and damaged my newly built fence. Oh, for a medicinal glass of wine, kindly provided by neighbours Sue and Alister James. Once the weather cleared and all was righted, I was truly happy to be home. There was a chance that the familiar spirit of the place could perhaps have disappeared, even though it looked exactly the same, but that did not happen. My dear house still had all its inviting warmth and traditional elegance.

CHAPTER 18

A Born Survivor

In February 2010, the Minister for Arts, Culture and Heritage, Chris Finlayson, announced a review of the Historic Places Act that would include the disestablishment of all New Zealand Historic Places Trust branch committees and elected board representatives. A ripple of disquiet, and in many instances anger, went through the heritage volunteer sector. Historic Places Trust members resigned in protest. The proposed legislative change would alienate the invaluable grassroots input of volunteers who had worked cooperatively with trust staff for some 50 years and affect hundreds of heritage advocates throughout the country. Half a century of hours spent, energy and enthusiasm would be wiped out with one stroke. I felt so strongly about what was happening that I pushed at board level, and received funding for, a Wellington meeting to be attended by two delegates from each branch, to decide on a way forward for the disestablished branches. At the July 2010 meeting Finlayson said he was willing for the ministry to support the transition phase and was also open to negotiation on several matters, including resources for the transition.

This, however, did not happen. From the meeting came a decision to start a replacement organisation. The delegates did not want to lose the momentum of having a strong local voice for heritage in the regions. But where do you start with no membership and no funding? That's a big mountain to climb. Despite the massive challenge ahead, the group resolved to form a steering committee. With me as chair, there were David Kiddey from Wellington, David White from Central Otago, Jimmy Wallace from South Canterbury, Peter Dowell from Wellington and James Blackburne from Tairāwhiti. Individually and collectively, through our respective talents and skills, we were in a position to lay the foundation for a solid and credible new non-government organisation. After more than two years of hard work, with regrettably negligible financial and human resource support from Historic Places, and relying totally on limited self-funding and goodwill, the steering group took Historic Places Aotearoa from an idea to a reality.

The new organisation was launched in grand style at Government House on 14 August 2012. As patron Dame Anne Salmond put it, there would now be 'two powerful voices for the protection of historic sites and buildings in New Zealand': the Crown entity, the New Zealand Historic Places Trust (to be renamed Heritage New Zealand), and Historic Places Aotearoa, a non-government organisation 'able to advocate for historic sites and buildings without fear or favour'. The two would 'almost certainly work closely together'. In my address as inaugural president, I emphasised that Historic Places Aotearoa would retain the eyes and ears of those hundreds of regional volunteers who could have been lost. A strong voice to advocate for vulnerable heritage, not just from earthquakes and other natural disasters but also from destruction through inappropriate development, was immediate and necessary.

It was a turning point for New Zealand's heritage and marked a new beginning for local advocacy. The opportunity for communities to have a louder say in preserving their heritage for future generations was a return to the original spirit of heritage protection in this country. I was president of Historic Places Aotearoa from 2010 until 2013 and remained on the executive until 2015. Although the workload took its toll on me while I was coping with the aftermath of the earthquakes, I am proud to have been a co-founder of an organisation that is still thriving.

When my role on the board of the New Zealand Historic Places Trust ended in 2014, after 11 years, I and other retirees, former chair Shonagh Kenderdine, Māori Heritage Council chair Sir Tumu Te Heuheu, together with board members Dr Apirana Mahuika, Gerard O'Regan, Allan Matson and David Kiddey, were given a formal farewell at the trust's Antrim House headquarters in Wellington, to thank us for our work and make us honorary life members of the newly minted Heritage New Zealand.

On 17 September 2012, Hugh Bromley Bower, HB, the last of my six 'parents', died. The funeral, a low-key affair, gave me time to reflect on how he had

affected and influenced both my and Dorian's lives. He had been good to us and I was pleased that I had kept in regular contact, particularly when he was less active. We had enjoyed discussing the old days at the factory, lamenting the failure of the plastic recycling pilot scheme that was well before its time, as well as his favourite subject of crop circles and politics. He was well read and enjoyed a good debate.

Both my mother and my father had ultimately moved from their second to their third 'life' partners. After leaving Joan, his second wife, my father met Kathleen, and until their respective divorces came through, the two lived quietly in the little North Canterbury town of Domett. There they eventually married in 1990 and built a house where they lived until serious health problems brought them back to Christchurch and nearer the hospital. I gave them the downstairs flat next door at 88 Chester Street East until my father died. I then bought Kathleen a little house after her return from Scotland, where she lived happily until her death in 2009. My mother, after her split from HB, met Sam and they eventually relocated to live together in Queenstown in 1981 in a state of either restrained or drunken bliss, interspersed with bursts of happiness and misery until my mother's death. Once he was alone, Sam's health deteriorated and he died 10 years later.

I continued to find solace in travel. In May 2013 I left for Britain to stay with my old friend Kathy, whom I had not seen for many years. We explored – or rather I said where I wanted to go and kind Kathy made the arrangements. It took a day of nightmare travel to south-east London to visit the William and Jane Morris's famous Red House in Bexleyheath. The uniqueness of Philip Webb and Morris's pioneering Arts and Crafts design, and the decorated interior, sited in the equally important garden, made the trip worthwhile. Another day involving a trek of train catching was to South London to visit the Dulwich Picture Gallery, designed by Sir John Soane and opened in 1817 as the first purpose-built public art gallery in England. I had referred to it in my PhD thesis and was keen to see it. The design of its magnificent top-lit gallery spaces was echoed by architect Edward Armstrong for the lantern roof lights at the Robert McDougall Art Gallery in Christchurch, and both galleries were designed in the neo-classical style. A two-day excursion requiring train and taxi to reach Vita Sackville-West's Sissinghurst in Kent was also a dream finally realised.

For our eight days in France, Kathy chose the picturesque village of Isle-sur-La-Sorgue in Provence, which had few modern eyesores and even fewer tourists. The rail journey from London with the white-knuckle (for me) 20-minute ride under the Channel brought us to Lille. From there we took a train to distant Avignon and another to our destination. We stayed on the first floor of the private home of Madame Claudine, who was an excellent host and insisted on taking us, over several days, to see neighbouring villages perched on hillsides or standing atop rocky spurs, their narrow winding streets and small squares with fountains and outstanding views. Tout à fait charmant.

We also managed four days in Amsterdam, where Kathy sighed but generously went along with my interests in art and architecture. At the Rijksmuseum, only three months after a fabulous revamp, I was delighted to see Rembrandt's *The Night Watch* returned to its own room at the end of the Hall of Fame. The painting was much larger than I realised and the throng of people made it difficult to study from further back. I was bubbling with excitement to get to the nearby Van Gogh Museum, which contains the world's largest collection of his paintings and drawings. To see *The Potato Eaters*, *Bedroom in Arles*, *The Yellow House* and *Sunflowers* brought back so many superb memories of my art history days and my 1991 visit to Arles.

I was devastated, on my return to Christchurch, to learn that Lynda Patterson, who had been installed as Christ Church Cathedral's first female dean in 2013 after Peter Beck resigned and was happily entrenched in her new life, had died on 20 July, aged only 40. I was thankful to be back in time for her funeral, which was held at the Transitional Cathedral. She was mourned by many. Sheena was invited to participate in the service. Both women were called to Christchurch and both became successfully integrated into the city's religious life, Lynda happy to discuss theology and worship and Sheena as a protector and advocate for the less fortunate. Both transformed lives; Lynda's own, alas, was far too short.

I had gone without a dog for too long since Ziggy's death. Mark was not particularly happy about having one but he would relent if I gave up travelling and took responsibility for it. Once the feisty Hester, a four-month-old Cairn terrier, had bonded with Mark, I felt I could tell him that I was going overseas again.

'Only for a month or so,' I said.

'You lied to me. You said you wouldn't travel again.'

'I know, sorry. I leave in September.'

Travelling the 11,226-kilometre Silk Road from Beijing to Moscow by train was the journey of a lifetime. Once again, Barbara was my travelling companion and we shared the very comfortable cabin accommodation, which had an en suite and two beds that converted to a couch during the day. When not leased out for private travel, the luxurious Shangri-la Express was the train of choice for Xi Jinping, the General Secretary of the Chinese Communist Party, and other high-ranking party officials. China had always fascinated me, especially after my first trip there with Barbara in 1999, and I had hankered to return and study the more serious historical and cultural aspects of this enormous country. As an undergraduate, I had taken a course on traditional Asia taught by Professor S. A. M. Adshead, a quaint and unworldly Englishman who dressed in clothes that had seen better days, but was a brilliant scholar and world-renowned authority on China. Many thought him forbidding (mistaking this for his shyness), but though in awe of his intellect and knowledge, I was thankful he opened my eyes to the wonders of China's history. I was also aware writer and political activist Rewi Alley, a Cantabrian who had dedicated 60 years of his life to improving the lives and working conditions of the Chinese people and establishing schools.

After crossing the Gobi Desert we arrived at Urumchi, a major hub on the Silk Road and the border with Kazakhstan. Here we changed trains under the eyes of an armed guard escort because of the recent bombings and ethnic tensions with the local Uyghurs. We then travelled through three of the five Central Asian independent 'Stan' countries that had been part of the Soviet Union: Kazakhstan, Uzbekistan and Turkmenistan.

The ancient city of Merv, in Turkmenistan, had a long, complicated and fascinating history. Briefly the largest city in the world and an important stop on the Silk Road, it was left to 'die' in 1794 after the Emir of Bukhara destroyed the dam on which the population depended for water. We visited one of the five walled cities contained within the 13-hectare area.

After the train left Ashgabat, the capital of Turkmenistan, for Khiva, it made a brief stop at Ichoguz while crossing the Karakum Desert. At 2 a.m. those brave enough for an adventure left the train. Barbara and I were, and we went to hell. Parked alongside the train was a row of old cars. They had no seats but rugs were spread over the floor and there we crouched, not knowing what our destination was. It was rather spooky and we were very trusting. There was no road; the convoy of cars simply headed over the sand dunes into the distance. After 20 minutes we reached Darvaza's famous burning gas crater, located in an area rich in gas, which explains the wealth of Turkmenistan. A New Zealand health and safety officer would have had a field day there. The crater was huge and unfenced, with no warning signs about not going too close to the edges, which crumbled away quietly if you neared them. No wonder the locals referred to the 70-metre-wide crater as the 'Door to Hell'.

In Uzbekistan our last stop before Russia was the desert town of Khiva, one of the most intact Silk Road settlements. It is truly a living museum. The Itchen Kala (inner town), surrounded by high walls, contains eye-watering treasures: the fourteenth-century tomb of Shaikh Sayid Alauddin, the Kunya-Ark Fortress, the former palace of the khans and 16 historic mosques and madrasahs. After this glory it was almost a relief to travel with no stops until we reached Volgograd (once Stalingrad). I had read a scholarly history of the siege of Leningrad, which I found gruelling and it affected me deeply, but not one of Stalingrad. I was, therefore, totally unprepared for the assault on my senses when visiting the sobering war memorial complex on top of Mamayev Kurgan, which overlooks the city. As I climbed the 200 steps representing the days of the siege and the Battle of Stalingrad, to pay homage at the feet of the 85-metre sculpture, *The Motherland Calls*, I could only be awestruck and overwhelmed by the courage, sacrifice and sheer bloody-mindedness of over a million soldiers and civilians who fought to protect their city and homeland. Art historians are inclined to sneer at the war memorial and *The Motherland Calls* as reactionary Soviet realist kitsch. Obviously they have not been there.

As we concluded our odyssey in Moscow, I had not quite filled my Russian heritage tank and vowed to return and visit St Petersburg. I flew home exhausted but also invigorated after experiencing so much history and many architectural wonders – all within a month. And Mark and Hester had survived my absence.

In 2015, there was another celebration, this one for the launch of a book based on my PhD thesis, and with the same title. The mayor opened proceedings and Mark Stocker, now at Te Papa, flew down from Wellington to give a speech along the lines of the foreword he had penned for the publication. I was amused by his summary: contemporary museology meets Anthony Trollope. I have never seen the book on sale anywhere – even the Christchurch Art Gallery shop did not stock it – and I do not think it has ever been reviewed, but I am pleased I saw it through. I was chuffed, too, by Mark Stocker's remark that were I 45 years younger, with the same PhD and book under my belt, I would be destined for a great academic career as an art historian or museologist.

In December 2017, my boy made the crucial decision to leave his marriage of 20 years. I had witnessed his growing unhappiness for some time and was saddened but not surprised. The enormous consequences of his decision would soon become evident and the following weeks were emotionally difficult and Christmas a sad occasion. Seeing in the New Year at sunrise on New Brighton beach, a tradition I followed each new year, heralded the start of a different life for Dorian – and for me. I no longer felt so welcome at the family home where I had been used to popping in to see the girlies. They celebrated my January birthday with me as usual, but it was not quite the same.

In late June, Dorian and his new partner, Jeanette Kwant (aka J), were flying to Ho Chi Minh City in Vietnam for an annual international accountancy conference. When I called in to get last-minute instructions for when they were away and to confirm arrangements for taking them to the airport, Dorian was very quiet. He said, 'Sit down, Mum', and pulled out a chair for me. He then explained that he had visited the doctor the day before and she informed him that he had cancer in his left kidney. This had been discovered when a scan of his liver revealed he also had Stage 4 cirrhosis. Words cannot begin to even touch the shock of this news. Both Dorian and I have an Anglo-Saxon propensity to go quiet when we are not sure how to cope with emotions. I drove them to the airport in silence. When I got home I found it impossible to carry out even the simplest tasks. Until their return, I sat mute and impassive in the armchair in the kitchen for hours and hours. The thought of losing my beautiful boy was unbearable. Mark, patient and understanding, left me to my solitude, for which I was grateful.

I somehow roused myself from time to time. J and Dorian video-called me every day when they were away and J's upbeat personality, and seeing Dorian, sustained me for brief moments. I was thankful J was there for him. Then I made two visits that I thought would help me – and did to some degree. One was to my doctor to ask if it was possible for me to donate part of my liver to my son. She looked at me kindly and said that it was not as simple as that. But at least it was an answer. My second visit was to clinical psychologist and friend Olive Webb. She listened quietly to my outpouring and then asked the obvious question, 'Has Dorian had a second opinion?' The answer was 'No'. She then gave me advice on physical, emotional and practical ways to continue coping, plus a list of questions that needed medical answers. This helped me enormously.

On his return from Vietnam Dorian promptly sought a second opinion from a specialist who saw him in July. Oh, how right Olive was. The specialist revealed that his condition was not so bad, though he was not out of the woods yet. The scarring of Dorian's liver was caused by prescribed medication that he had been taking for years. He was told to stop taking it immediately. Then, in October, he underwent surgery to remove the cancer in his kidney. After further operations and prescribed medication he has subsequently been given a clean bill of health. May it stay that way.

When I hit my seventies I felt I had lived a full life, but I asked myself, What next? There were only two things that I had not yet achieved: experiencing the culture of the land of my ancestors by spending time in a little French village, and returning to Russia to visit St Petersburg. So, I did both. And what could be better, to help Dorian recover physically, mentally and emotionally from his marriage break-up and his recent five-hour cancer operation, than a month relaxing in a little village in the south of France? My boy and I were off on another adventure.

Dorian and I – Lesley and J joined us later – escaped to the quietly charming medieval town of Céret in the foothills of the Pyrénées, just two hours' drive over the border from Barcelona. It was perfect: fewer than 8000 residents and very few tourists. The cottage I had rented for a month was bijou, charming and typically French, with its shuttered windows and doors, and within walking distance of the village centre. There was a small supermarket at one end of the street, opposite the fourteenth-century Pont du Diable (Devil's Bridge), and an excellent butcher's shop at the other. The cobbled streets, shady trees and appealing stone buildings, many of them listed, satisfied my appetite for architectural history. We shopped locally, Dorian and J joined the gym and went each morning, I found a hairdresser, we purchased fresh croissants for breakfast and quaffed briskly chilled Veuve Clicquot at any opportunity. Our French improved daily. The Saturday farmers' market at Céret, one of the best in the region, stretched right along Boulevard Aragon and around the corner along Boulevards la Fayette and Jean Jaures. J and I shopped there every week.

Céret was exceptional in another way, as a cultural heart. It became known as the 'Mecca of Cubism' because of the constant flow of artists who went there. Pablo Picasso (think *Paysage de Céret* in the Guggenheim New York), Picasso's friends Manolo Hugué, Frank Burty-Haviland, Georges Braque, Juan Gris, Auguste Herbin, Max Jacob, André Masson, Raoul Dufy, Jean Cocteau, Jean Dubuffet, Joan Miró and Marc Chagall, to name only a few, all arrived in Céret at some stage between 1910 and 1922 to live and paint. Picture panels are installed at each point where a view of the town was painted by one of those famous visitors. The Museum of Modern Art of Céret opened its doors in 1950 with works donated by many of these artists, including 14 sketches drawn in nearby Collioure by Matisse and a collection of 28 pieces of ceramic art by Picasso. It is an extraordinary gallery and collection for such a modestly sized town. Wherever I went, art and architecture assailed me. It was intoxicating.

We knew the idyllic adventure must come to an end but I did not want to leave. Our departure on the leisurely four-day road trip to Paris coincided with the opening of the cherry festival – Céret is known as the national capital for growing the fruit – and so we stocked up with some luscious red cherries for snacking as we drove. These we washed down with a swig of holy water from our overnight visit to Lourdes.

Dorian and J flew home from Paris but I was off to Moscow. This time I took a day pass to explore the grandiose marble and gilded stations of the Moscow Metro. Opened in 1935, it was part of Stalin's plan for the reconstruction of the city and is rich in the art of Socialist Realism, that expression of glorified Communist values. However, it bore more than a passing resemblance to the neo-baroque movie palaces of 1930s Europe. As the art historian and Soviet spy Anthony Blunt noted on his visit to

Moscow in 1935, the Metro had a 'Parisian chic and one almost expects a top-hat to emerge from its doors'. Muscovites navigate their city in this palatial subterranean world graced with sculptures, mosaics and richly hued stonework illuminated by chandeliers. I rode to some of the most decorative stations to view the bas reliefs of Dynamo, the mosaic vaulted ceiling of Mayakovskaya and the white marble of Teatralnaya and admire this higher phase of Soviet architecture.

I made my way from Moscow to St Petersburg aboard the *Viking Helgi* via the 'Waterways of the Tsars', sailing along the Moscow Canal, then through the locks of Uglich, Rybinsk and Sheksna to the Volga–Baltic Canal. From there the route went to Lake Onega, along the Svir River to Lake Ladoga and finally the Neva River to St Petersburg. The first stop was at Uglich, a magnificent city to behold from the river. During the sixteenth century, Ivan the Terrible used the town kremlin, not far from the jetty on the steep riverbanks, as a place of exile for his last wife, who lived there with their son Dmitry, who was destined to be the next tsar. The boy was brutally murdered. We visited the magnificent Church of St Dmitry on the Blood, built on the site where his body was found. The frescoes in the interior tell the story of his terrible death.

Further south, we sailed over a market square and saw a belfry rising from the river. In 1939–40, as part of the construction of the Uglich hydroelectric power station, part of the old town of Kalyazin, including all its significant historical and architectural monuments, was flooded. One of those was the belfry erected in the late eighteenth century as part of the monastery of St Nicholas, the richest in Russia, which stood in Kalyazin's Market Square. This was not the only flooded religious building we saw. At the mouth of the Upper Sheksna River is the remains of the Church of the Nativity of Krokhino, a village that was obliterated by inundation resulting from the creation of the Volga–Baltic Waterway. The price of progress, destroying heritage.

I will never forget 21 May 2019. That was the day I got horribly lost in Yaroslavl. Part of what is known as the Golden Ring, a group of historic cities north-east of Moscow, it straddles the Volga amid a region of forests. Founded in 1010, it is dotted with the onion-shaped domed churches of Russian Orthodoxy. My destination was the Volkov, Russia's first public theatre, built in 1750. The local tour guide explained where I could find it and I set off on my own. I finally found the theatre but when the time came for me to rejoin the tour group, I could not remember how to get back. I started walking but after half an hour realised I was hopelessly lost. The street signs in Russian were indecipherable and nobody spoke English. People shrank from a worried, lost 75-year-old trying to ask for directions and there was not a policeman in sight. I felt extremely isolated and almost ready to panic when, miraculously, I found myself back at the theatre. I tried walking in the other direction this time and after another hour located the bus and was reunited with my group.

Situated at the north end of Lake Onega, Kizhi Island is home to the famed open-air Museum of Architecture, a UNESCO World Heritage site, with an incredible collection of traditional timber structures, some moved there for preservation from various parts of North Karelia, Karelia and Pudozhsky. Dozens of buildings, including farmhouses, barns, mills, bell towers and two eighteenth- century churches, illustrate Russia's unusual and visionary architecture, which relied on wood rather than stone. Churches were crafted without the use of a single nail, using a special notching technique. Their exteriors rise to a mass of clustered domes: the three-tiered Transfiguration Church has 22, the Intercession Church a more modest nine.

People live on the island of Kizhi in timber houses, always with the traditional banya (sauna) close by, where families, friends and even business associates cleanse themselves and socialise. You sit naked in a room heated to more than 95°C. Aromatic herbs are added and you wear a felt hat and mitts to prevent your head and hands from overheating. Birch or oak switches are provided to hit and massage your skin and open the pores, improving circulation. You scrape off the dirt and sweat, then either plunge into a cold bath or roll in the snow. I now wished I had taken a banya, if only as a reminder of my days at Maruia Springs all those years ago.

Once in St Petersburg, the bold and lavish showcase of the might of its founder, Peter the Great, I spent hours in the Hermitage Museum, once the royal Winter Palace, then an enriching evening attending the ballet – this is the city of Baryshnikov and Nureyev – followed by a drive through the glittering canal-lined streets. I saw, too, the neo-classical Pavlovsk Palace with its understated elegance and rich collection of lush paintings, period furniture, carpets and antiques second only to those found in the Hermitage. Then there was the extravagant Peterhof, the palace designed by Peter himself and often referred to as the Russian Versailles, thanks to its French-inspired interiors, spectacular landscaping and magnificent gardens with grand cascading fountains. Taking a boat cruise provided the most romantic views from the granite-lined waterways where I gained a perspective of St Petersburg unachievable on land. Then, in the town of Tsarskoe Selo (Pushkin), there was the Catherine Palace, a stunning example of baroque architecture. The sheer ambition of the restoration of the palace was nothing short of miraculous: 30 halls and rooms recreated after the palace was left in ruins, were available for public viewing, including the famous Amber Room, once described as the eighth wonder of the world and presented to Peter the Great in 1716. Its amber decorations were carried away to Konigsberg by Nazi troops in 1942 during the Siege of Leningrad, never to be found, but the panels were remade from black and white photos, taking 5.7 tonnes of raw materials and many years to complete.

In complete contrast to the resplendent palaces and dazzling onion-domed churches, and as a former registrar, I enjoyed privileged access to the off-site storage facility for the overflow of the vast number of works from the Hermitage and other state collections not on display. The Hermitage boasts some 3 million works of art and historical artefacts precious to Russia's heritage. Like most museums around the world, only a fraction of their collections is on display, the rest locked away from visitors. I have always been convinced that purpose-built off-site storage facilities are the answer for precious and ever-growing public historic collections. When I was a member of the Canterbury Museum Board, I presented this option most strongly. It would mean that the restricted site on which the museum stood could be used entirely for exhibitions and exhibits, with the remainder of the collection in storage. Visiting the carefully monitored storage facility in St Petersburg, built in 2012, confirmed my opinion. I will concede that Christchurch would not require such a large building.

With a historian/registrar I visited some of the many secure vaults, where displays of imperial carriages, treasured sculptures, priceless art and Romanov furniture were jumbled into a 'planned' viewing area roped off for visitors. Included was a huge gold-embroidered tent from a Turkish sultan and gifts presented to Russian royalty by countries throughout the world. Every door to each large storage area had a security code and there were cameras everywhere. I noted they used Halon gas for fire protection, rather than a sprinkler system. Halon gas was originally installed in the basement of the McDougall but later removed because it was believed to be lethal and dangerous, not for the art but for the staff. It was changed to a sprinkler system, which was not good for the art, because of potential water damage, but safe for the staff. The 'behind closed doors' viewing was enlightening and thrilling at the same time. The tour had held my attention and fed my curiosity for eight hours.

How had the splendours of St Petersburg, later named Leningrad, survived? I had read Anna Reid's narrative of the epic Second World War siege, which lasted two and a half years, during which some 750,000 Leningraders died of starvation. But the gilded city of St Petersburg survived that last attempt to bring it down. The grand boulevards, a lacework of canals, elegant baroque and Palladian architecture, imposing palaces and astonishing onion-domed churches were made even more gorgeous with the addition of priceless art and artefacts, frescoes and icons, gilding and glorification, fountains and follies and manicured parks and gardens. I was happy that I had finally seen the wonders of St Petersburg with my own eyes.

A few months after I returned home, on a warm day in late September 2019, a letter arrived. It displayed a gold crown and the words 'Government House New Zealand' along with the phrase 'Personal and Confidential'. I had received such an envelope in 2005, containing a letter informing me that I had been recommended for a Queen's Service Order, for services to arts, culture and heritage. I was completely overwhelmed then, and now I felt unsure. This time the letter told me that I had been recommended for appointment as a Dame Companion of the New Zealand Order of Merit in the New Year Honours 2020 for services to heritage preservation and governance. My first reaction was that it had to be a mistake, even a hoax. I was filled with doubt and bewilderment. This could not possibly be happening to me. Inconceivable. But it was real.

When my damehood was announced, I was deluged with phone calls, emails, texts, cards, visitors, flowers and letters from all quarters. I was warned by another honours recipient that it is always interesting to note those people you would expect to hear from, but who say precisely nothing. This was only too true. Sometimes, refreshingly, it could be the opposite. The usual interviews for radio and TV predominated and took up a lot of time and energy. It was an exciting time but the bewilderment persisted. That is, until the investiture ceremony at Government House in July. I shared my honour with Dorian, J and my friend Barbara. When the korowai was put around my shoulders and the breast star and insignia were attached by Governor-General Dame Patsy Reddy, I had no control over the silent tears of joy that started to flow.

Last Word

In 2020, when Covid-19 locked us in and curtailed all travel, I decided to write my story. I felt compelled to do so for my son, Dorian, and my granddaughters. I have lived through times so different from theirs and the world has changed immeasurably in those years. I have experienced adversity and tragedy and transcended both. I encourage Olivia, Alice and Harriet to take opportunities, never give up and always be true to themselves. I hope they will not be subjected to the unfair sexism of my era, well before the advent of social media and Me Too, and that patronising and superior male attitudes have had their day. Throughout my life, many people have underestimated me and my abilities, and because of this I have often felt an outsider. Despite this, I made it in my own way, refusing to surrender to a diminished existence and avoiding self-pity at all costs. So, with more years behind me than in front of me, with my demons banished and self-respect established, finally fulfilled and content, I live for the now and the ordinary.